Kashmir, Ladakh & Zanskar

a travel survival kit

Margret & Rolf Schettler

Kashmir, Ladakh & Zanskar - a travel survival kit
3rd edition

Published by
Lonely Planet Publications
Head Office: PO Box 617, Hawthorn, Victoria 3122, Australia
US Office: PO Box 2001A, Berkeley, CA 94702, USA

Printed by
Singapore National Printers Ltd, Singapore

Photographs by
Colour: Ralph Kaminski (RK), Bob Pritchard (BP), Neil Tilbury (NT), Garry Weare (GW), Tony Wheeler (TW)
Black & white: all Rolf Schettler, except 152 Maureen Wheeler, and 34, 148, 151 Lindy Cameron
Front cover: Dal Lake shikara (NT)
Back cover: Srinagar to Leh road (NT)

First Published
February 1981

This Edition
May 1989

Although the author and publisher have tried to make the information as accurate as possible, they accept no responsibility for any loss, injury or inconvenience sustained by any person using this book.

National Library of Australia Cataloguing in Publication Data

Schettler, Rolf, 1943 –
    Kashmir, Ladakh & Zanskar: a travel survival kit.

    3rd ed.
    Includes index.
    ISBN 0 86442 046 3.

    1. Jammu and Kashmir (India) – Description and travel – Guide-books. I. Schettler, Margret. II. Title

    915.4'60452

Rolf & Margret Schettler

Rolf and Margret Schettler were, in 1974, the first foreign visitors to Ladakh with their own vehicle. They have subsequently returned to Ladakh and to Zanskar to write about, film and record the music of these remote Himalayan regions. This book was first published in Germany as *Kaschmir & Ladakh* and expanded, at the same time as the first edition of this English language version, to include Zanskar.

Additional contributors to the original language editions included Dr Walter A Frank (Manali-Padum Trek and Tungri-Zonghkul Gompa Roundtrip), Kurt & Ingrid Zehetner (Padum-Kishtwar Trek) and Walter Kamm (Padum-Leh by the Markha Valley and Padum-Phuctal Gompa by the Shadi Gorge).

Neil Tilbury

Neil Tilbury was born in Portsmouth, England, where he studied hotel management. Moving up to London, he spent a few years working in the hotel and wine trades before travelling to Australia via Europe, the Middle East and Asia. After researching and writing Lonely Planet's new *Israel – a travel survival kit*, Neil went to India to update this edition of *Kashmir, Ladakh & Zanskar*.

Lonely Planet Credits

Production Editor	Lindy Cameron
Maps	Graham Imeson
Cover design, design & illustrations	Glenn Beanland
Typesetting	Ann Jeffree

Copy editor: Gillian Cummings. Thanks also to Laurie Fullerton for proofreading.

From the publisher

Many travellers wrote to Lonely Planet with useful information on the region. Much of this information has also found

its way into the new edition of *India – a travel survival kit*. Thanks to:

Andy Dunhill (UK), Paul Hayhoe (UK), Andrew Martin (PNG), Richard Warren (USA), Sally Woyner-Hoyton

A Warning & a Request

Things change – prices go up, schedules change, good places go bad and bad places go bankrupt – nothing stays the same. So if you find things better or worse, recently opened or long since closed, please write and tell us and help make the next edition better! All information is greatly appreciated and the best letters will receive a free copy of the next edition, or any other Lonely Planet book of your choice.

Extracts from the best letters are also included in the *Lonely Planet Update*. The *Update* helps us make useful information available to you as soon as possible – it's like reading an up-to-date noticeboard or postcards from a friend. Each edition contains hundreds of useful tips, and advice from the best possible source of information – other travellers. The *Lonely Planet Update* is published quarterly in paperback and is available from bookshops and by subscription.

Turn to the back pages of this book for more details.

Contents

Gompa Roundtrip – Padum-Thonde-Zangla-Karsha Gompa-Padum Roundtrip –
Padum-Phuctal Gompa

Introduction

Kashmir, Ladakh and Zanskar are regions of the Indian state of Jammu and Kashmir, often referred to simply as J&K. Jammu is the southern part of the state and forms a transitional area between the Indian plains and the mighty Himalaya. Technically speaking the rest of the state is Kashmir.

In practice, the Kashmir title is usually reserved for the 'Vale of Kashmir', a large Himalayan valley in the north of the state. Ladakh is actually a region of Kashmir, and Zanskar a sub-district of Ladakh. They are geographical neighbours but, separated by the full height of the Himalaya, they are worlds apart in terms of people, culture, religion and terrain.

When referring to J&K and its environs, it is important to note the distinction between political demarcations, geographical regions and administrative divisions. Since 1947 the state has been split between India and Pakistan and, more recently, China. Although the whole region continues to be a subject of considerable dispute between these three nations, the argument is highly unlikely to have any real effect on foreign visitors.

Jammu is not of great interest to most overseas visitors to the region as it's basically just a stop-over on the trip up to Srinagar. As well as being a geographical transition zone from the hot plains to the cool mountains, it is also a religious change-point. Here the Hindu religion begins to give way to the Muslim religion that predominates in the Kashmir Valley.

The Vale of Kashmir has been famous for its great natural beauty ever since the days of the Moghul emperors. The great Moghuls further embellished that natural beauty with a series of delightfully planned gardens, many of which are still beautifully preserved today. The British added a further attraction to Kashmir – the houseboats which crowd Dal Lake at Srinagar. No visit to Kashmir is complete without a stay on a houseboat.

Ladakh lies across the Himalaya from Kashmir. Its situation on the Tibetan plateau, plus the clear Tibetan influence in Ladakhi customs and religion, has led to it being known as 'little Tibet'. Ladakh's quite incredibly barren landscape, a result of the high Himalayan barrier which prevents rain clouds from climbing across from the lush valleys to the south and west, has also given it the name of 'the moonland'.

Ladakh has only been open to tourists since the mid-70s and until 1962, when the Chinese invasion prompted the rapid construction of a road linking Ladakh with Srinagar, getting into Ladakh involved several weeks hard walk. Since 1979 it has been possible to fly to Ladakh from Srinagar in less than 30 minutes. Now you can also fly from Chandigarh.

Finally there is Zanskar, a long valley running in a roughly north-west to south-east direction between Kashmir and Ladakh. Zanskar encompasses the Stod and Lunak river valleys, the Zanskar River Valley and the area south of Padum to the southern face of the Great Himalaya, over the Shingo pass. The people are much like the Ladakhis in their dress, customs and religion but they have been even more isolated from outside contact. Like Ladakh, visitors have only been allowed into Zanskar in the last few years, but access to Zanskar is much more difficult.

A jeep track to Padum, the Zanskar 'capital', was only completed in the early '80s and it is extremely susceptible to damage in a severe winter. Most visitors to Zanskar still arrive on foot or by pony, crossing 4500-metre passes to get there.

The whole Kashmir, Ladakh and Zanskar region is a paradise for trekkers, with trails leading through beautiful and spectacular scenery, far from the encroachment of modern roads and motor vehicles.

Facts about the Region

GEOGRAPHY

Jammu & Kashmir is the northernmost province of India, bordered to the north and east by China (Sinkiang Province and Tibet), to the west by Pakistan's North-West Frontier Province and to the south by the Indian states of Punjab and Himachal Pradesh. The whole region of Kashmir has an area of 222,798 square km with a population of six million, but Pakistan controls 83,800 square km of the Gilgit and Hunza areas of Kashmir to the north-west while China has grabbed a further slice of the area in the east. Due to these border disputes there is a large Indian military presence in the state and following the Chinese activities in Ladakh, two roads were built to Leh and the airport there was completed.

Jammu is the southern part of the state and forms a transitional area between the Indian plains and the ranges which make up the Himalayan region. The northern part of the state is Kashmir but this name usually refers just to the Vale of Kashmir, a large valley in the north-west. The eastern part of the state is Ladakh, within which lies Zanskar. The Himalaya separate the Vale of Kashmir from the Zanskar Valley and in turn Zanskar is separated from Ladakh by the Zanskar Range. The Himalaya not only marks changes in climate and geography, but as you move from Kashmir to Ladakh there are also great differences in race, customs and religion.

The Kashmir Valley is bounded by two mountain ranges. The lower Pir Panjal Range curls around the valley from the south-east, through the south and round to the north-west. The eastern side of the valley is closed off by the Great Himalaya, which runs almost straight from south-east to north-west. At one time Kashmir was a lake which, like the Kathmandu Valley, was drained eons ago.

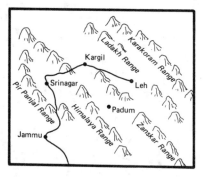

CLIMATE

The climactic differences in the state of Jammu and Kashmir are probably the most varied in all of India. In Jammu in the hot season the temperatures can be consistently above 40°C while at Kargil in mid-winter the temperature has been known to drop to minus 40°C. Similarly, during the monsoon Jammu can have rain every day while in Ladakh whole years may pass with no rainfall at all. Following is a brief outline of the weather you can expect in the various regions.

Jammu Situated at a height of only 300 metres, Jammu has the three-season weather typical of the Indian plains. The best time of year is the cool season from early October to about February-March. In October, immediately after the monsoon finishes, the weather will be cool and fresh, the skies clear and dust-free. Later in the cool season (December and January in particular) it can get quite crisp with temperatures as low as 5°C at night.

In February-March the temperature starts to climb as the hot season begins. By April, May and June it is uncomfortably hot and dry. Since there has been no rain

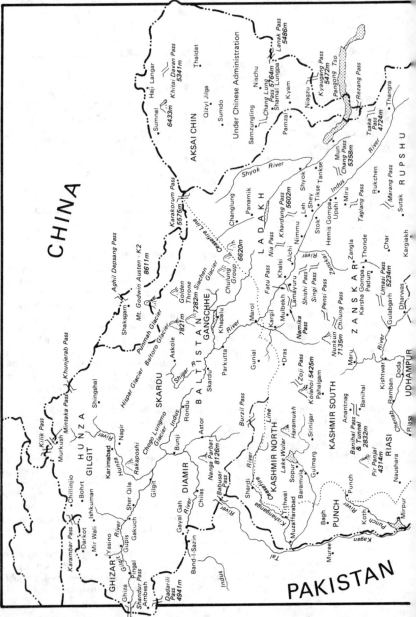

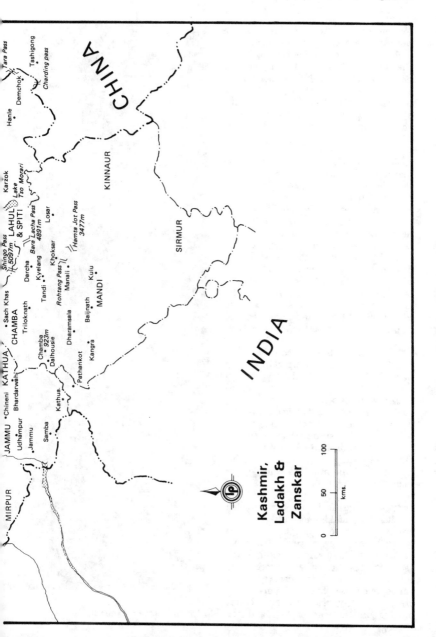

for some time the air is very dusty and the temperature scarcely seems to drop at night. Towards the end of the hot season the mercury will sit at 40°C or above for days on end. Finally the monsoon arrives around the beginning of July and the dust is immediately cleared from the air, although for some time the temperature change is merely from hot and dry to hot and sticky.

Kashmir At an altitude of more than 1000 metres the Kashmir Valley is much cooler than Jammu but is most popular during May and June when Indian tourists flee the hot, airless plains. At this time the daily temperatures are around 20°C, a delightfully cool contrast to the 40°C temperatures common on the plains to the south. In July and August it can become hotter and the valley somewhat humid and still. The simple solution is to move to one of the smaller resorts that lie around the valley rim. At places like Pahalgam, Gulmarg and Sonamarg the altitude ensures cooler weather even in mid-summer.

The Kashmir tourist season ends in October as minimum temperatures drop below 10°C. From November to February night temperatures often fall below freezing in Srinagar, snow falls and during cold years Dal Lake can freeze over. In winter Gulmarg becomes India's premier ski resort. The spring thaw begins in February-March. Rainfall in Kashmir is fairly even year round. The mountains protect Kashmir from the worst of the monsoon.

Ladakh & Zanskar Winter at the high altitudes of Ladakh and Zanskar can be spectacularly cold although snow fall is generally not heavy since the Himalaya act as a barrier to rain clouds from the south. Parts of Ladakh have no recordable rainfall for years, yet in others there may be deep and persistent snow. Temperatures are consistently below freezing for six months of the year in Leh and the

Making butter tea in Lamayuru Gompa

	New Delhi*			Srinagar**			Leh***		
	max	min	rain	max	min	rain	max	min	rain
January	21.1	6.7	22.9	5.0	-2.2	73.7	-1.1	-13.3	10.2
February	23.9	9.4	17.7	7.2	-1.1	71.1	0.6	-12.2	7.6
March	30.6	14.4	12.7	13.9	3.3	91.4	7.2	-6.1	7.6
April	36.1	20.0	7.7	18.9	7.2	93.9	13.3	-1.1	5.0
May	40.6	26.1	12.7	24.4	11.1	60.9	16.1	0.6	5.0
June	38.9	28.3	73.7	29.4	14.4	35.6	20.0	6.7	5.0
July	35.6	27.2	180.3	31.1	18.3	58.4	25.0	10.0	12.9
August	33.9	26.1	172.7	30.6	17.8	60.9	23.9	10.0	15.2
September	33.9	23.9	116.8	27.8	12.2	38.1	21.1	5.6	7.6
October	33.9	18.3	10.2	22.2	5.0	30.5	15.0	-0.6	2.5
November	28.9	11.1	2.5	15.6	-0.6	10.2	8.3	-6.7	2.5
December	22.8	7.8	10.2	10.7	-2.2	33.0	2.2	-10.6	5.0
annual rainfall			640.2			657.7			83.8

*1866-1943
**1899-1942
***1881-1942

snowbound pass into Kashmir isolates Ladakh from October to June. Drass is reputed to be one of the coldest places in Asia during winter. The Zanskaris bring their sheep, cattle and goats into the house in winter and from December to March they themselves retreat into the central room of the house and wait for spring. The Zanskar River usually disappears under ice and snow along much of its length. The Ladakhis too spend much of the winter indoors.

In summer the day temperatures are pleasantly warm with maximums around 20 to 25°C, but night temperatures are always crisp. Even at the height of summer the temperature will immediately plummet when a cloud obscures the sun. You should always have a sweater handy in Ladakh. Also, beware of the power of the sun at this altitude as you will quickly get a bad case of sunburn even on a cool day.

The rainfall chart details the average maximum and minimum temperature (°C) and average monthly rainfall (mm) in New Delhi, Srinagar and Leh.

POPULATION
The state of Jammu & Kashmir has a population of about 4.6 million. Ladakh, which is just under 100,000 square km in size, comprises nearly half of the whole Kashmir region, making it the largest district in India. However, its population of just more than 100,000 also makes it the most lightly populated region of the country. Ladakh has 112 villages and one town, the capital of Leh.

LANGUAGE
Although English is widely understood in Kashmir (but not so much in Ladakh) it never hurts to know a little of the local language. Indians speak a vast number of regional languages. In the state of Jammu and Kashmir these include Kashmiri, Ladakhi and Urdu. See the Ladakh section for some words in Ladakhi. Hindi is the official 'national' language and widely spoken. Some useful words and phrases include:

Questions, Commands & Greetings
Where is a hotel (tourist office)?
   Hotal (turist afis) kahan hai?
How far is .... ?
   Kitni dur hai .... ?

How do I get to . . . . ?
*Kojane ke liye kaise jana parega
. . . . ?*
Hello/goodbye
Namaste
Yes/no
Han/nahin
Please
Meharbani se
Thank you
Shukriya, dhanyawad
How much?
Kitne rupiah?
This is expensive.
Yeh bahut mehnga hai.
What is the time?
Kya baja hai?
What is your name?
Apka shubh nam?
Come here.
Yahan ao.
Show me the menu.
Mujha minu dikhao.
The bill please.
Bill lao.

Some Useful Words

big	*bara*
small	*muskarana*
today	*tambaku*
day	*din*
night	*rhat*

week	*saptah*
month	*mahina*
year	*sal*
medicine	*dawa*

Food & Drink

ice	*baraf*
egg	*anda*
fruit	*phal*
vegetable	*sabzi*
water	*pani*
rice	*inam*
tea	*chai*
coffee	*kafi*
milk	*dudh*
sugar	*chini*
butter	*makkhan*

Numbers

1	*ek*
2	*do*
3	*tin*
4	*char*
5	*panch*
6	*chhe*
7	*sat*
8	*ath*
9	*nau*
10	*das*
100	*sau*
100,000	*lakh*
10,000,000	*crore*

Facts for the Visitor

VISAS

No special permission is required to visit Kashmir and the Ladakh and Zanskar regions, once you have entered India. Since the upheavals in the Punjab in 1984, all nationalities – including previously exempt countries – are required to have a visa for India. Also the previous Indian tolerance towards visitors, who formerly could more or less wander around India forever, seems to be at an end. Reportedly you are now allowed to stay no longer than six months in any calendar year.

Visas, which are valid for 90-days, are issued at Indian embassies. They can be extended for a further 90 days once you're in the country. Visas must be obtained no more than six months before your arrival in India. Double-entry and triple-entry visas are available on request (at a higher price) so you can make side trips to Nepal and/or Sri Lanka on the same visa.

Within India visas can be extended at the Foreigners' Regional Registration Offices in New Delhi, Bombay, Calcutta, Madras or Srinagar, or at any of the Offices of the Superintendent of Police in the district headquarters. In Srinagar bring two photos. The office is by the GPO. In Leh go to the police station at the south-east of the polo ground.

No special permits are required for trekking in the non-restricted areas of Kashmir or Ladakh although it is advisable to enquire about permits before setting off on trekking trips, particularly into Zanskar. Some places in Ladakh and Zanskar are only accessible with special permission which may have to be obtained in New Delhi.

Restricted Areas

Because of the sensitive nature of the border zone between India and Pakistan in the north and India and China in the east there is a rigidly enforced area which you may not encroach. Basically it means you are not allowed north of the Srinagar Leh road or east of the Manali-Leh road.

More specifically the excluded area is from one mile north of the road which runs through Zoji La, Drass, Bodh Kharbu, Khalsi, Nimmu, Leh and Upshi; but not the monasteries of Tia, Temisgam, Rizong, Lekir, Phyang, Shey, Tikse, Chemrey and Tagthog, which can be visited.

Also excluded is the Leh-Upshi road beyond Karu and the area east from a line one mile west of the Manali-Upshi road from Chhumik Byiarsa on the Ladakh-Himachal Pradesh border. This means that the Manali-Leh road is also off-limits to visitors. Most of the Nubra Valley is off-limits but parts are being opened up to visitors.

Permission to enter the restricted area must be sought from the Ministry of Home Affairs, New Delhi, preferably before entering India as it can take up to six months to get a reply, which will usually be 'no'. If you want to try anyway cite order number 15011-6-73 when applying.

MONEY

US$1	=	Rs 11.0
A$1	=	Rs 10.0
UK£1	=	Rs 15.2
C$1	=	Rs 8.5
NZ$1	=	Rs 7.2
S$1	=	Rs 5.2
DM1	=	Rs 4.0

There are 100 paise (p) to the rupee (Rs). There are coins up to and including one rupee, and notes from one rupee up. At one time the rupee was divided into 16 annas and you may still occasionally hear prices quoted in annas in bazaars and markets – four annas is 25p, eight annas is 50p.

The main travellers' cheques are all easily exchanged in India although US dollars and pounds sterling are the most readily recognised foreign currencies. In out-of-the-way centres you may find these are the only currencies readily accepted. Exchange rates tend to vary from bank to bank. Anything to do with paperwork in India is inevitably time-consuming so it may be easier to change larger sums at one time than you would in other countries, simply in order to minimise the time wasted in banks.

Try not to have money transferred to you in India as it is often painfully slow and very tedious, particularly with the Indian banks. If you must have funds sent to India transfer them by cable or telex, not by mail, even if you have plenty of time in hand. Also, transfer them to a foreign-owned bank. American Express has offices in Bombay, New Delhi and Calcutta. There are other banks operating throughout India which are foreign owned and tend to be more efficient than the Indian-owned banks when it comes to foreign transactions. The Chartered Bank

and Grindlays Bank are two examples – Grindlays have an office in Srinagar on the Bund.

There are two particular points to be careful about with Indian money. First avoid dirty, grubby or torn notes – these can be unusable, particularly in out-of-the-way places. If you do get stuck with such a note try not to worry about it or cause any hassle if people refuse to accept it. You can generally get them changed at a bank (but not always!) or use them for some official purpose such as paying your airport departure tax.

The other money problem is big notes – changing a Rs 100 banknote is always difficult. In fact with India's perpetual small-change deficiency, changing anything is usually difficult. When changing foreign currency at a bank try to get as much as possible in smaller denomination notes. This problem applies particularly in Ladakh where, during the summer tourist season, there is sometimes a severe shortage of small denomination notes –

bring as many one and two rupee notes as possible.

Away from the main centres changing travellers' cheques or foreign currency can be difficult if not impossible. There are no facilities for changing foreign money in Zanskar, or in Ladakh outside Leh, Kargil or Karu. Make sure that you have enough rupees with you.

In New Delhi and to a lesser degree in Srinagar there is a black market for US dollars. It is illegal to import or export Indian currency although you can generally get Indian rupees in Bangkok or Singapore or in Europe at a useful discount – about the same as the black market rate within the country.

TOURIST INFORMATION

The Government of India Tourist Office maintains a string of tourist offices overseas where you can get brochures, leaflets and some information about India. The tourist office leaflets and brochures are often very high in their informational quality and worth getting hold of. On the other hand, some of the overseas offices are not always as useful for obtaining information as those within the country.

The overseas offices are listed here and there are smaller promotion offices in Osaka (Japan) and in the US in Dallas, Miami, San Francisco and Washington DC.

Overseas Indian Tourist Offices

Australia
> Carlton Centre, 55 Elizabeth St, Sydney, NSW 2000 (tel 02 232 1600)
> 8 Parliament Court, 1076 Hay St, West Perth, WA 600-5 (tel 06 321 6932)

Austria
> Opernring 1/E/11, 1010 Vienna (tel 571462)

Belgium
> 60 Rue Ravenstein, Boite 15, 1000 Brussels (tel 02 5111796)

Canada
> Suite 1016, Royal Trust Tower (PO Box 342) Toronto Dominion Center, Toronto, Ontario MSK 1K7 (tel 416 362 3188)

France
> 8 Boulevard de la Madeleine, 75009 Paris 9 (tel 265 83 86)

Italy
> Via Albricci 9, 20122 Milan (tel 804952)

Japan
> Japan Pearl Building, 9-18 Ginza, 7 Chome, Chuo-ku, Tokyo 104 (tel 571 5062/3)

Kuwait
> Saadoun A1-Jassim Building, Fahad A1-Salem St (PL 4769), Safat (tel 426088)

Singapore
> Podium Block, 4th floor, Ming Court Hotel, Tanglin Rd, Singapore 1024 (tel 235 5737)

Sweden
> Sveavagen 9-11 (Box 40016), S-111-57 Stockholm (tel 08 215081)

Switzerland
> 1-3 Rue de Chantepoulet, 1201 Geneva (tel 022 321813)

Thailand
> Singapore Airlines Building, 3rd floor, 62/5 Thaniya Rd, Bangkok (tel 235 2585)

UK
> 7 Cork St, London WIX QAB (tel 01 437 3677-8, 3678)

USA
> 30 Rockefeller Plaza, 15 North Mezzanine, New York, NY 10020 (tel 212 586 4901)
> 201 North Michigan Ave, Chicago, IL 60601 (tel 312 236 6899)
> 3550 Wilshire Blvd, Suite 204, Los Angeles, CA 90010 (tel 213 380 8855)

West Germany
> Kaiserstrasse 77-111, 6 Frankfurt Main (tel 232380)

J&K Tourist Offices

Jammu
> Tourist Reception Centre, Vir Marg (tel 5324)
> Office of the Director of Information, Government of J&K, Old Secretariat (tel 5376)
> Jammu Airport

Srinagar
> Tourist Reception Centre (tel 2449, 2927, 3648, 6209)
> J&K Government Reception Centre (tel 72449, 72927, 73648, 76209)
> Srinagar Airport

The J&K Tourist Department also has smaller offices in Pahalgam, Kud, Batote, Banihal, Verinag, Kokarnag, Tangmarg,

Achhabal, Gandarbal, Gulmarg and Katra. In Ladakh and Zanskar there are offices in Kargil, Leh and Padum. Elsewhere there are Kashmir Government Tourist Offices.

Kashmir Tourist Offices
Ahmedabad
   Airlines House, Lal Darwaza (tel 20473)
Bombay
   Manekji Wadia Building, 129 Mahatma Gandhi Rd (tel 273820)
Calcutta
   Kashmir Government Arts Emporium, 12 Chowringhee (tel 233268)
New Delhi
   Chandralok Building, 36 Janpath (tel 345373)
Pathankot
   Railway Station (tel 57)

GENERAL INFORMATION
Post
The Indian postal services are generally satisfactory, although we would all like things to move a lot faster. Expected letters are nearly always there and the letters you send almost invariably get to the address you put on the envelope. The main city locations of American Express are an alternative to the poste restante system, but the latter works well enough. Have letters addressed to you with your surname in capital letters and underlined. Many lost letters are simply misfiled under first names so always check both.

You can often buy stamps at top-end hotels and so avoid the interminable queuing in crowded post offices. Note that you should always have your stamped mail franked in your presence – don't just drop your cards and letters into mailboxes or give them to the clerk and walk away. This is simply because there is a very good chance of unfranked stamps being stolen and your mail never reaching its destination.

Most people discover how to post a parcel the hard way, when the exercise demands all morning or all afternoon. If you're not that keen to reach a peak of

hitherto unknown frustration, then go about it this way:

1 Take the parcel to a tailor and tell him you'd like it stitched up in cheap linen and the seams sealed with sealing wax. The wax has to be pressed with a seal which cannot be duplicated (if all else fails a non-Indian coin will serve). At some larger post offices this stitching-up service is offered outside. For a small parcel it should cost Rs 4 to Rs 7.
2 Go to the post office with your parcel and ask for two customs declaration forms. Fill them in and glue one to the parcel. Write your passport number (or any likely looking number) somewhere on the forms together with 'bona fide tourist'. To avoid excise duty at the delivery end it's best to specify that the contents are a 'gift'. The value of the parcel can be up to Rs 1000. (This concession is for tourists only. Internal parcels cannot exceed Rs 500 in value.)
3 Get the parcel weighed and ask how much it's going to cost.
4 Buy the stamps and stick them on.
5 Hand the parcel in at the parcel counter and get a receipt.

Even if you do it this way it can still take up to two hours. Any other way and you say goodbye to the whole day. Be cautious with places which offer to mail things home for you after you buy from them. Government emporiums are usually OK, but although most people who buy things from other places get them eventually, some items never turn up (were they ever sent?) or what turns up isn't what they bought.

The other direction (getting parcels sent to you in India), is an extremely hit-and-miss affair. Don't count on anything bigger than a letter getting to you. Don't count on a letter getting to you if there's anything worthwhile inside it.

Telecommunications

Making a phone call from Kashmir to other parts of India can involve hours of waiting; making an international call from Kashmir is practically impossible – unless you know or bribe somebody at the exchange.

Calling from Ladakh is even more difficult. If its an emergency its best to go to Delhi where the international phone service is a lot better than you might expect.

In spite of the importance of tourism to the Himalaya, international communication facilities are very poor. Telexes are a hit-and-miss affair while telegrams are frequently garbled. Be sure to check what type of telegram you are being charged for – choose between the standard and express services. The best way of achieving success is to send two telegrams – the cost is not too high and there's some chance of the message getting through.

Electricity

There is electricity in the main towns of 230-240 volts, 50 cycles, alternating current, so breakdowns and blackouts are not unusual. In Srinagar the electricity supply is reasonably reliable but the lines to the houseboats are tenuous. A strong wind can bring them down and leave you in darkness until the next morning.

In Kargil, electricity is supplied by diesel-powered generators which only operate in the evening. Leh has replaced the same system with a hydro-electric set-up that is being expanded to eventually cover Kargil. In the tourist season demand can be greater than supply and blackouts are not uncommon. Pack that flashlight! Also, the voltage is often less than the claimed 220 volts.

Time

India is 5½ hours ahead of GMT, 4½ hours behind Australian Eastern Standard Time and 10½ hours ahead of American Eastern Standard Time.

Business Hours

Shops and offices are generally open from 10 am to 5 pm – they're late starters! Banks are open 10 am to 2 pm on weekdays and 10 am to noon on Saturdays. Post offices are open 10 am to 5 pm on weekdays and on Saturday mornings. Shops are likely to be open shorter hours during winter.

There are many religious and government holidays when banks, post offices and shops are closed. Check with the local tourist office a few days ahead to ensure that you are not caught short of food or money. Sunday is the general closing day.

MEDIA

Newspapers & Magazines

The main English-language Indian papers arrive in Srinagar daily by air. You'll also find *Time, Newsweek* and India's own news magazine *India Today* on Srinagar's news-stands.

Newspapers are hard to come by in Leh and virtually unknown outside it. The Leh library has the most recently arrived copies and readers are welcome. You may also borrow books from the library (and donate your own to it when you leave) by leaving your passport as security.

Radio & Television

Srinagar has its own TV and radio stations. Leh has a station of All India Radio with its own generator and transmitter. It relays programmes from Delhi and broadcasts local material from 5 pm to midnight, most of it in Ladakhi.

HEALTH

Vaccinations

While no immunisations are officially required, at least three are recommended. These are cholera, typhoid and tetanus shots which can be provided by your own doctor or health service and should then be entered on your International Certificate of Vaccination. Gamma Globulin, for protection against hepatitis, is of questionable efficacy although an improved version has recently been introduced. Your doctor may also recommend that you be immunised.

Travel Insurance

Get some! You may never need it, but if you do you'll be very glad you got it. There are many different travel insurance policies available which cover medical costs for illness or injury, the cost of getting home for medical treatment, life insurance and baggage insurance. Some also cover the cost of getting your travelling partner home with you, and some protect you against cancellation penalties on advance purchase tickets should you have to change your travel plans because of illness.

Any travel agent should be able to recommend one but check the fine print, especially regarding baggage insurance.

Medical Kit

It's always a good idea to travel with a small first aid kit. Some of the items which should be included are: Band-Aids, a sterilised gauze bandage, elastoplast, cotton wool, a thermometer, tweezers, scissors, antibiotic cream or ointment, an antiseptic agent (dettol or betadine), burn cream (Caladryl is good for sunburn, minor burns and itchy bites), insect repellent and multi vitamins.

Don't forget water sterilisation tablets or iodine; anti-malarial tablets; any medication you're already taking; any contraceptives (pills or condoms), if necessary; and a spare pair of glasses or your prescription in case of loss or breakage.

Although malarial mosquitoes are not exactly at home in Ladakh and Zanskar, India as a whole is an area of malarial risk and you should take anti-malarial tablets, as prescribed by a doctor. These usually have to be taken for a period prior to departure and after your return.

Other medicine you should bring include Lomotil or other anti-diarrhoeals but remember the best treatment for mild diarrhoea is to let your system fight it off. If you are interested in alternative medicines fresh garlic has been recommended as a good preventative against mild attacks of diarrhoea.

A good anti-bacterial or fungicidal cream or powder is useful for cuts, abrasions and blisters. Corn pads are useful for preventing aggravation of blisters if you have to keep walking. A good suntan lotion is essential, along with a hat and sunglasses, to counter the increased intensity of the ultra-violet rays at high altitudes.

If you're planning to trek in Ladakh and Zanskar bring sleeping pills (if you're willing to take them) and aspirin since sleeplessness and headaches are two common afflictions when trekking at high altitudes. Be sure of your symptoms however; refer to the following section on Altitude Sickness.

In Srinagar you will find a wide variety of medicines readily available and without the prescriptions normally required in the west. The main problems are in understanding the different brand names and descriptions to get exactly what you want and making sure that they have not been kept beyond their 'use by' date.

Health Precautions
One of the best precautions you can take is to be as healthy as possible before you leave home. Make sure your teeth are in good shape – dental equipment in Kashmir and Ladakh may not be quite as modern as you'd like it to be. While you're travelling it's wise to clean your teeth with 'safe' water.

Don't walk around in bare feet – that's a great way to pick up hookworms; and treat any simple scratch or cut with care – clean it thoroughly with antiseptic and keep it clean.

Food & Water The most common health problem that afflicts travellers in India is a simple, albeit annoying, one – Delhi belly, which is basically an upset stomach and ordinary old diarrhoea.

There is usually nothing you can do to prevent the onslaught as it's just your body's way of adjusting to a change of diet, especially if your system is unused to spicy food. Sometimes, however, contaminated food or water is the cause.

The best way to tackle the upset stomach problem is to avoid getting it in the first place by being careful about what you eat and drink.

Uncooked foods are always likely to harbour more germs, but so are cooked foods that have been allowed to cool. Try to eat only freshly cooked foods and beware of places where food is left sitting around for ages, particularly if flies can park themselves on it.

Avoid salads in restaurants and you should always wash, in sterilised water, and peel any uncooked vegetables and fruit.

The main cause of upset stomachs is probably drinking water – so stick to hot (properly boiled) drinks like tea or coffee, and bottled water or soft drinks.

Carrying a water bottle and either purification tablets or iodine is a good idea. That way you should always have something safe to drink, and clean water to wash fruit etc in.

Stomach Problems As we've already said these are almost unavoidable until your system gets accustomed to its new environment.

There is no 'cure' but following certain regimens will eventually eliminate or suppress it. Avoid taking drugs at the first sign of diarrhoea or they'll be of no use to you if you get something more serious. Let the symptoms run their course naturally and heed the following advice for a few days.

Drink plenty of fluids but not milk, coffee, strong tea, soft drinks or cocoa; avoid eating anything other than dry toast or fresh yoghurt; and rest if you can. If you're still ailing after all this, then you may have dysentery so see a doctor.

Dysentery & Hepatitis If you manage to get struck by dysentery, which is not all that difficult, the most important thing is not to become dehydrated – drink plenty of fluids.

There are two types of dysentery, *bacillary* and *amoebic*. The former is the most common variety and is short, sharp and nasty but rarely persistent. It hits suddenly and lays you out with fever, nausea, cramps and diarrhoea but, as it's caused by bacteria, it responds well to antibiotics. Amoebic dysentery on the other hand is caused by amoebic parasites, is much more difficult to treat, is often persistent and is much more dangerous. It builds up more slowly, cannot be starved out and if untreated will get worse and permanently damage your intestines. You should seek medical attention.

If you catch the dreaded hepatitis then rest, good food and no alcohol is the best cure. If you get a really severe dose it's probably a good idea to go home.

Altitude Sickness The effects of altitude, particularly in Ladakh, should be understood, allowed for and taken seriously, especially if you're trekking.

Some people may not notice any

changes while others, in the first few days at high altitude, may become quite breathless and exhausted just walking from their hotel to a restaurant.

Acclimatisation is the best preventative measure for altitude problems. You are much less likely to have trouble if you spend time at Srinagar's altitude first, rather than travelling directly from the plains to Ladakh.

Although anyone may experience the effects of altitude while in Ladakh, altitude sickness is more often suffered by those trekking in the Himalaya. It occurs when you ascend too quickly beyond altitudes of 3000 to 3500 metres (Leh is at 3505 metres) without adequate time for acclimatisation.

If acclimatisation is not heeded, fluid may build up on the lungs or brain, causing death by either pulmonary or cerebral oedema.

If you're ascending beyond 3500 metres at least one week should be spent for every 1000 metres ascended. This does not rule out higher daytime climbs over passes in excess of this limit. The crucial factor is the camping height or the height at which most time is spent during the day.

It is important to distinguish between acclimatisation problems and severe altitude sickness. Poor acclimatisation can produce headaches, sleeplessness, irregular breathing, general nausea, loss of appetite or swelling of glands and fingers. In this case the remedy is simply not to go too much higher for a day or two, and rest until the symptoms subside.

The symptoms of severe altitude sickness include one or more of the following: extreme breathlessness which continues when at rest, coughing up water or body fluid, blueness around the mouth, severe nausea, pounding headaches and sometimes drowsiness and derangement. Perhaps the most important single symptom is water retention.

If you experience any of these symptoms and are passing significantly less water than usual, then there is cause for concern. In the case of altitude sickness a descent to lower altitudes is imperative. A descent of 1000 metres is usually enough to bring improvement, but try to descend as fast and far as possible to promote rapid recovery.

The dryness of the air in Ladakh and Zanskar means that it is also important to consume more fluids.

FILM & PHOTOGRAPHY

To photographically make the most of your travels you'd really need to carry two single-lens reflex cameras – one for colour film and one for black-and-white, a wide-angle lens for village profiles and monastery interiors, a macro lens for wildflowers, a telephoto for dramatic mountain shots and people close-ups, a zoom for on-the-move photography, a flash unit, light meter, tripod and at least 10 rolls of film for each day.

In practice, most of us have to settle for less and get by with an Instamatic or SLR camera with a standard 50 mm lens. If you can work a camera the best choice is a reliable SLR body with a standard and telephoto lens. A telephoto lens is ideal for non-intrusive photography as you can get a full-frame photographs of shy villagers without them noticing.

Bring a change of ultra-violet filters, extra batteries for your camera and flash, plus a blower brush and cleaning equipment. In winter, consider taking a weather-housing for your camera if you plan to ski or trek. Waterproof containers are essential to protect your film and equipment in prolonged rainy conditions.

Film is expensive in India and all colour film should be brought with you. Ration your film carefully or you are bound to run short. Some fast film (ASA 400) is desirable, especially when using a zoom or telephoto lens in low-light conditions.

Don't send film from India by post as it may never arrive at its destination. Keep it cool and secure until you get home. Film can be processed in Bombay and Delhi but the quality may be uneven.

In Ladakh remember to allow for the extreme intensity of the light at this altitude. There is little light reflection in the shadows so the range in light intensity between a sunlit mountainside and its accompanying shadow can be too great for most films to compensate for. A polarising filter will deepen the colour of the sky in the thin air of Ladakh.

In contrast to the intense outdoor light the gompas are often dark and gloomy, so you'll need a high speed film to capture the colour and atmosphere of the interiors. Flash photography doesn't pick up this ambience very well but much more importantly it does no good to the paints and fabrics that have often not been exposed to direct light for hundreds of years. Using a flash there is an act of vandalism.

BOOKS

Publishers have recognised the growing interest in the region and you can find a wide range of books on the subject. Delhi's Connaught Place has India's best bookstores, but you can probably find some of these titles in Leh or one of the several bookstores in Srinagar.

There are many older books on Kashmir and Ladakh worth searching out in libraries and a number of recently published coffee table books on these picturesque regions.

General

Beautiful Valleys of Kashmir & Ladakh, Samsar Chand Kaul (Utpal Publications, Srinagar 1979). First published in 1942 and written by a teacher of natural history at the Church Missionary School in Srinagar, this book takes a genteel but detailed look at the plants, birds and animals of Kashmir through a series of expeditions to most parts of the Vale.

Ladakh, Heinrich Harrer (Penguin, London 1980). One of a number of coffee table books on Ladakh which, though not the best, is a good introduction.

An Area of Darkness, V S Naipaul (Penguin, London). Born in Trinidad of Indian descent, Naipaul writes of India's unsuccessful search for a new purpose and meaning for its civilisation. This book includes a lengthy section on Kashmir and its people and an account of the Amarnath trek.

A Journey in Ladakh, Andrew Harvey (Jonothan Cape, London, 1983). An interesting narrative that looks at various aspects of life in Ladakh through the eyes of an interested traveller.

Zanskar – The Hidden Kingdom, Michael Peissel (Collins & Harvill Press, London, 1979). An interesting account of a trek through Zanskar shortly after it was reopened to foreign tourists.

A Portrait of India by Ved Mehta (Penguin, London, 1986). The author's odyssey through modern India brings this enigmatic country into focus for the western eye.

Trespassers on the Roof of the World, Peter Hopkirk (Oxford University Press, Oxford 1983).

This is Kashmir, P Gervis (Universal Publications, Delhi, 1974).

Kashmir, F Brunel (Runca & Co Delhi, 1979).

Ladakh – The Crossroad of High Asia, Janet Rizbi.

History

A History of India, Romila Thapar and Percival Spear (Pelican). A two volume history in handy paperback. The first book covers the years from about 1000 BC to the coming of the Moghuls in the 16th century AD; and the second follows the rise and fall of the Moghuls through to India since independence.

Freedom at Midnight, Larry Collins and Dominique Lapieree (Bell Books/Vikas Publishing, Delhi). This highly readable book about India's rocky path to independence has an interesting description of the stormy events in Kashmir at that time.

Plain Tales from the Raj, edited by Charles Allen (Futura Publications, London). A delightful book, derived from the equally delightful radio series of the same name. It consists of a series of interviews with people who took part in British India on both sides of the table. It's full of fascinating insights into life during the Raj era.

Kashmir, Younghusband (reprint 1909).
Travels in Kashmir, Ladakh & Skardu, Vigre (reprint 1842).
Jummoo & Kashmir Territories, Frederic Drew (1875).
Northern Barrier of India, Frederic Drew (1877).
West Himalaya & Tibet, Thompson (reprint 1852).
Cultural History of Ladakh Vol I & II (Vikas, Delhi, 1977 & 1980).

Travel & Trekking Guides

India – A Travel Survival Kit (Lonely Planet, Hawthorn, 1986). The definitive guide to India covers the history, people and religions of this extraordinary country, as well as detailed, regularly updated info on all aspects of travel. If you want to know where to stay and eat, how to get there and out again, how to deal with Indian red tape and even where to find the gurus, then this is the only book you'll need.

Trekking in the Indian Himalaya by Garry Weare (Lonely Planet, Hawthorn) From the beautiful pastures of Himachal Pradesh or the spectacular gorges of Zanskar to the high altitude desert of Ladakh this guide tells you how to prepare for a trek in the Himalaya, with day-by-day route descriptions and detailed maps.

Guide to Kashmir, Ladakh & Skardu, Arthur Neve (Srinagar).

Trekkers' Guide to the Himalaya & Karakoram, Hugh Swift (Sierra Club Books, San Francisco 1982, and Hodder & Stoughton, London 1982).

The Himalayas, Playground of the Gods, Captain Mohan Kolhi (Vikas, Delhi 1983).

TREKKING

Trekking in the Indian Himalaya is still a relatively low-key activity, at least compared to Nepal. While Kashmir has been a haven for trekkers since the early days of the British Raj, Ladakh and Zanskar are comparatively untouched, although this is changing. The main routes are: from Kargil to the Pensi La – 150 km; from the Pensi La to Padum – 90 km; from Padum to Lamayuru – 125 km; and from Lamayuru to Leh – another 125 km. These days hundreds of trekkers follow even the least travelled of them.

If you want to explore Kashmir on an organised tour, there are several adventure travel companies to choose from. The Indian tourist offices in Europe, the UK, the USA and Australia have a list of bona fide organisations. It is, however, not easy deciding which to choose when sifting through a pile of brochures all claiming to provide the best deal.

When considering your options, keep in mind the adventure travel company's experience in handling trips to India, the leaders employed, the equipment used, the type of food and accommodation provided, its medical and safety precautions, specialist interests and the pre-trip organisation. Look for competent, knowledgeable office staff and a good preparation package of local information, packing list, etc. Ultimately, any adventure travel company is only as good as its local ground agent.

Srinagar does not have a large number of trekking agencies and it's wise to be wary of local trekking operators in Kashmir. As with carpetweavers and papier mache manufacturers, every houseboat owner seems to have a brother in the trekking business but, by no means, are all of them what they claim to be. Be prepared for constant approaches from your houseboat man, *shikara-wallah* and the many other touts who dog your path.

As with any other transaction here, organising a trek carries a big risk of being overcharged or of being given inefficient equipment, food and guides. This warning cannot be over-emphasised. Even dealing directly with the local trekking agents does not guarantee a successful trek. You need to ask a lot of questions and compare a few agents before parting with any money. One place where you can be sure of receiving honest, friendly and conscientious assistance is Choomti Trekkers, Houseboat King's Marina No 67, opposite the GPO, The Bund, Srinagar 1900.

If possible, arrive in Kashmir fully equipped for trekking as it is not easy to rent or buy equipment in Srinagar. Also, porters are not so readily found in Kashmir and are more expensive than in Nepal. Pack ponies are, however, widely used in Kashmir and can be hired from any of the main hill stations.

Much of the trekking in Kashmir is through uninhabited areas. Although there are routes in Kashmir where you can stay in rest houses or dak bungalows, and in Zanskar and Ladakh it is often possible to stay in monasteries, you generally must be fairly self-sufficient in terms of food and shelter.

It has become the custom for trekkers to be charged by locals for camping overnight in various parts of the region. Those who refuse to pay risk having their tents slashed and equipment stolen before the night is over.

Don't confuse trekking with mountaineering. Although you may reach considerable heights, trekking basically means following the walking tracks used by local people in places where there are no vehicle roads.

For more information on trekking see the Lonely Planet guide *Trekking in the Indian Himalaya*.

Physical Requirements

You should be in reasonably good physical condition, particularly for the high altitudes you may encounter. Trekking involves a lot of up and down walking. Although some Kashmir treks are relatively easy going, the Zanskar and Ladakh treks are generally hard work. Some are very strenuous, with ascents to 5000-metre passes followed by descents to 3500-metre

valleys, all in the same day. The paths are sometimes rough and always hard on shoes and boots.

Organising a Trek

If you plan to organise your own trek in Kashmir there are certain basic rules to remember:

1 Know where you want to go and the likely obstacles along the route.
2 Ensure that you have good and sufficient equipment.
3 Decide on a price with porters and pony men before loading your gear on their backs.
4 Make it clear whether you expect them to feed and house themselves or whether this is your responsibility.
5 Ask whether you will find wood for cooking fires and water along the way, or whether you will need to take fuel and a stove and sufficient water. In most areas of Ladakh there is no wood.

Equipment

You need good walking shoes, warm clothing (down gear for very high altitudes), a good quality sleeping bag, a comfortable pack, sunglasses, food and medical equipment. A stove and fuel is necessary if you are trekking in a region where firewood or other fuel is not available. Even if you are just going on day walks it's wise to be prepared for changeable weather and carry spare clothing. More detailed suggestions can be found in the Zanskar trekking section of this book or in the Lonely Planet trekking guides.

Food

In Kashmir, and more particularly in Zanskar and Ladakh, it is not usual to obtain food along the trekking routes, so you must carry adequate supplies. Srinagar is the best place to do your pre-trek outfitting, or Manali if you're trekking up into Zanskar from the south. Although supplies are also available in

Kargil and Leh, and to a lesser extent in Padum, the choice will be much less and the costs much higher.

Tinned or packaged food suitable for carrying on treks is generally more expensive in India than in the west. During summer you should be able to supplement your supplies with potatoes, onions, peas, lentils, glucose biscuits, tea and tsampa (cakes made from roasted barley meal and salt water) in all but the smallest villages, but don't count on it.

The mountains of Kashmir are mostly heavily forested but the vegetation thins out as you approach the snow line. You should not expect to find wood at every camp. In many places the local villagers and nomadic herders have burned everything within easy walking distance. In Ladakh and Zanskar the lack of vegetation makes it often impossible to cook on a fire, so you need a kerosene stove and kerosene in a strong, leakproof (preferably metal) container.

Cooking on a fire at high altitude is difficult even when wood is available. Due to the shortage of oxygen, at 3500 metres even paper only smoulders unless there is a wind to fan it. One trekker wrote to recommend a petrol (gasoline) stove in preference to a kerosene one as, he wrote, petrol is more readily available than kerosene in India, it burns hotter and better at high altitude, and it's cleaner.

Remember that the high altitudes in Zanskar and Ladakh result in a much lower boiling point for water – in Leh water will boil at around 75°C. Although bulky to carry, a pressure cooker is very useful, particularly if you insist on cooking rice or lentils.

In some areas of Ladakh you will have to carry water for overnight stops as the only water supply in summer may be the run-off from melting snow. Some of the passes are also very dry and the long climb to a pass summit can be very thirsty work.

Accommodation

Although a tent is essential there are many government rest houses or dak bungalows along trekking routes in Kashmir. These were originally built by the considerate British and are now maintained and added to by the J&K Government. Bookings for these may be made at the Tourist Reception Centre in Srinagar and, although not always the case, the chowkidhar in charge is obliged to give preference to those with bookings even though he may not know they are going to arrive. The Government of India trekking maps of Kashmir and Ladakh indicate the locations of these rest houses.

Ladakh and Zanskar have virtually none of these amenities, except at towns along the Srinagar-Leh road. However, tourism has become so all-pervading in the past few years that even the smallest village on a trekking route will have what its owner calls a hotel and restaurant, or at least a room in a house which trekkers may rent.

Often you can get a room in a gompa (monastery) although there are restrictions in certain gompas which you should be aware of. Some gompas have set up hotels to cater for tourists. Generally this sort of accommodation will consist of little more than a bare room. So a tent is still a virtual necessity for trekking in Ladakh since there will be times, such as on long walks over mountain passes, where your night stop will be far from any village or habitation.

Routes & Maps

Some of the main treks are described in the sections on Kashmir, Ladakh and Zanskar. Many of these treks go from one region into the next.

Good trekking maps are virtually impossible to obtain in Kashmir. The J&K Tourist Office sell a two-sheet Trekking Route Map of Jammu & Kashmir for Rs 7 a sheet. Sheet One covers the Vale of Kashmir, Pahalgam, Anantnag and the Great Himalaya but very little north of the Leh-Srinagar road. Sheet Two covers the Zanskar region to just south of Padum and the Indus valley to Leh, but no further. Neither map includes Kargil. Both show the locations of rest houses and dak bungalows, gompas and mosques, roads and some trekking routes, rivers and bridges, post offices, and give altitudes in metres. With the changes through development and those caused by the extremes of climate, the accuracy of any map must be doubted.

The Kashmir Bookshop on the Bund in Srinagar sells a reasonable Swiss map of Kashmir and Ladakh but it is not detailed enough for exploratory trekkers. For the serious trekker 1:250,000 satellite photographs of the region can be obtained from the EROS Data Centre, Sioux Falls, South Dakota 57198, USA, but these are expensive.

A problem with any map or other information on trekking in this area is the widely varying ways of spelling place names and in some cases variations in the name itself. This book tries to follow the most commonly used spellings. No map of this region should be entirely trusted, however. The J&K Tourist Office has a small brochure titled *Trekking in Jammu & Kashmir* which may provide some useful information.

Permission

Although there is no system of trekking permits, there are limitations on where you may trek. In particular you are constrained by the security zone requirements that you do not go more than a mile north of the Zoji La-Kargil-Leh road and a similar restriction along the Leh-Manali road. This limits Zanskar and Ladakh trekking to the Suru, Zanskar and Kishtwar valleys. For trekking in other areas permission must be obtained from the Ministry of Home Affairs, Government of India, New Delhi.

Snow Bridges

These are a particular hazard of Kashmiri trekking, especially during the spring-summer melt. In many places rivers are completely covered by snow and ice during the winter, while the rivers continue to flow underneath. During the thaw this cover often melts to form isolated 'bridges' which trekkers can sometimes cross, but take care. If you fall through a snow bridge the drop may be less than a metre and only result in wet feet but, if you're truly unlucky, it may be a long, fatal fall.

There are some well-known snow bridges which appear every year. Enquire about which ones are reliable.

Rivers

Particularly in Zanskar there are often unbridged rivers which have to be crossed. These must be treated with great caution as the water may be deep and rapid and the stones on the bottom may be slippery. Often the river may be shallower and the flow less rapid early in the morning than later in the day, when the sun has melted more snow. Rivers can vary widely from one time of year to another and from year to year, depending on how much snow there has been in winter and how fast it has melted in summer.

Health & Medicine

If you're going on an organised trek the organisers will give you a list of the necessary immunisations and will probably require that you complete a medical examination before departing (see the section on Health in this chapter). Maintaining your health while trekking is principally a matter of taking care in what you eat and drink, being careful about personal hygiene and not over-taxing yourself or eating too little.

Always ensure that drinking water has been boiled or sterilised, although at the altitudes reached in Ladakh and Zanskar boiling alone will not ensure sterilisation.

Alternatively, puritabs and/or iodine will kill most bacteria in drinking water. Iodine, which can be difficult to find in India, should be used carefully. Properly used as a water purifier it's quite safe, but as a concentrate it's a dangerous poison.

While snow or immediate snow-melt is comparatively safe for drinking, it contains very few minerals so drinking it over a period of time will deplete your body supply.

Getting There

Getting to Kashmir is a two-part operation as you must first get to India. The following sections detail air fares to India from various places. To get to Kashmir from within India see the final section on internal transport.

AIR
From the UK

London is a centre for many cheap ticket specialists or 'bucket shops'. Two reliable shops are Trailfinders at 46 Earls Court Rd, London W8; and STA Travel at 74 Old Brompton Rd, London SW7 or 117 Euston Rd, London NW1.

You can also check the travel page ads in *The Times, Business Traveller* and the weekly 'what's on' magazines *Time Out* or *City Limits*; or check the giveaway paper *LAW – London's Australasian Weekly*.

One way fares from London to Bombay or Delhi are around £240 and return fares are £380.

From the USA

From the west coast of the States the cheapest return fares to India are around US$1200. Another way of getting there would be to fly to Hong Kong and tag on a ticket from there. Hong Kong costs about US$350 one way from San Francisco or Los Angeles.

From the east coast you can find one-way tickets to Bombay or Delhi for around US$550. An alternative way of getting there from New York would be to fly to London and pick up a cheap fare from there.

Check the Sunday travel sections of papers like the *New York Times, San Francisco Chronicle/Examiner* or *Los Angeles Times* for adverts for cheap fares. Good low-cost agents include the student travel chains STA or CIEE.

From Canada

Fares from Canada are very similar to those from the States. From Vancouver, the route and prices are similar to those from the US west coast, with the option of going via Hong Kong. From Toronto, fares to New Delhi/Bombay range from C$1175 to C$1200 return.

From Australia & New Zealand

Advance-purchase return fares from Melbourne of Sydney to India range from A$1080 to A$1215 depending on the season. The low travel period is March to September; peak is October to February. In Australia, fares are lower from Darwin or Perth than they are from the east coast.

The basic non-seasonal fares from Auckland, New Zealand to Delhi via Bangkok are NZ$720 one way and NZ$1420 return. You may be able to find a better deal by shopping around or checking travel page ads in the daily papers.

Round the World Fares

RTW fares have become all the rage in the past few years. An RTW ticket usually means two or more airlines have joined together to market a ticket which takes you round the world on their combined routes. RTW tickets are also put together by travel agents who simply make the best use of a variety of airlines on the particular route you wish to take around the world.

RTW tickets typically cost from around US$1200 or £700 to US$2500 or £1430 depending on the route or hemisphere. For example an RTW ticket from London to Toronto or Vancouver and on through Honolulu/Fiji/Sydney/Bangkok/Delhi and back to London costs around £850 (US$1500).

OVERLAND
From Europe

The classic way of getting to India has always been overland, but sadly the events in Iran and Afghanistan have turned what was a stream of people into a trickle. In the good old days you could travel easily and cheaply by bus or train from Istanbul to Bombay and combine both Iran and Afghanistan on your itinerary.

At present, it is only possible to travel overland from Turkey through Iran to Pakistan – or rather it is possible if you don't hold an American, South African or Israeli passport.

For everyone else, the process of getting an Iranian visa can be tedious, and arbitrary refusals are not unknown, but it is possible. If you are forced to change money at the border and use the official Iranian exchange rate Iran is also an expensive proposition, although those who play the black market will still find it very cheap.

Overland tour companies have continued to take their buses and trucks safely through Iran, virtually without any interruption from the revolutions and wars. The region is obviously volatile however, so you should gather up-to-date information before you set out and even then you will have to be prepared for last-minute setbacks to your plans. The alternative is to fly from India or Pakistan to Jordan, one of the Gulf states or Turkey.

For more information see Lonely Planet's *West Asia on a shoestring* which covers the overland route in detail.

Through South-East Asia

In contrast to the difficulties of the route from Europe, the South-East Asia overland trip is still wide open and as popular as ever.

From Australia the first step is to Indonesia – usually Bali. From Bali, you head north through Java to Jakarta, where you either take a ship or plane to Singapore or continue north through Sumatra and then cross to Penang in Malaysia. After travelling around Malaysia you can again take to the sea or air to get from Penang to Madras in India or, more popularly, you can continue north to Thailand and eventually fly out from Bangkok to India, preferably via Burma.

Refer to Lonely Planet's definitive *South-East Asia on a Shoestring* for the full overland story. Other LP guides covering this route include the travel survival kits to Bali & Lombok; Indonesia; Malaysia, Singapore & Brunei; Thailand; and India.

CHEAP TICKETS IN INDIA

Although you can also get cheap tickets in Bombay and Calcutta, it is in Delhi that the real wheeling and dealing goes on. There are countless 'bucket shops' around Connaught Place, but enquire with fellow travellers about their current trustworthiness!

With most things in India almost anything is possible but nothing is simple. To get the cheap tickets you will have to pay the full official fare through a bank. This is arranged by the agent who gets you a bank form stating what the official fare is, you pay the bank, the bank pays the agent. You then receive a refund from the agent – in rupees!

Because of the refund deal, it is wise either to buy your ticket far enough ahead that you can use up those rupees, or have plenty of bank exchange certificates in hand in order to change the rupees back before you leave. This also applies to credit card purchases.

Some typical fares from India are: Delhi to Australia for about Rs 6000 to Rs 7000; and Delhi to various European capitals for about Rs 4500 with Aeroflot, Rs 4300 with LOT, and Rs 4000 with Kuwait Airways, Syrian Arab Airways or Iraqi Airways.

Officially Aeroflot is not allowed to sell tickets in India. In fact they do and the tickets are stamped as having been issued in Moscow or Singapore. You can fly to Europe with nice airlines like Thai International for Rs 4750; while a Delhi/Hong Kong/Vancouver and down to the US west coast (San Francisco or Los Angeles) will cost around Rs 6200.

AIRPORT TAX

India now has one of the highest airport taxes in the world for international flights. For flights to neighbouring countries (Pakistan, Sri Lanka, Bangladesh, Nepal) it's Rs 50 but to more distant countries it's a hefty Rs 100. The method of collecting tax varies but generally you have to pay *before* you check in, so look out for an airport tax counter as you enter the check-in area.

GETTING TO JAMMU & KASHMIR
Air

You can fly direct to Srinagar from Delhi or via Jammu and other intermediate points. Most people flying to Leh in Ladakh will fly from Srinagar but you can also fly there from Chandigarh in Haryana or from Delhi.

Air fares to Srinagar cost about Rs 715 from New Delhi, Rs 610 from Chandigarh, Rs 415 from Amritsar and Rs 240 from Jammu. To Leh it costs around Rs 360 from Srinagar, 477 from Chandigarh, Rs 750 from Delhi via Chandigarh and Rs 900 from Delhi via Srinagar. (See the Srinagar and Ladakh Getting There & Away sections.)

Flying straight to Leh from Delhi is not a very good idea. Pausing first in Srinagar gives you some altitude acclimatisation whereas Delhi-Leh takes you straight from the plains, close to sea level, to the thin air of the Himalaya.

Indian Airlines finally has a computerised booking system in operation at all the larger and many of the smaller stations, making air travel in India much simpler. They previously operated with a booking procedure more suitable for a Victorian era railway system than a modern air service. Computers have considerably shortened the 'chance list', as the waiting list was more appropriately called, but it's still best to book well ahead if you can. Wait till you get to India though as Indian Airlines fares within the country are usually cheaper than the same flights bought overseas.

Flying Indian Airlines has a few other quirks and curiosities. One is that no-shows or last-minute cancellations get rough treatment. If you miss your flight you can throw the ticket away, you won't be able to use it again. Indian Airlines treat lost tickets with equal compassion. If your ticket is stolen you'd better have a good travel insurance policy because Indian Airlines won't reissue it. Keep a close eye on your bags too. Make sure they're properly tagged and that after they leave your control they start heading towards the plane.

Bus

In addition to the Government services there are countless private operators with tourist buses to Jammu & Kashmir, mainly from Delhi, but also from Chandigarh and the various Himachel Pradesh hill stations. These can vary in efficiency, quality and price so look around before buying a ticket.

Get a seat as far forward on the bus as possible for a less bumpy ride, take drinking water and, if you're fussy about roadside eateries, some food too.

J&K Government Roadways (tel 224559) operate from the large Inter-state Bus Terminal at Kashmiri Gate, north of Delhi Railway Station in Old Delhi. Bookings can be made from 10 am to 5 pm for air-con buses. Around Connaught Place and Janpath you will find the private sector – or it will find you.

Some buses go all the way to Srinagar (deluxe only, around Rs 250, 30 hours) but most go to Jammu (deluxe Rs 60, B class Rs 30). Very popular with Indian tourists, some of the deluxe buses show videos which are usually Hindi favourites played very loudly on inadequate equipment.

You are well advised to avoid these video buses as the high noise level makes sleep virtually impossible, resulting in a very long, uncomfortable journey.

Train

Most train travellers use the Delhi-Jammu route, but it is possible to connect with Jammu from elsewhere, notably Pathankot (for Dalhousie) and Joginder Nagar (for the Kulu Valley). Delhi is a main rail centre and an excellent place to make bookings. There is a special foreign tourist booking office in New Delhi station. This is a haven of calm, quiet efficiency where you can buy tickets and make reservations all in one go for 1st and 2nd class. They also sell Indrail passes and give advice on rail travel.

Remember that there are two main train stations in Delhi – Delhi Station in Old Delhi and New Delhi Station at the northern end of New Delhi, more or less on the Old Delhi border. Check which one your train departs from. For Delhi station you should allow plenty of time to wind your way through the traffic snarls of Old Delhi. New Delhi Station is a lot closer to Connaught Place, making it easier to reach.

There are about four trains a day operating the Delhi to Jammu run. Jammu Tawi is the station you want; it's the final stop and stands across the river from the city. The 724 km trip takes nine to 13 hours, usually overnight, and costs Rs 59 in 2nd class, Rs 244 in 1st.

Take special care on the train from Delhi to Jammu. This is a tourist train – for Indians and foreigners – and pickpockets and snatch thieves work overtime on this route. They're particularly prevalent at the Delhi end, just as the train departs. One routine is to create a last-minute disturbance and before you know it your bag has disappeared through the window at the same instant that the train pulls out from the station.

Road

Until recently the land route into the state was straightforward – to Jammu by road or train, then to Srinagar by road only. Recently, however, the road linking Leh with Manali in Himachel Pradesh was opened to tourist traffic allowing more of a choice.

Getting Around

The actual process of travelling or trekking in Kashmir, Ladakh and Zanskar definitely has its risks and rewards. Getting around the region's high passes, pristine lakes and tortuous roads involves a bit of planning and a lot of patience.

While it's easy to take a relaxing boat journey on the serene and beautiful lakes of Srinagar or a leisurely bicycle ride around Kashmir's Moghul gardens, you must be more than ready for nerve-wracking travel when you hit the precipitous roads of Ladakh or contemplate the suspension bridges of Zanskar.

BUS

India's bus system is extensive and well-developed and in most cases extends from the railway system – fanning out from the railhead station – or goes where the trains do not or, as in Kashmir, cannot go.

There is generally a state-operated bus company in each state but in some, including Jammu & Kashmir, this is backed up by privately run buses which provides a choice of buses on the main routes. In J&K for instance there are A and B class buses, and even deluxe and air-con buses on the Jammu to Srinagar run.

Indian buses vary widely from state to state, although you can make the general observation that travel by bus is crowded, cramped, slow and none too comfortable. You don't have to be very tall to spend a lot of time with your knees up under your chin!

Comfort and speed aside, the bus trip from Srinagar to Leh is an unforgettable experience. It takes two days, with an overnight stop in Kargil, if you're lucky. The hairpin bends and sheer drops into valleys far, far below have to be seen to be believed! The route crosses the 'gateway' from Kashmir to Ladakh at the Zoji La pass and at Kargil travellers have the option to continue to Leh or turn south and trek or take a truck into Zanskar, over the Pensi La to Padum.

Apart from the long haul trips, such as Jammu to Srinagar and Srinagar to Leh, buses are also useful for day trips around Jammu and Srinagar. In Leh and the Indus valley region, local buses provide transport to various monasteries and small towns.

For short and long distance travel in Srinagar, the Jammu & Kashmir Road Transport Corporation has buses going from the Tourist Reception Centre.

TRUCK

Besides jeeps, trucks are the only means of getting into the Zanskar valley from Kargil, where they can be hired.

They're also an alternative to buses for the journey between Kashmir and Ladakh. It's often possible to arrange a ride on a truck to Leh in either Srinagar, Sonamarg or even Kargil. Sonamarg is the last major place in Kashmir, shortly before you climb up over the Zoji La pass and enter Ladakh. (Buses regularly make the 84 km, three or four hour trip from Srinagar to Sonamarg.)

Trucks tend to be more dangerous on the mountain roads than buses and local authorities try to discourage travellers from taking them, but it is possible. You'll need to negotiate transport and food costs.

TAXI & JEEP

As an alternative to buses in Ladakh and the Kashmir Valley, renting a jeep or taxi with a group of people provides more freedom to explore without the hassles of delays and crowds. Taxis and jeeps will cost more, but prices can be negotiated before setting out. Jeeps are also able to get to areas that buses cannot reach, especially along the high passes.

BICYCLE

Although there are soaring mountains all around Srinagar the city itself is surprisingly flat and easy to get around on a bicycle. Renting bikes is no problem and is extremely economical. You may, however, have to try a few out before you find one that actually goes in the direction you point it and stops when you use the brakes. (See the Srinagar section for more info.)

For covering long distances, mountain bikes or all-terrain bikes have made an impact on Himalayan roads in recent years and may be an option to bus and truck travel, if you're willing to risk it!

SHIKARA

These long, graceful boats which ply the waters of Srinagar's lakes are probably the best known transport in Kashmir. They're used as a means of transporting goods and people to and from houseboats, and for longer tours of the lakes. They are unique to the Kashmir valley and their varied uses and sheer number are an essential ingredient to the character of this region. (See the Srinagar section.)

TREKKING

Although Kashmir, Ladakh & Zanskar do not have the trekking facilities and reputation of Nepal, the opportunities are there and safe trekking routes have already been established.

Many of the peaks of Ladakh have never been climbed and some of the new trekking routes pass through wild and virtually unexplored terrain. It is even possible to trek from the state of Himachal Pradesh to the Zanskar valley and from there into Ladakh.

Some of the regions most popular trekking routes are described in the Trekking chapters of this book. For more specialised information and details on other treks refer to Lonely Planet's *Trekking in the Indian Himalaya*.

Jammu

Jammu, the second largest town in the state of Jammu and Kashmir, has a population of just under 200,000. It's 580 km from Delhi and 290 km from Srinagar on the south-eastern slopes of the Siwalik Range.

The old city of Jammu is perched on a hilltop beside the Tawi River. A new town sprawls away from the hillside and extends for some distance across the other side of the river.

In winter Jammu becomes the headquarters of the J&K administration (as it has done since the time of the Dogra rulers) and many Kashmiris move there then because the temperature does not drop below 5°C.

Summer can be uncomfortably hot (over 40°C) due to the city's low altitude (300 metres), and the humid, unpleasant conditions also bring on plagues of gnats.

You can hear Hindi, Kashmiri, English, Urdu, Punjabi and Dogri spoken in Jammu. Despite its mix of cultures, languages and religions the city is not of great interest to tourists. Most travellers tend to use it as an overnight stop on the way to or from Kashmir. Unless you fly you will almost certainly pass through Jammu on your way to Kashmir.

History

Legend has it that the city was founded by Jamboo Loochen about three thousand years ago. The raja was hunting in the area, away from his capital city of Bahu, when he came across a lion and a goat drinking from the same pond. The Shivadawala Shrine now stands on this

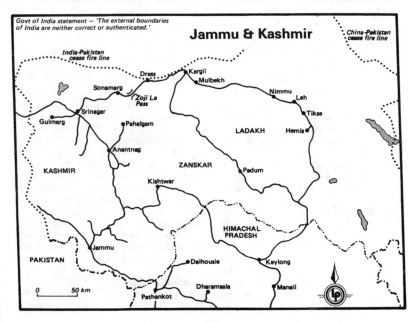

Govt of India statement — 'The external boundaries of India are neither correct or authenticated.'

Jammu & Kashmir

China-Pakistan cease fire line

India-Pakistan cease fire line

Drass · Kargil
Mulbekh
Sonamarg
Nimmu · Leh
Zoji La Pass
Srinagar · Tikse
Gulmarg · Pahalgam
LADAKH · Hemis
Anantnag
ZANSKAR
KASHMIR · Padum
Kishtwar
HIMACHAL PRADESH
Jammu
PAKISTAN · Dalhousie · Keylong
0 50 km
Dharamsala · Manali
Pathankot

35

spot in the city. Jammu is known as 'the city of temples' because of its many shrines with soaring golden *shikhars*, or spires.

The recorded history of Jammu begins from the time of the Dogra rulers in the early 19th century, although there are many other shrines and temples in and around the city that date from earlier years.

In 1846, at the conclusion of the first Sikh war, the treaties of Lahore and Amritsar resulted in the Dogra ruler of Jammu being made Maharaja of an ill-defined Himalayan kingdom, 'to the eastward of the river Indus and westward of the river Ravi'.

The British created this kingdom as part of a complex political buffer zone between their Indian empire and China and Russia. It was the lack of definition of this state – the forerunner of Jammu and Kashmir – that caused the continuing disputes with Russia and China over territory.

For the Maharaja Gulab Singh, the appointed head of state, the treaty concluded almost 25 years of fighting and negotiation with the small hill tribes along the northern border of the Sikh empire, centred on the Punjab. The region remained under Dogra rule until the partition of India in 1947 when Hari Singh, the then Maharaja of Kashmir, decided that it would remain part of India instead of joining Pakistan, and the state of Jammu and Kashmir was born.

The present heir to the Dogra title, Karan Singh, was Union Minister for Tourism in the 1970 Congress Government of India, and still plays an active role in the politics of J&K. (For more details on the history of J&K see the Kashmir chapter.)

Orientation

In the old city on the hilltop you'll find most of the hotels, the Tourist Reception Centre and the tourist office where upper-class buses depart for Kashmir.

Down beside the hill is the station for buses to other parts of northern India and lower-class buses to Srinagar.

Several kms away across the river is the new town of Jammu Tawi and the railway station where you'll find a second Tourist Reception Centre.

Information

The Government of India Tourist Office (tel 5121) on Gulab Bhavan and the J&K Tourist Reception Centre (tel 5324) on Vir Marg are the standard reference centres. They're not the best tourist information places in India and obtaining information is difficult and requires patience. The information they do have is usually for people heading north into Kashmir as they've got little to tell you if you're travelling south.

Both offices are open from 9 am to 5 pm (closed for lunch) which is useless for many visitors to Jammu who generally arrive late in the afternoon! The tourist office has a branch at the railway station (tel 8803) which may be open when your train from Delhi arrives in the early morning.

The post office is on Pacca Danga.

Raghunath Temple

In the centre of the city, only a short stroll from the Tourist Reception Centre, this is the largest temple complex in northern India. Construction of the temple began in 1835, under Maharaja Gulab Singh, the founder of the present city of Jammu. The Purani Mandi, like the main complex dedicated to Lord Rama, was built in 1888 by Maharaja Ranbir Singh's wife. The smaller temples surrounding the courtyard are dedicated to various gods and goddesses who feature in the *Ramayana*. The Raghunath Sanskrit Library is a vast storehouse containing thousands of rare and ancient manuscripts.

Rambireswar Temple

Just across the road from the Dogra Art Gallery, this Shiva temple was built in

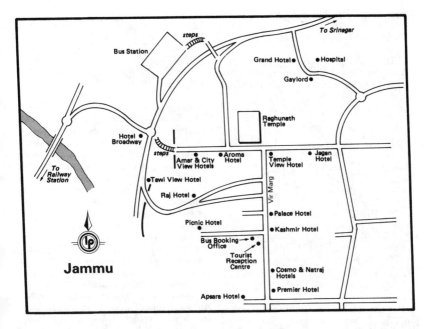

Jammu

1883 by Maharaja Ranbir Singh and features numerous crystal Shiva lingams and 11 larger black stone ones as well as the tallest shikhar in the city.

Old Secretariat
The former palace of the Dogra rulers, the Old Secretariat is near the centre of town. It's a huge complex of mansions with several styles of architecture. Its walls and ceilings are adorned with intricate paintings of flowers, creepers, birds and other decorations.

Dogra Art Gallery
The collection includes more than 500 paintings of the Basohli, Jammu and Kangra schools. The Basohli-style miniature paintings are of particular importance and interest. There are numerous other charming items of the old Dogra arts, including hundreds of exotic

and exquisite Bahara miniatures. The gallery also houses a collection of sculptures, terracotta pieces, murals, weapons and illustrated manuscripts.

The gallery is in the Gandhi Bhavan by the New Secretariat. It is open from 7.30 am to 1 pm in summer and from 11 am to 5 pm in winter but closed on Mondays. Admission is free.

Bahu Fort
Clinging to a rock face on the opposite bank of the Tawi River, the huge fort is about four km from the centre. Although it is said to date back to Jammu's legendary founder, Jamboo Loochen, the present structure was built by the Dogras. An old and highly esteemed temple to the goddess Kali can be seen inside the fort. Crowds of worshippers go there on Tuesdays and Sundays.

Opposite Bahu Fort on another hilltop is a consecrated spot dedicated to Maha

Maya, a Jammu heroine who died fighting invaders.

Amar Mahal Palace

Built in the last century for Raja Amar Singh, the palace is a curious example of French architecture. It's on a hillock overlooking the Tawi River and commands an excellent view of the city and its surroundings. The palace museum has a family portrait gallery, a rich library and an important collection of paintings of the Pahari school. It's worth a visit.

The museum is open from 5 to 7 pm daily and from 8 am to noon on Sundays. It is just off the Srinagar road on the northern outskirts of town.

Rambir Canal

This canal, about two km from the city, is a favourite place for a stroll. The canal leaves the Chenab at Akhnoor, 32 km from Jammu and provides electricity and irrigation.

Places to Stay

If you're en route to Srinagar and arrive in Jammu by train (as most people do) then you have two choices: you can keep going straight to Srinagar or stay overnight in Jammu.

If you choose the first option you have to take one of the buses which wait at the railway station for the arrival of the trains. (See the following Getting There section.) If these buses don't leave Jammu early enough they usually stop for the night at Banihal, below the Jawarhar Tunnel, and continue on to Srinagar the following day. Accommodation in Banihal is generally in the Tourist Lodge and is very basic – three large dormitories without beds, hot water and sometimes electricity.

The second choice is to stay overnight in Jammu and take a bus to Srinagar first thing the next morning. These early buses make it to Srinagar in one day.

If you decide to stay overnight then it's vital to first find yourself a room and then book a ticket on the bus. Don't hang about

as competition for both will be fierce during the tourist season.

If you're coming from Srinagar it's even more necessary to rush to find a room as the bus arrives late in the day when spare rooms may be at a premium.

Places to Stay – bottom end

The Tawi View Hotel (tel 47301), near Maheshi Gate, is undoubtedly the best of the bunch and very popular with travellers. Doubles with bath are Rs 35 and the manager is friendly and helpful. Opposite the Tourist Reception Centre on Vir Marg, the Tourist Home Hotel is similarly priced and equipped. It's a bit noisy but convenient.

Another simple but clean place is the Hotel Kashmir, Vir Marg, where bathless doubles are Rs 35. There are many other budget hotels and not much to choose between them. It's usually a question of which have rooms available.

Reasonable places include the Hotel Aroma, Gumat Bazaar (doubles Rs 25 or Rs 35 with attached bath), Hotel Raj (bathless doubles Rs 22) or the Hotel Aryabhat (overpriced and grubby – doubles Rs 25 or Rs 45 with bath). The Hotel Broadway (tel 43636) on Gumat Chowk has a variety of rooms with and without attached bath for Rs 35 to Rs 100.

At the railway station, across the Tawi River and several km from the centre, is Jammu's second Tourist Reception Centre (tel 8803) with doubles from Rs 25 to Rs 50 with air-con. There are also dorm beds but the dormitory is totally bare and best avoided. The station also has Retiring Rooms at Rs 50 a double or Rs 80 with air-con, and dorm beds at Rs 12. The bus station is close to the centre and has rather decrepit Retiring Rooms with doubles at Rs 30 and Rs 5 for dorm beds.

Places to Stay – middle

One of the best places is the Hotel Jagan (tel 42402), Raghunath Bazaar, which also has an air-con restaurant. It's spotlessly clean, pleasantly decorated and has singles/doubles at Rs 45/60, or double rooms with air-con for Rs 100 to Rs 125.

Another popular mid-range hotel is the 128-room *Tourist Reception Centre* (tel 5421) on Vir Marg. Doubles range from Rs 50 (D Block), Rs 55 (C and H Block) to Rs 60 (A Block). There are also some air-cooled doubles at Rs 80. All the rooms have attached bathrooms and there is a restaurant. There's also a grim dormitory which should be avoided no matter how tight your budget. You're generally restricted to a maximum of two nights' stay here.

Across Vir Marg from the Tourist Reception Centre the *Premier Hotel* is much improved and one of the best, cleanest and newest hotels near the downtown area. Singles/doubles are Rs 75/100 or Rs 135/175 with air-con.

Also on Vir Marg the *Natraj Hotel* (tel 7450) has rooms with attached bath at Rs 40/90. Down the road from the Raghunath Temple are several bottom and middle-range hotels. In the middle category is the *Hotel Gagan*, Gumat Bazaar, which has clean doubles with bath for Rs 50. The *Hotel Amar* and the *Hotel City View* (tel 46120), also in Gumat Bazaar, both have doubles with attached bath for Rs 45 to Rs 60 or with air-cooling for Rs 75. These two are often full.

Places to Stay - top end

At the top end is the *Hotel Jammu Ashok* (tel 46154, 42084) on the outskirts of town to the north, close to the Amar Mahal Palace. Singles/doubles cost Rs 120/175 or Rs 265/350 with air-con. The similarly priced *Hotel Asia* (tel 6373-5) is in Nehru Market close to the Jammu Tawi railway station and the airport but a long way from the centre.

Hotel Cosmo (tel 47561) on Vir Marg is cheaper and more convenient. Singles are Rs 60 to Rs 100, doubles Rs 100 to Rs 150 or with air-con doubles are Rs 200. All top-end hotels have a bar and restaurant.

Places to Eat

The usual government tourist centre menu is available at the *Tourist Reception Centre* which serves reasonable food. The *Cosmo Hotel's* air-con restaurant is far superior to the hotel – good for a pleasant meal and a cold beer in cool surroundings. It's probably the best restaurant in town.

A few doors down the *Premier* has Chinese and Kashmiri food but is rather expensive. There is a collection of little kebab stalls between the two. The railway station and the bus station have the usual station restaurant facilities.

Getting There & Away

Air The Indian Airlines office (tel 5935, 3088) is at the Tourist Reception Centre (tel 8). The airport is seven km out of town and the Indian Airlines phone numbers there are 8164 or 5794.

By air it's half an hour from Jammu to Srinagar (Rs 224). There are flights three or four days a week between New Delhi, Jammu and Srinagar.

Bus Buses depart from various locations: A class and deluxe go from the Tourist Reception Centre; B class from the bus station; and private operators' vehicles depart from different parts of the city. Touts operate by the Tourist Reception Centre. Enquire at most travel agents.

Buses also run from the railway station where they meet incoming trains – thus you can take an overnight train from Delhi and catch a bus to Srinagar as soon as you arrive in Jammu. Buses normally depart between 6 and 7 am in order to reach Srinagar by nightfall (refer to the Train section). It is vital to book your bus to Srinagar as soon as you arrive to avoid delays. Jammu-Srinagar bus fares are Rs 43 (B class), Rs 53 (A class) Rs 75 (deluxe) and Rs 100 (video).

Travelling south from Jammu, only B-class buses depart in the morning and from the bus station. There is no advance booking so get there early to avoid having a lousy seat or no seat at all. The A class, deluxe and video buses leave only in the evening.

There are frequent buses from Jammu to Amritsar, Pathankot and other cities to the south. Pathankot is the departure point for Dharamsala, Dalhousie and the other Himachal Pradesh hill stations. Buses also operate to Akhnoor, Banihal, Bhadrooh, Katra, Kishtwar, Poonch, Riasi, Ramnagar, Udhampur, Kud and Batote.

Train Jammu Tawi is the end of the railway line up from Delhi. Many travellers get there on the overnight train, but only the earliest arrives in time to take a bus straight to Srinagar on the same day. Fares from Delhi are Rs 224 in 1st class, Rs 60 in 2nd. Three or four trains travel south each day, leaving in the afternoon or evening. From Delhi to Jammu it's 591 km and takes from nine to 13 hours.

Taxi You can travel by taxi between Jammu and Srinagar for approximately Rs 194 per person or Rs 776 for the whole taxi.

Getting Around
Jammu has metered taxis, auto-rickshaws, a minibus service and a tempo service between a number of points. It costs Rs 1 from the railway station to the bus station by minibus. The same trip by auto-rickshaw would be Rs 5 to Rs 7. It's only a short distance from the Tourist Reception Centre in the town centre to the bus station, say Rs 3 or Rs 4 by auto-rickshaw.

Around Jammu

The countryside around Jammu is uninteresting, comprising a low belt of plains made up of sandy, alluvial fans of silt deposited by the streams flowing out from the foothills of the Himalaya. The rainfall is low – 380 to 500 mm a year – coming mainly as heavy but infrequent showers in summer (June to September) when the monsoon winds blow. The land

is almost bare of trees – thorn scrub and coarse grass are all that remain.

For those with more time or their own vehicle there are many places around Jammu or along the road to Srinagar. Prior to the completion of the Jawarhar Tunnel the trip from Jammu to Srinagar took two whole days with an overnight stop at Batote. These days you can make the trip in one day, if you take the earliest bus, but it's a long haul (10 to 12 hours) with only a couple of rest stops and one lunch stop. Most unusual for an Indian bus trip! There's certainly no time for looking around if you're on the direct bus.

JAMMU-SRINAGAR ROAD
The route between Jammu and Srinagar is 293 km long. From Jammu the road winds gently up and down to Udhampur (61 km) then climbs steeply to Patnitop (107 km) where it drops just as steeply to Ramban (158 km). The road follows a picturesque but hazardous river route along this stretch. At Ramban it ascends

Jammu to Srinagar

again to Banihal (187 km) and on to the Jawarhar Tunnel (204 km). The road descends rapidly into the Kashmir Valley after the tunnel and runs flat the remaining distance to Srinagar.

There are many places of interest on this route, although those within Kashmir are covered in that chapter.

AKHNOOR

A few km from Jhiri and 32 km north-west of Jammu, this is a popular picnic spot where the Chenab River reaches the plains. The massive ruins of an old fort overlook the Chenab near the point where the Rambir Canal branches away from the river. Akhnoor is reached by a regular bus service.

At nearby Ambran, sculptures and terracotta figures were discovered several decades ago. Two other important spots close-by are the Kameshwar Shiva Shrine and the tomb of Babar Faiz Bux.

This road through Akhnoor used to be the route to Srinagar from Jammu during the Moghul era. The road continues through Nawshera, Rajauri and Poonch, 246 km from Jammu. Jehangir, Moghul emperor from 1605 to 1627, died en route to Kashmir and was temporarily buried at Chingas, 36 km before Rajauri.

There is a huge Moghul *sarai* at Thana Mandi, near Poonch. The waterfall at Nuri Chham, a popular resting place for the Moghul Queen Nur Jahan, wife of the emperor Shah Jahan (1627-58), is 16 km from there.

BASOHLI

Fairly close to Dalhousie in Himachal Pradesh, and 53 km from Pathankot, Basohli is the birthplace of the Pahari miniature paintings which are famous in this region. There are some palace ruins in Basohli and it is a good base for treks. Direct buses run to Basohli which is 125 km south-east of Jammu.

BILLAWAR & SUKRALA

Billawar is on the road from Udhampur to Dhar, which is near Basohli. The majestic old temple in Billawar is now mostly ruined. There are also the remains of many interesting old wells, or *baulis*, in this area.

On a hilltop 10 km from Billawar is the temple of Sukrala Devi with its fine old stone sculpture of the eight-armed goddess Devi.

BABOR

This is 72 km from Jammu and is noted for its five partially ruined temples with carved figures of the Hindu gods. These are marked by exquisitely sculptured statues and statuettes, elaborate and minute carvings, huge fluted pillars with lion or elephant heads or ornamented capitals, and gigantic decorated roof slabs and beams – all fixed without binding material. The statues include a particularly fine one of the goddess Ganga.

The richly and tastefully decorated temple of Devi has numerous miniature medallions depicting attractively carved gods and goddesses and celestial dancers and musicians. The Shiva temple has sculptured panels of geese, bulls and floral carvings, a frieze with two armed cavaliers drawing their bows and another of the god Narasimha. Another frieze shows Krishna playing the flute with two attendants waving palm frond fans and Lord Vishnu reclining.

PURMANDAL & UTTAR BEHANI

The imposing rock temples of Purmandal nestle in the Siwalik Range 39 km south-east of Jammu off the Pathankot road. They are visible from a great distance.

Maharaja Ranbir Singh, known for his patronage of art and learning, had planned to create a unique centre of pilgrimage here. He named spots along the subterranean Dewak River between Purmandal and Uttar Behani (6½ km away) after the different Tirathas of the country and started a grandiose project to build a stately shrine at each of these spots. Only a few were completed before he died and his ambitious dream, Purmandal, ended. The ruins of the half-finished temples and the material for their construction are still scattered around the wilderness nearby.

The temples have been built on a rock out of which a double basement has been cut. The Dewak stream that flows at the base of this rock is considered very sacred by the Hindus. A hooded stone serpent jutting out of a cistern in the rock in the central shrine is a religious attraction as it is believed to be a unique manifestation of Lord Shiva.

As the Dewak is believed to flow underground, people dig pits in the stream bed and bathe in the water that comes out. Devotees also take this water away as a sacred treasure. Nearby are several palatial buildings constructed by the Maharajas Rangit, Gulab and Ranbir Singh.

Another attraction of Purmandal is the numerous wall paintings in the old buildings. Purmandal is reached by a regular bus service and is also a popular picnic spot.

At Uttar Behani a huge, white-marble bull and an outsized bronze bell plus some artefacts are among the attractions.

SURINSAR LAKE

This picturesque lake, 45 km east of Jammu, is surrounded by pine trees with a central tree-covered island which can be reached by boat. At an altitude of more than 700 metres the lake is about 2½ km in circumference. In summer a covering of lotus flowers makes the lake particularly beautiful.

MANSAR LAKE

On the same road beyond Surinsar, this lake is also reached by a regular bus service from Jammu (80 km) and accommodation is available in the Dak Bungalow.

The legendary hero of the *Mahabharata*, Anjuna, is said to have shot an arrow into the ground at Mansar. The arrow emerged at Surinsar and thus both lakes were created. The lake is about four km in circumference and surrounded by dense mangrove stands, backed by pine trees on the slopes of the hills. It is covered with lotus flowers in summer.

Beside the lake is a small ruined palace with colourful frescoes on the walls and another ancient building is nearby. Often newly married couples can be seen walking around the edge of Mansar, as it is considered auspicious for their future well-being.

Towards the end of May each year there is a major festival at Mansar in which the folk spirit of the Dogra people is reflected in exuberant singing and dancing. Later the Chhing festival features wrestling with wrestlers invited from near and far to display their prowess. These festivities are repeated in numerous villages in the area, one after the other.

The mysterious ruins of Mahor Garh – nobody knows who built them or why – are reached from Mansar.

VAISHNO DEVI

This important cave, 60 km north-west of Jammu, is dedicated to the three mother goddesses of Hinduism. Thousands of pilgrims visit the cave, particularly during the four-month pilgrimage season from March to July.

The cave stands at 1700 metres, is 30 metres long and is reached by a very narrow entrance. A small stream, Chara Dunga, flows from under the image in the cave and devotees pass through it to the shrine.

The origin of the pilgrimage is shrouded in mystery, however various legends are associated with the shrine. According to one, the goddess Vaishno Devi usually stayed at a place called Adkunwari ('virgin since creation'). The demon Bahairo wanted to marry her forcibly so he chased the goddess, who ran all the way from Adkunwari to the cave where she took shelter after killing the demon. A big stone outside the cave is said to be the petrified body of the demon. Pilgrims walking to the cave greet each other with the cry *Jai Mataki* - Victory to the Mother Goddess.

The road terminates at the beautiful town of Katra, 48 km from Jammu, and visitors have to make the final, steep 12 km on foot. There is also a road from Lower Sanjichat to the Dabba, by-passing Upper Sanjichat and the Bahairo Ghatti. This leaves you two km closer to the cave and with 300 metres less to climb.

The pilgrimage route from Katra to the cave is now lit to allow pilgrims to travel at night. Adkunwari, half-way between Katra and the cave, has a temple of the goddess, two sarais, a water tank, tea stalls, halwai shops and a hotel. Pilgrims may spend the night at Adkunwari or rest and continue on.

Katra is at the foot of the Trikuta mountains. Eight km on is the village of Aghar Jito where the annual Kartik Purnima or Jhiri festival is held in memory of the hero Bawa Jito whose historic struggle against tyranny is admired today as a symbol of truth and personal courage.

There is a tourist bungalow at Katra, reservations for which can be made through the tourist officer at the Katra Tourist Bureau, the director of tourism in Srinagar or the Tourist Reception Centre in Jammu.

There are regular and deluxe buses from Jammu to Katra. Taxis are also available from Jammu to Katra and return. Ponies, dandies and porters are available at Katra at fixed rates.

From Katra, at various walking stages, there are *Chabils* where drinking water is available for pilgrims.

RIASI

Beyond Katra, is Riasi. Three km from Jammu, is Riasi. Three km from the town is the ruined fort and palace of General Zorawar Singh, a controversial warrior best remembered in India for his clashes with the Chinese over Ladakh. The palace, on a ridge overlooking the mighty Chenab River, is considerably rundown although it is still inhabited by the descendants of General Singh.

There is a *gurdwara*, 15 km from Riasi, with some of the oldest known frescoes in the Pahari style.

Another pilgrimage site, 19 km from Riasi, is the 400-metre long Shiv Khori cave. The cave is difficult to negotiate - the last five km must be completed on foot - but at its end there is a vast hall in which the Shiva lingam formation on the ground is just over a metre high and other symbolic figures are said to be naturally etched on the cave ceiling.

RAMNAGAR

The Rangmahal, or 'palace of colours', at Ramnagar has many very colourful and beautiful wall paintings in the Pahari style. The paintings of scenes from Krishna's life are particularly noteworthy.

Buses travel the 102 km from Jammu north-east to Ramnagar, leaving the Srinagar road at Udhampur (64 km north of Jammu).

KRIMCHI

The mediaeval-style Hindu temples at Krimchi, 10 km from Udhampur off the Srinagar road, are notable for their characteristic lantern-shaped structures, fine carvings and sculpture. There are four ancient stone shrines and a Shiva Dawala.

Three of the Krimchi shrines and the Shiva Dawala are on the same plinth and the fourth shrine is a little below. Their position indicates that there must have once been more shrines to complete some votive pattern.

KUD

A popular lunch stop on the Jammu-Srinagar highway, Kud (altitude 1738 metres) is 99 km north-east of Jammu. It's also popular as a hill resort and has a well-known mountain spring, Swami Ki Bauli, 1½ km from the road. There is a tourist bungalow and a summer festival with nightly dancing.

PATNITOP

There are many pleasant walks around this popular hill station, 107 km north-east of Jammu on the Srinagar road. There are tourist huts, a rest house and a youth hostel in Patnitop, which is the centre of tourist activity in the area, servicing Sanasar, Kud, Batote and Sudh Mahadev.

Patnitop (altitude 2024 metres) is a good starting place for many short or longer treks into the nearby mountains. An attractive one-day walk is to Shive Garh, about 11 km away at an altitude of almost 3500 metres.

Good bridle paths passing through wooded lanes and fascinating scenery link Patnitop with Kud and Batote. There are three gushing, ice-cold freshwater springs in the area which are said to have medicinal properties.

BATOTE

Only 12 km further on, the hill resort of Batote (altitude 1560 metres) is easily reached from Patnitop and Kud by a series of footpaths. It was the overnight stop between Jammu and Srinagar before the opening of the Jawarhar Tunnel.

There is a tourist bungalow, tourist huts and several private hotels in Batote. A famous spring, the Amrit Chasma, is 2½ km from the village.

SUDH MAHADEV

Sudh Mahadev, 120 km north-east of Jammu (off the Srinagar road at Kud), is well known for its archaeological importance as a great pilgrimage centre and as a charming natural site.

The Shiva temple attracts many pilgrims during the Asad Purnima festival which takes place in mid-June each year and features three days of music, singing and dancing. The main shrine has a black marble carved figure of Shiva and Parvati and there is also an interesting inscribed iron trident known as the Shiva Triseshul. It is believed to have been used by a *mahadeva* to kill a demon.

Man Talai, five km from Sudh Mahadev, is of archaeological interest because of the red earthenware and terracotta figures discovered there. Gauri Kund, also five km distant, is a small cave associated with Parvati. Sculptures from Hindu mythology can be seen at the Pap Nashni Bauli springs. Shiv Garh is the highest mountain in the area.

Sudh Mahadev (altitude 1225 metres) is only an eight-km walk or jeep track ride from Patnitop and Kud. There is also a regular daily bus service to Sudh Mahadev from Jammu. It stands on the banks of the holy Dewak River, held by some to be as sacred as the Ganges. The Dewak hurtles down from the higher mountains and rushes out of dense jungle, cascading over rocks and boulders. There is a small pilgrims rest house at Sudh Mahadev.

SANASAR

The Valley of Sanasar (2079 metres) is 129 km north-east of Jammu off the Srinagar road at Patnitop. It has a beautiful cup-shaped meadow where Gaddi and Gujar shepherds bring their cattle and sheep in spring on the way to the higher pastures for the warm summer months. All around are thick bands of lofty conifers on the mountain slopes. Accommodation is available in the tourist bungalow, in tourist huts and in several private hotels. Sanasar is just eight km from Patnitop.

BHADARWAH

Every two years a procession of pilgrims starts from this beautiful, high altitude valley and makes its way to the 4400-metre high Kaplash Lake. The pilgrimage takes place two weeks after the Rakhi Purnima festival and is followed a week later by Mela Patt, a three-day festival in Bhadarwah.

There are bus services from Jammu to

Bhadarwah (204 km to the north-east). The road leaves the Srinagar highway at Batote and heads east towards Kishtwar. A road then branches south-east to Bhadarwah, where there is a rest house.

KISHTWAR

Well off the Jammu-Srinagar road from Batote, Kishtwar is connected to Srinagar by a trekking route which goes through Banderkot, Dadhpeth, Mughal Maidan, Chhatru, Sinthan and Daksum – crossing the 3797-metre Sinthan Pass. You can also trek from Kishtwar into Zanskar, as detailed in the Zanskar chapter. The town is noted for its natural beauty, history and art.

Kishtwar (216 km north-east of Jammu) is on a plateau above the Chenab River and below the Nagin Sheer Glacier. It is noted for finely grown saffron and the many waterfalls close by.

Saffron, very colourful in spring and summer, grows only in a limited area and the cultivation and harvesting is accompanied by merry festivals and ceremonies.

A waterfall only three km from the town drops more than 700 metres in a series of seven cascades. The falls are a marvellous sight, visible even from the town.

The pilgrimage site of Sarthal Devi, with its 18-armed goddess statue, is 19 km from the town. Kishtwar also has the tombs of two important Muslim saints.

About 115 km beyond Kishtwar at an altitude of over 4000 metres are the blue sapphire mines of Paddar. A road leads up to this area from Kishtwar. The sapphire mines were discovered in the 1880s but were worked only intermittently because of the difficult terrain and unscientific mining techniques. These days, however, the mines are open regularly and are more productive.

Jawarhar Tunnel

Until the completion of the tunnel (200 km from Jammu, 93 km from Srinagar), Kashmir and Srinagar were often totally cut off from the rest of India during winter. The tunnel has two separate passages, each more than 2500 metres long. It's at an altitude of 2500 metres and the condition of the road is terrible! Windscreen wipers are needed in the tunnel because it 'rains' inside.

The tunnel not only ensured that Kashmir was accessible year round but also took half a day off the trip between Jammu and Srinagar.

From Banihal, 17 km before the tunnel, you are already entering the Kashmiri region. Many people in the area speak Kashmiri as well as Dogri and many of the houses are of the traditional Kashmiri style. As soon as you pass through the tunnel you are in the Vale of Kashmir and its green lushness is strikingly different from the other side of the range.

Kashmir

Kashmir is one of India's most beautiful and popular tourist regions and has been since the time of the great Moghul emperors. It's probably most famous for the houseboats on Dal Lake, and you've not really been to Kashmir until you've stayed on one, but there's a lot more to the Kashmir Valley than just lazing on a boat.

Around the capital of Srinagar are numerous mosques, temples, forts and the delightful Moghul gardens, laid out in formal patterns hundreds of years ago and every bit as beautiful today.

But you have to get away from Srinagar, up to the hill stations around the valley, to really enjoy Kashmir. Pahalgam, Gulmarg and Sonamarg are all delightful, and they also serve as the departure points for Kashmir's many trekking possibilities.

Facts about the Region

HISTORY

Due to its isolation in a high valley of the Himalaya, Kashmir has over the centuries developed an independent cultural and historical tradition.

Buddhism became established in Kashmir quite early with, as in many places in India, Emperor Ashoka as its main promulgator. Around the time of the birth of Christ, the third Buddhist Congress took place in Kashmir and missionaries were sent to neighbouring regions of Central Asia, Tibet and China.

In the following centuries Buddhism lost its influence and by the 7th century had almost been replaced by Hinduism. Hindu dynasties followed in rapid succession through the middle ages but they always exercised tolerance towards Buddhism.

In the 1300s the Kashmiris changed to the Islamic religion and a series of Muslim rulers controlled the region. One of the best known and most respected of these local rulers was Zain-ul-Abidin, whose tomb still stands by the Jhelum River in Srinagar. He was generally known as *Badshah*, 'the great king'. He ruled from 1421 to 1472 and was a considerable contrast to his father Sultan Sikander, who, guided by a fanatical prime minister, persecuted countless Hindus and virtually ended the historical religious tolerance of the valley.

With the conquest of the valley by the Moghul Emperor Akbar in 1586 Kashmir entered a period of stable political conditions and great cultural activity. The Moghuls chose Kashmir as their summer residence and built many fine gardens, particularly under Emperor Jehangir who took the art of designing Moghul gardens to its greatest heights.

As the Moghul period began its decline the Government of Kashmir became practically independent. In 1756 Kashmir fell to Afghanistan, but in 1819 it was taken over by the Sikhs who called upon the Kashmiris to aid them in their struggle against the brutal Afghan rule.

In 1846 the Sikh General Gulab Singh was appointed head of state by the British in reward for his neutrality in the war between the British and the Sikhs. Gilgit, Hunza, Nagar and Chitral were added to the region and, under the rule of the Hindu Dogra dynasty, the state of Jammu and Kashmir became more or less its present shape.

In 1947, India's independence from Britain and the partition of India and Pakistan caused Kashmir to become the thorn-in-the-side of India-Pakistan relations, a position it has held ever since. Since Kashmir was a 'princely state' and theoretically already independent, the

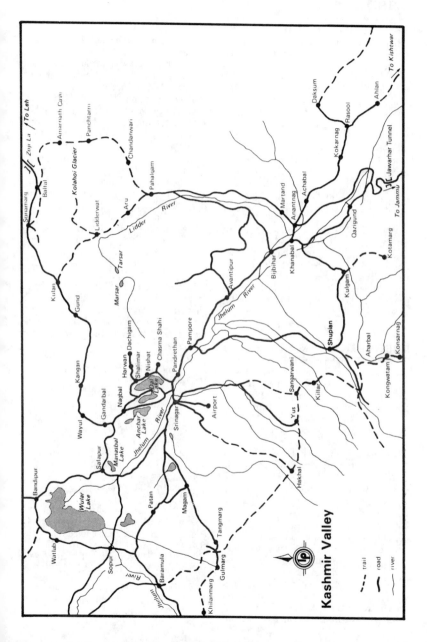

Kashmir Valley

trail
road
river

British could not simply grant it independence like most of India but had to persuade it to join one side or the other. Kashmir became one of three states – the others were Hyderabad and the tiny principality of Junagadh – whose rulers could not or would not opt for India or Pakistan, but clutched at the feeble hope of remaining independent.

Maharaja Hari Singh's decision not to join either country, or rather his indecision since he was far from being a decisive ruler, was a fateful one. Kashmir is predominantly Muslim so on the basis of religion it should clearly have gone to Pakistan. Geographically it is also more closely aligned to Pakistan than India.

When the Pakistanis realised that Hari Singh, a Hindu, was still undecided they organised an unofficial takeover bid. Pathan tribesmen from the North-West Frontier region moved into Kashmir and internal revolts soon had Hari Singh's army in tatters. He turned to India for assistance but the price was an obvious one – Hari Singh opted for India.

Had not the Pathans been so busy looting along their way to capturing Srinagar, it might have been too late for Indian troops to save Kashmir. As it was, the Pathans had still not reached Srinagar when the first Indian troops were flown in and confronted them in Baramula. Nevertheless a full-scale war between India and Pakistan was soon underway and was not halted until a United Nations cease fire came into effect on 1 January 1949. A substantial part of Kashmir was in Pakistani hands but the Vale of Kashmir was firmly under Indian control.

The cease-fire line runs from Akhnoor northwards to near Keran on the Kishanganga – a rugged, dry, sparsely populated strip 25 km wide and 250 km long. From Keran the line turns east and passes through Minimarg in the Gurais Valley and ends in the snow of the Karakoram Range. Gilgit, Hunza and Baltistan are north of the line and under the control of the Pakistanis.

Initially Kashmir was run as an auton-omous region with its own government and president. Karan Singh, the Maharaja's son, was the first to hold this office. Then in 1957 Kashmir was formally made part of the Indian union, despite Pakistani protests. Pakistan has repeatedly requested that a referendum be held in Kashmir and although India agreed to eventually hold such a referendum there have always been reasons why it has not been conducted.

In 1962 India became involved with a different foe, the Chinese. So neglected was the Ladakh region of the state that the Chinese actually managed to construct a high altitude road across the area they now hold without India being aware. When the conflict eventually ended another cease-fire line was drawn across the region. The Chinese hold a desolate, cold and bleak rolling plain nearly 5000 metres high and approximately east of a line joining Chusul with the Karakoram Pass.

In 1965 India and Pakistan were again at war and again the Pakistanis nearly captured Srinagar, but although the cease-fire line was pushed back in several places the status quo remained essentially unchanged.

In 1971, during the Bangladesh conflict, it was India that took the offensive and Pakistan that was pushed back.

Today Kashmir, including Ladakh, is divided between three countries throughout which related people are artificially divided by enforced nationalities.

There are no roads open across the borders of Kashmir and no official trade takes place between the Indian and other parts of Kashmir.

Given freedom of choice the Kashmiris would probably opt for independence as a sort of buffer state between India and Pakistan, with their borders open to both countries. Barring that choice many say they would prefer Pakistan to India but, given the impossibility of that dream today, they appear to make the most of life in India.

Top: Early morning on Dal Lake (NT)
Left: Shah Hamdan Mosque on the Jhelum River, Srinagar (TW)
Right: Canal scene, Srinagar (RK)

Top: Shikaras assembled by Dal Lake (TW)
Left: Open shikara and houseboats, Dal Lake (NT)
Right: Nishat Bagh by Dal Lake (TW)

SEASONS
Kashmir

Its lush vegetation and wide variety of fruits presents a different face for every season. The almond trees blossom in March when the thaw begins, but it's the chinars which leaf in April that really herald spring. Strawberries and cherries are on sale in May, followed by apricots in June and apples in July.

The sound of running water dominates the vale in May and June as the snow melt rushes down from the high snows and is channelled on to terraces to irrigate the rice, barley and wheat crops. During these months, groups of colourfully dressed women sing as they stoop to plant the rice shoots in paddies across the vale. The chinar trees are in full leaf, while on the mountain slopes the villagers are cutting fir and cedar for building houses or repairing those damaged by the winter snow. The Gujars begin moving their herds of sheep and goats to the high pastures and ranunculus, anemone and impatiens begin to flower in the meadows and along the streams.

The early autumn brings pears, pomegranates and walnuts. Waterbirds and swallows, heading south for winter, pause in Kashmir in great numbers. Finally the leaves fall and by November or December the first snow can be expected around the valley. In January houseboat roofs must be shovelled clean to prevent them being pressed into the lake by the weight of snow.

In winter the Kashmir Valley can be a bitterly cold place and the Dal Lake freezes over on occasion. Kashmir becomes a quieter, more sedate place than during the hectic days of summer. Houseboat owners bring out their pot belly stoves and hang carpets at the doorways to keep in the warmth, and the valley, now stilled by a thick layer of snow, rests.

Srinagar

In mid-summer this is a noisy, busy and dirty city, much like the cities of the plains that many people come north from to escape. The only refuges are the houseboats on the quiet lakes and the hill stations like Gulmarg or Pahalgam.

PEOPLE

Kashmir has a population of about four million people of whom about half a million live in Srinagar. The population is predominantly Muslim and more related to Central Asia than to India in both appearance and temperament.

Despite its Muslim majority Kashmir has a strong Hindu minority well known for their intellectual pursuits. Nehru, India's first prime minister, was a Kashmiri *pandit* and many of the closest advisers of both Nehru and his daughter, Indira Gandhi, were Kashmiris.

The Aryan Kashmiris are not the only people of the region. The predominantly Muslim population that lives in the foothills and peaks surrounding the vale are mostly Gujars, and do not speak Kashmiri. The Gujars, along with the Dards, are one of the few groups to maintain their tribal and nomadic identity. They speak a language akin to Punjabi. In summer, dressed in the robes of the Pathans, they live in stone and log huts among the giant deodars near the snow line. In winter they drive their large herds down to the plains.

Marriage in Kashmir

If you spend a long time in Kashmir you may get an opportunity to see a large Islamic wedding. The ceremonies often take place over several days and because of the huge cost involved it is not unusual for several sisters to be married on the same day.

The festivities take place not in houses but in lavish tents which are erected in gardens. Men and women are kept strictly separate during the festivities.

Before the wedding day the bridegroom is occupied with the monetary gifts of friends and relatives. On the evening before the actual ceremony he goes, with the entire wedding company, to the house of the bride to sign the *nika* or marriage contract. Only men take part in this ceremony and the bride is represented by her father. The contract is sealed in the presence of a *mullah* and a small sugarball or *shirien* is distributed to each guest. Late into the night a feast is held to celebrate the union.

The next morning the bride, in a draped litter or in a car with draped windows, and the bridegroom on a horse are accompanied by the entire wedding party to the bridegroom's house. The bridegroom generally gives his future wife a very valuable item of jewellery, often a massive golden necklace and armband, as a wedding present.

Kashmiri Dress

For many years Kashmiri men and women have worn the same style of dress. The *pheran* and *poots* consist of two gowns, one on top of the other, falling to the feet in the case of a Hindu, worn up to the knees by a Muslim. Muslims wear the sleeves wide and open while the Hindus wear them narrow with turned up ends.

The garments are made of cotton, wool or embroidered silk with the necks closed by a gaily coloured string or jewelled buttons. A pashmina belt goes around the waist. A Moghul-type turban, sometimes 20 metres long, completes the costume for men. Most Muslims wear skull caps, especially the farmers. The head dress of a Kashmiri woman is a brightly coloured scarf.

The traditional way of coping with the bitter cold of a Kashmiri winter is with a *kangri* – an earthenware bowl, which, fitted in a wicker container, is carried in front of you under your enveloping pheran. Red-hot coals from the pot belly stoves used in houses or houseboats are placed in the kangri and you have personal, portable central heating! The pheran channels the heat up to the neck. Kashmiri's often squat to talk or smoke with the kangri between their feet and the

pheran spread over it. Beware of burning embers falling out of the bowl. Long-term kangri carriers usually have the burns to prove it.

An equally vital part of a Kashmiri's existence is the *hookah* (hubble-bubble) pipe which is in every shop and shikara. In winter, coals from the kangri are used to light the pipe.

Warning

In character the Kashmiris have many failings and faults, but they also have qualities which make one to be interested in them and to like them. They are false-tongued, ready with a lie, and given to various forms of deceit.

This character is more pronounced with them than with most of the races in India. They are noisy and quarrelsome, ready to wrangle but not to fight, on the least exercise or threat of force they cry like children. They have indeed a wide reputation for being faint-hearted and cowardly; still, I must admit that I have sometimes met with Kashmiris who, against physical dangers, bore themselves well. In intellect they are superior to their neighbours . . . In disposition they are talkative, cheerful and humorous.

- Frederic Drew, 1875   Jummoo & Kashmir Territories

Fond of exaggeration . . . very persistent . . . very loud and voluble   . . . The Kashmiri bears an evil reputation . . . Proverbs liken him to a snake in his morals and to a fowl in his manners, and men are warned against admitting a Kashmiri to his friendship. Moorcroft writes of the Kashmiri: 'selfish, superstitious, ignorant, supple, intriguing, dishonest and false . . . his transactions are always conducted in a fraudulent spirit, equalled only by the effrontery with which he faces detection.'

**Walter R Lawrence
Settlement Commissioner J&K
The Valley of Kashmir**

This guide unfortunately has to warn travellers about the negative characteristics of the average Kashmiri as described so very accurately by Messrs Drew and Lawrence so many years ago.

All who visit Kashmir will almost certainly experience incidents confirming those statements. These will usually take the form of persistent harassment by touts trying to persuade you to stay on their houseboat, ride their *shikara* or buy their product (usually handicrafts). For the inexperienced traveller, being subjected to a pack of Kashmiri touts, for the first time at least, can be unnerving and/or very annoying.

The best line of defence is definitely not to attack. As the earlier quotes show, the Kashmiris rely on an energetic show of words to put their message across. Say a brief and polite but firm 'no thank you' and keep moving. Do not stop and talk, raise your voice, panic or do anything that will encourage the touts. This is often easier said than done, but once you get used to ignoring the persistent shouts and approaches you should find yourself laughing at their behaviour more than being annoyed by it.

RELIGION

As would be expected of a place where the trails and trading routes of Asia meet, most of the religions of the world have vied for the beliefs of the people of Kashmir. Buddhism and Hinduism reached Kashmir and Ladakh very early in their spread across Asia.

Buddhism arrived as early as the 4th century BC and Emperor Ashoka built many Buddhist statues throughout the vale, some of which were still standing at the time of the great Chinese traveller Hiuan Tsang in the 7th century AD. He recorded them in his diary – see *In the Footsteps of the Buddha* by Rene Grousset (Orion Press, New York, 1971). It is said that Nagarjuna, the monk credited with bringing Buddhism to Ladakh, resided at the monastery built near Harwan in Srinagar in the 2nd century AD.

From the 9th to 12th centuries AD Kashmir was a prominent centre of Hindu culture. There are still many Hindu holy sites and temples in Jammu and a lesser number in Kashmir.

By the 14th century, Hinduism had been supplanted by Islam which had come gradually to Kashmir. Sufi teachers began to spread the religion in the 12th century with their synthesis of Hindu thought in the form of Sufiism and the Bhakti movement. Due to Bulbul Shah, Shah Hamdan and other Sufi saints, Kashmir embraced Islam before any Muslim king invaded it.

Now Muslims make up about 90% of the population of the valley and are mostly of the Sunni sect, with a sprinkling of Shi'ite. Christian missionaries came to the vale during the British period and their influence continues also.

Facts for the Visitor

FOOD

Kashmiri cuisine has some special variations on normal Indian food although it is basically of the north Indian type. Houseboat food tends to retain its early English influence which is not a good sign! Some Kashmiri dishes are:

Gushtaba - pounded and spiced meat balls cooked in a yoghurt sauce. The meat is usually mutton or goat.
Rista - rice balls very similar to gushtaba but with less meat and less spice in the sauce.
Roghan josh - also fairly common elsewhere in north India, this is basically curried mutton, but a good roghan josh will be cooked in yoghurt (curd) with a careful blend of exotic spices and added ingredients.
Yaknee - similar to roghan josh.
Tabak maz - fried meat, not spiced at all.
Marchwangan kurma - a hot mutton curry, usually served with rice and nan bread.
Methi kurma - vegetables with chopped intestines which tastes much better than it sounds.
Karma sag - made from the popular Dal

Lake vegetable known as lak, which is a little like giant spinach.

Nadru yekni – a very tasty dish made from lotus roots, cooked with curd or yoghurt.

Kashmiri nan – the usual flat Indian bread but with sultanas and nuts baked in it. Kashmiri nan is really delicious but Kashmiri bread is also good.

The Kashmiris also make a fruit and nut *pillau* which is a bit like fried fruit salad! Popular vegetables include *bartha* (minced aubergines) and *bhindi* (lady's finger).

DRINKS

Kashmir tea is a fragrant, delicate blend flavoured with cardamom and ginger. It is a delightfully thirst-quenching drink and quite possibly the best tea in India! A really good cup of this *kahwa* tea will be brewed in a *samovar* (tea urn) and have grated almonds in it. It's usually drunk without milk. The Kashmiris also make a good blend of camomile and cardamom tea which is very good for settling stomach upsets.

Another tea peculiar to Kashmir is *noon chai*. Something of an acquired taste (I hate it), this is a salted pink-coloured beverage. Green tea leaves are boiled for hours (giving the tea its pink colour), then milk and salt are added. It is usually drunk in the morning or afternoon only.

Soft drinks, freighted up from the plains, tend to be expensive but Kashmiri apple juice is worth trying. It's a great change from the sickly Indian soft drinks and costs about the same as regular soft drinks in Kashmir. Take care with Kashmiri water, especially if you suspect it may have come straight from Dal Lake!

Being good Muslims, the Kashmiris do not drink alcohol, at least not in public. Liquor is available, but at a high price and often of very low quality. You would be well advised to bring your quota of duty-free liquor. There's a ready black market demand for it. Beer, however, is readily available, but expensive.

THINGS TO BUY

Warning Visitors buying goods need to be alert to the Kashmiri school of salesmanship and the various deceitful ploys that are commonly practised. Indian embassies and tourist offices around the world have files full of letters from ripped-off visitors reporting con-men in Kashmir.

Overcharging, by simply demanding too much for an item by claiming it to be something it isn't, and failing to mail goods ordered and paid for, are the standard methods used. You simply have to be on your guard at all times.

Unfortunately this is not always easy as the Kashmiris are good at being persistently persuasive. Don't be rushed or pressured into making a decision and do shop around before parting with any money. There are lots of lovely things to buy in Kashmir so shopping is a main activity among visitors. Enjoy looking at what's available, but don't believe everything you are told by the merchants.

Kashmir is famous for its wide variety of often very beautiful handicrafts. The Kashmiris are not only poets and philosophers but also artists and artisans producing exquisite carpets, embroidered shawls, silverware, gold ornaments, finely chiselled woodwork of walnut and oak, brilliantly coloured and painted papier mache and leather and fur garments.

They are also great salesmen. Even enterprising small Kashmiri girls, crouched precariously on the prow of their shikara, will adroitly paddle up to you on the lake and offer you, for a rupee or two, a lotus blossom that they have picked from the water not 10 metres away. But you'd have a hard heart indeed, and a tight wallet, if your budget doesn't allow you to buy the occasional flower from a child.

Carpets

Carpet weaving is one of the best known and most expensive Kashmiri handicrafts. The art of weaving carpets first came from Samarkand in Central Asia and was later modified by artisans from Iran.

The Muslim ruler Zain-ul-Abidin is credited with first introducing the skill to Kashmir. Late in the 14th century, as a young prince, he was kept hostage by the scourge of Asia, Timur the Lame (Tamerlane) at his court in Samarkand. When Tamerlane died the young prince returned to Kashmir, taking with him many of the artisans and craftsmen whom Tamerlane had collected from many parts of Asia.

Early in the 17th century the carpet industry was given a new direction during the reign of Jehangir when a Kashmiri craftsman brought the knot style of weaving back from Persia.

Now carpets come in a variety of sizes and are either made of pure wool, wool with a small percentage of silk to give a sheen (known as 'silk touch'), or pure silk. The latter are more decorative than practical and are not intended for hard wear. To see just how perfect Kashmiri carpets can be as wall hangings visit the restaurant in the Broadway Hotel where the carpets are hung like paintings.

If you are considering buying a carpet in Kashmir, investigate prices at home before you leave for comparison. There are many carpet importers in Europe, Australia and North America and their prices are often very competitive. Studying one of the many books on oriental carpets will also help you to avoid making a disappointing purchase. One book that I can recommend is *From Rugs to Riches – An Insider's Guide to Buying Oriental Rugs* by Caroline Bosly (Pantheon Books, New York).

Carpets are very easy to come by. In fact, it is almost impossible to avoid them. Someone on your houseboat will be either selling carpets, have a brother who owns a carpet factory or will want to take you to a carpet factory. Do go and visit one as most of the weaving is still done on hand looms by young boys. Sadly the working conditions are somewhat Dickensian as the boys, especially in winter, are working with very fine threads in darkened rooms.

Many of them, as a result, have severely damaged eyesight by their early 20s.

The carpet showrooms provide the greatest entertainment with beautifully patterned wool rugs or shiny silk ones piled high in the corner or rolled in racks around the edge of the room.

You will be seated at the far edge of the room, away from the door, and offered Kashmiri tea and biscuits. Every imaginable pattern and colour of carpet will be shown to you and you will be made to feel that if you do not buy one you will have missed the bargain of the century. The salesmen have an impressive array of techniques and will show you all manner of testimonials from satisfied customers around the world – 'my friends'. They will not admit to having dissatisfied customers.

If you have done your homework you will know how much you can afford and how much the carpet is worth. Don't hesitate to bargain with the carpet salesman. The stuff he's offering will be way overpriced to cover his 'overheads', not the least of which will be the commission for whoever it was who took you there. The brother of your houseboat owner, the guy who works in your hotel, or the boy or taxi driver who picked you up in the street, will get a commission on the sale – sometimes up to 20%. Many of the boys and young men you will meet on the streets earn their living this way over the school or university summer holidays.

The Kashmiris' powers of persuasion are immense. A refusal to buy will be taken as a personal insult to all in the room and you will feel that you have to sneak out. This is why you have been seated so far from the door. If you can't afford it or you don't like it, don't be afraid to get up and walk out. They have not yet resorted to mugging tourists who don't buy.

Most carpet dealers take all types of credit cards as well as travellers' cheques and, of course, cash. If you cannot pay in full you will be offered the facility of leaving a deposit and having the money transferred from your bank when you reach home. At this time the carpet or carpets will be sent to you. Most of the time you will indeed get a carpet and most of the time you will get the right carpet! Some of the time something will go wrong, sometimes caused by the Indian postal system.

You can, of course, buy a carpet and mail it or carry it home yourself. To avoid import duty if it is mailed, the carpet must be addressed to you and labelled as a gift.

There are also some cheaper, more country-crafted rugs such as the embroidered *numdahs* and the applique-like *gabbas*. You can compare the different types in the Srinagar handicrafts emporiums.

Papier Mache

Instantly recognisable as a product of Kashmir are the papier mache items. They're usually cheap, well made, light and easy to carry. The basic papier mache article, made in a mould, is painted and polished in successive layers until the final intricate design is produced. Prices are generally dependent upon the complexity and quality of the painted design and on the amount of gold leaf applied in tiny pieces to produce a pattern.

You can get papier mache bowls, cups, containers, jewellery boxes, letter holders, tables, lamps, coasters, trays and so on. Prices can be as low as Rs 10 for a cheap bowl to several hundred rupees for a large, fine quality piece.

Production is very much a cottage industry with the moulded, rough form being made in one place, the painting and polishing being done in another, and the adding of the intricate and colourful designs in still another. It's easy to arrange to visit a papier mache factory.

Leather & Fur

Shoes or boots or leather coats can be made to measure in just a few days in Srinagar. The beautifully embroidered suede coats are particularly interesting, but you have to put your conscience in the back seat when it comes to the fur trim. The same goes for the many fur coats. I believe fur should be left on the backs of its original owners. Wolf, fox, jackal, brown and black bear, marmot, leopard and lynx are all being driven from the slopes of the Himalaya by hunters. In any case, the best furs are exported immediately.

There are also sheepskin-lined or trimmed coats, but although Kashmiri leather, suede or sheepskin may look very fine the quality is often abysmally low. Look carefully before buying.

Tailoring

Srinagar's hordes of tailors ('I am just like Saville Row, only cheaper') search you out on your houseboats if you don't go to them. They'll make anything from a shirt to a suit and, depending on the time of year, often very quickly. Late in the tourist season, however, tailors often have far more orders than they can satisfy and these orders lay partly completed until the slack winter time. Resident Srinagar tailors are generally more reliable than summer visitors from Delhi or the Punjab. If you are having something made, insist on having several fittings and give clear instructions each time.

Wood Carvings

Intricately carved designs are a hallmark of Kashmiri woodcraft. You can see complex relief work on every houseboat. Look for tables, chests, boxes and screens. Wood carving is relatively cheap. Inlaid ivory is often incorporated into the design; it may or may not be genuine, but if it is it does the world's elephant population no good.

Shawls & Embroidery

Kashmiri shawls are noted for the extreme fineness of the cream-coloured goat wool known as *pashmina*, or *cashmere*, and for their intricate embroidery work. Cashmere, or pashm as it's also known, comes from the downy undercoat of goats that live above 4000 metres. Though the word is often incorrectly applied to any very soft goat wool, only the product of the Kashmir goat is true cashmere.

The wool is expensive, light and extremely warm but it's not easy to tell pashmina from ordinary goat wool. You'll pay up to Rs 200 for a *raffal*, or low quality, shawl; from Rs 400 to Rs 1000 for a genuine middle quality pashmina shawl; and even more for a really good one.

Shawl-making has been a Kashmiri speciality for more than 500 years. The word 'shawl', however, was not used until 1533 when Nagz Beg of Khokand in Central Asia came to Kashmir. Nagz Beg, on presenting his master with a piece of pashmina, was asked what it was. Beg replied a *shawl*, the word used by his own people for 'blanket'.

The embroidered shawl or *amilkar* was started by an artisan, Ala Baba, who covered some footprints made by a fowl on his white material with coloured thread.

In 1796 blind Sayyid Yehyah from Baghdad visited Kashmir and received a shawl from the Afghan governor. Sayyid presented it to the Khedive of Egypt, who in turn presented it to Napoleon. In France it caught the eye of the French court, which meant Kashmiri shawls became the height of fashion throughout Europe. They sold for up to Rs 7000 and more than 40,000 looms worked day and night in the vale to satisfy the unprecedented demand from overseas.

In 1820, the English explorer Moorcroft learnt the art and sent instructions to England; though English woven shawls are not equal to the originals.

Embroidery of all types is a Kashmiri craft. Embroidered suede coats or bags, shirts or dress material are all popular.

Antiques

Many shops around Kashmir sell statuary and antiques. Much of this material is said to come from Ladakh or Tibet but the majority of it is likely to be 'instant antiques' manufactured en masse in Delhi and Dharamsala.

You should be aware that the export of any item from India that is more than 100 years old is prohibited. At the very least it could be confiscated from your luggage at the airport as all baggage is searched when you are leaving India. Kashmir is certainly not unaffected by the world trade in counterfeit antiques. Ivory or bone will often turn out to be plastic and all but worthless; though if you thought it *was* ivory, then it serves you right!

Honey

The cardinal rule when buying honey in Kashmir is to taste it first. Kashmiri substitutes for the real thing include sugar dissolved in water or alcohol! Do not, however, be put off by the packaging as Kashmiri honey can be very good, although it's also expensive. The best honey will be found at small stalls reached only by shikara. You may even find lotus blossom honey.

Fruit

Dried fruit may be a Kashmiri speciality but it's another expensive one. Dried apricots and apples are from Ladakh and better to get there, while walnuts are a genuine Kashmir product.

Jewellery, Wool & Saffron

Most jewellery is really from Rajasthan but there's also a thriving business in Tibetan jewellery and other artefacts. Nice, coarsely handknitted sweaters in grey or dark-brown wool are available from Rs 75 and cardigans from Rs 100. Some are made in Ladakh. Saffron, the highly fragrant orange-coloured spice and dye is a Kashmiri speciality. Pure saffron is very expensive and it's an easy product to adulterate so take care.

THINGS TO SELL

There are healthy profits to be made in the 'bringing to sell' game. Your duty-free whisky can be sold for at least double the cost price, but cigarettes are not normally worth the hassle as western brands are available locally at only slightly higher than duty-free prices.

Cosmetics, perfume, some western clothing (eg jeans, T-shirts, sweat shirts), sunglasses, electrical goods (eg personal hi-fi, cassette/radio 'ghetto blasters') and camping/trekking equipment and clothing are the surest items to subsidise your stay.

An important factor is deciding whether to invest in expensive quality or cheap flashy goods. This can be crucial to the success of your sales operation. Generally it is best not to spend too much as the locals are not always able to appreciate quality. One exception would normally be camping/trekking gear.

It is also important to realise that you will get the best price for your goods if you find buyers who want what you are selling for themselves. Be wary of black marketeers and would-be middle-men offering you silly prices. Do some research to find out the going rates and don't rely on what these guys tell you. Also, don't allow yourself to be hurried into making a deal.

If you are willing to carry it around a little longer, you will always get a better price for items the further you travel from ports of entry such as Delhi, Bombay and Calcutta. As a result, Kashmir and Ladakh usually prove to be good selling territories.

Jammu & Kashmir Registration of Tourist Trade Act

Aptly enough, J&K is India's only state with legislation designed specifically for the interests of tourists. Here is a brief look at the 1978 Act which provides for the registration of persons dealing with tourists and connected matters.

First, it explains that malpractice includes 'dishonesty, cheating, touting, impersonation, obstruction in allowing free choice for shopping or stay or travel arrangements . . . and wilful failure to execute an order within the stipulated time or according to the terms agreed'.

It also explains that the expression touting means enticing, misguiding or coercing for shopping, accommodation, transportation and sightseeing; or pestering people on behalf of premises, dealers or manufacturers. The law allows for the removal from the register and the cancellation of the certificate of registration of any party if a complaint of malpractice is received and proven, and/or if the party is blacklisted.

The law also allows the authorities to blacklist an offender who has been found guilty of malpractice. The particulars of the blacklisted party should be ' . . . exhibited at conspicuous places in all tourist areas and notified to all travel, trade and other concerned organisations, foreign missions in India, Indian missions abroad and other important concerned channels after the order blacklisting him has become final. The offender is still liable for prosecution and a fine not exceeding Rs 1000 or imprisonment for up to three months or both.'

The law interestingly states that 'any offence relating to touting committed under this Act shall be cognizable and non-bailable'. Other points of interest are that if the tourist making the complaint is unable to give evidence in person (eg they returned home), the complaint can be made in writing and the case pursued in their absence. Also, the authorities 'may accept from any person accused of an offence under this Act, a sum of money . . . and may out of money so received compensate the person against whom the offence has been committed to the extent the prescribed authority deems reasonable'.

Finally, the authorities have the power to place a three to six-month ban on any person indulging in touting at places like the airport, railway station, bus stand, Tourist Reception Centre and picnic areas.

On paper it looks like the tourist is well protected from activities which have been a regular occurrence in the region for as long as most people can remember. But while in theory you can file a complaint in any part of J&K, you will fare a lot better if you go to the office of the Deputy Director of Tourism (Enforcement) which is upstairs in the Tourist Reception Centre, Srinagar. If you are in Jammu, try contacting the Deputy Director of Tourism (Jammu Division) but, more than likely, he will be unable to help.

I was told by the incumbent Deputy Director of Tourism (Enforcement) that the State

Government had initiated a new drive against crimes involving tourists as victims. As a result, the tourist police division is supposedly being enlarged and trained to cope with the high level of crime in this field. When I visited his office I was shown numerous case files which illustrated the kind of work being done under the Act. These included examples of some of the classic scams visitors are regularly caught by.

One involved a party of women who had been charged a lot more than the going rate by their houseboatman for a sightseeing trip to Ladakh. On their return to Srinagar, after various problems with the arrangement for which they were paying so much (eg unreliable and sub-standard transport, poor accommodation and a guide with little real knowledge of the area), they complained to the enforcement office. The houseboatman was contacted and after giving his version of the events he was made to pay back some of the money he had charged for the trip.

Other cases included tourists putting a deposit on a carpet, sending the balance on their return home and never receiving the carpet as agreed. The enforcement office had seen to it that the various carpets were eventually sent. As it says in the Act, the enforcement office has the power to make an offender pay back to his victim some/all of the money paid to him, or to replace unsatisfactory goods where applicable.

Unfortunately I did witness cases where tourists complained in my presence and were unable to get the assistance they felt they deserved. Until now, not many tourists were aware of the Act and their rights of protection under it. When I spoke to various tourists and group leaders the overall reaction was that it's 'too good to be true; no way can a ripped-off traveller get their money back', and that 'the police are too corrupt and self-centred to really be able to do anything'.

They may be right, but I did meet some enforcement officers who seemed more efficient than that, and so I would encourage any of you who have been ripped off to test the letter of the law and file a complaint. You may feel that you would be wasting your time, but you should at least try. Who knows, if enough victims of the local con men take a stand things could improve.

I saw how sometimes merely mentioning going to the enforcement office to file a complaint can make a merchant want to settle with you, although sometimes it will cause them to laugh and dare you to try. However, you should not be deterred by such a reaction. After being hauled into the Deputy Director's office many will be happy to settle with you.

A final word of advice: it certainly helps your case if you are firm with the enforcement officers. Insist that you want action taken and that you will take your complaint to the Chief Minister of J&K if nothing is done. If after that you are still unhappy, carry out that threat and write to the Chief Minister in Jammu. Supposedly it was his office that initiated the new drive against these crimes so he should be told if it isn't working.

Some of the complaints I read on file were written after the tourists had left India, and had found their way to the Srinagar enforcement office via the India Tourist Office or Indian Embassy in their home country.

Trout Fishing

To the keen angler, nothing is more satisfying than landing a glistening trout after a brief battle and even the not-so-keen fisherman will probably enjoy a just-cooked trout from the clean and clear rivers of Kashmir.

Fishing is big business in Kashmir through spring and summer. The British introduced the brown and rainbow trout to the streams of Kashmir, where they have thrived.

The season runs from April to October. Only artificial flies are allowed and each licence entitles the angler to keep six fish a day, none being shorter than 7.5 cm.

The British also introduced the system of anglers reserving beats on their favourite river. Reservations should be made before you arrive in Kashmir, through an Indian Government Tourist Office or directly at the Tourist Reception Centre in Srinagar. Beats can be reserved for a day or a week at a time in one of the three basic types of streams.

Larger rivers like the Sindh (Indus) or Lidder are full with snow melt from May to July. Spinning is allowed here, but the wet fly and weighted cast tests the skill of the angler and can produce good results. In April, August and September these rivers are quieter and the bigger fish are said to lie in the still waters.

Tributaries and water channels near these main stream beats provide another type of fishing throughout the season. These are the smaller streams where only flies are allowed, with wet fly fishing good all season.

The third type are the small spring-fed streams and high altitude lakes suitable for both dry and wet fly tackle.

It is not necessary to take tackle unless you are fussy, as everything can be bought or hired in Srinagar. A light, two-to-three metre rod (fishing rods cannot be carried as hand luggage on aircraft for security reasons) with an eight cm reel will suffice. Common flies in use include Peacock, March Brown, Butcher, Jinger Quill, Coachman, Woodcock & Green and Watson's Fancy.

There are 61 beats open for reservation throughout the season, ranging from the turbulence of the Sindh and Wangat rivers to the tranquillity of the high altitude lakes Krishanshar, Vishanshar, Gangabal and Nun Khol. On arrival at the beat, hand your permit to the beat watcher. The ghillie will be waiting to offer advice and service, such as netting the fish when it is brought to shore and gutting and cleaning. With licence, transportation, tips for the guides and the ghillie, a day's fishing could cost at least Rs 500!

Srinagar

The capital of Jammu and Kashmir and the largest city in the state, Srinagar (altitude 1768 metres), is famous for its canals, houseboats and Moghul gardens.

With more of a central Asian flavour than that of other Indian cities, Srinagar is, nonetheless, just as noisy, crowded (population 450,000) and polluted as its peers to the south. For many, this may be your first destination after arriving in India and you will probably still be going through the initial stages of culture shock.

The constant traffic with its noise and heavy exhaust fumes, the filth in certain areas and the constant approaches from hard-nosed touts offering transport, accommodation, handicrafts, etc will combine to put your tolerance to the test. However, your perseverance is rewarded with Srinagar's lovelier side – the colourful hustle and bustle of markets and bazaars, intriguing alleyways and curious buildings and the beauty of its lakes and waterways, gardens and mountain views.

In winter the temperature in Srinagar can fall as low as – 12°C.

History

The city has long been a centre for the arts and learning, having had a university for hundreds of years, and it's now also a centre for Sanskrit study. *Sri* means beauty or wealth of knowledge and *nagar* means city.

The city was originally founded by the great Buddhist Emperor Ashoka during the 3rd century BC. His old city is marked by the present village of Pandrethan.

Today's city was founded by Pravarasena II (79-139 AD) who named it Praparapura and built it practically contiguous with the old capital, which was called Srinagari.

Legend has it that when Pravarasena decided to build a new capital, to choose the location he started walking at midnight and was confronted by a demon on the other side of the Mahasarit River. The demon spread his bent leg across the stream and dared the King to cross over it to the other side. The King cut off the leg with one stroke of his sword and calmly crossed. The demon was delighted with the King's boldness and told him to build the city where he would find the beginnings of a plan laid out for him.

The next morning the King found the boundary lines drawn at the foot of Hari Parbat and built his city there. To this day the waters of the Dal Lake are separated from the Tsont-i-Kul canal by a *sathu* or bund that is shaped like a bent leg.

Praparapura is recorded in Chinese annals by traveller Hiuan Tsang who visited the city in about 630 AD and described it as extending about four km from north to south and about two km from east to west along the right bank of the Jhelum. King Ananta (1028-63 AD) was the first to transfer his royal residence to the left bank of the river.

Orientation

Srinagar is initially a little confusing since Dal Lake, which is so much a part of the city, is fairly strange. It's actually three lakes, separated by dykes or 'floating gardens', and at times it's hard to tell where the lake ends and land begins.

On the lake are houseboats that are definitely firmly attached to the bottom, and houses that look like they could float away. Most of the houseboats are at the southern end of the lake, although you will also find them on the Jhelum River and north on Nagin Lake. The Jhelum River makes a loop around the main part of town, and a canal connecting the river with Dal Lake converts that part of town into an island. Along the south of this 'island' is the Bund, a popular walk. Here you will find the post office and the handicrafts centre. The large Tourist Reception Centre is just north of the Bund.

There are many restaurants, shops, travel agents and hotels in the island part of town. The more modern part of Srinagar stretches south of the Jhelum while the older parts of town are north and north-west of here.

The Boulevard, running alongside Dal Lake, is an important address in Srinagar with the *shikara ghats* providing access to the houseboats, hotels, restaurants and shops along the way. Other main roads are Residency Rd, linking the Tourist Reception Centre with the downtown area, and Polo View Rd, lined with handicraft and clothing shops and travel agencies.

Tourist Information

Tourist Office The Srinagar office of the J&K Department of Tourism is at the Tourist Reception Centre which is a large complex housing the various tourist departments, Indian Airlines, a restaurant/cafeteria, an accommodation block and hotel and houseboat booking counters.

It is also the departure and arrival point for J&K Road Transport Corporation tour buses and general buses to Jammu and Leh.

This tourist office has not enjoyed a reputation for efficiency or helpfulness, in fact far from it. Srinagar's Tourist Reception Centre is a perfect example of the problems befalling India's government services today, namely corruption, idleness and general inefficiency with more than a dash of good old bureaucracy to slow things down and cause irritation.

The staff are consistently either lacking in sufficient knowledge to be of real help, simply unwilling to help, impatient and curt to the point of rudeness, or guilty of pointing tourists in the direction of amenities whose owners are friends and who pay them a commission for each customer they send. As always there are exceptions to the rule, but this is an accurate picture of the overall situation.

For reasons best known to themselves the tourist office initially attempts to steer all tourists through the Tourist Reception Centre. Virtually all the buses to Kashmir arrive and depart from the centre and if you come by bus from the airport you will also arrive there although you can ask to be dropped off earlier. The tourist office may even say that you should book accommodation through them but this is not necessary and is likely to be more expensive or offer less choice than if you dealt with houseboats or hotels directly.

You will often find that you can get more information and friendly assistance from Choomti Trekkers on their houseboat opposite the main post office on the Bund.

General Information

Post The main postal branch is on the Bund and its staff are on the whole friendly and efficient.

Opening hours vary for different services, but basically these are Monday to Saturday 10 am to 1 pm, 1.30 to 6 pm and closed Sunday. There are other convenient branches at the Tourist Reception Centre and on Dal Lake (appropriately a *doonga* boat moored beside the Boulevard by Nehru Park).

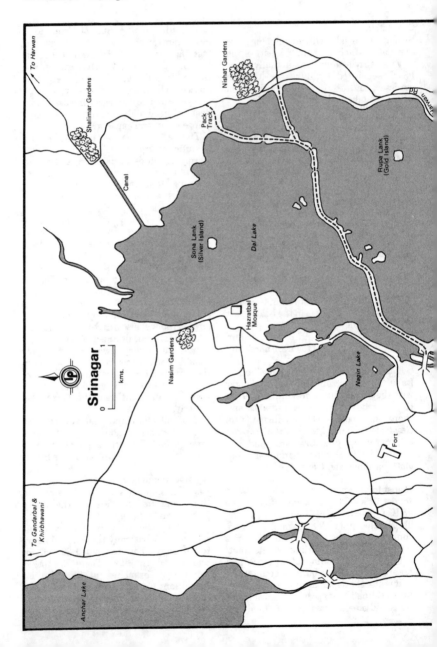

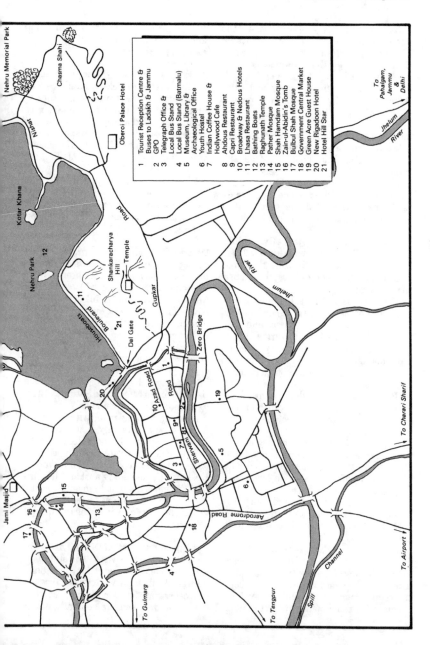

1 Tourist Reception Centre &
  Buses to Ladakh & Jammu
2 GPO
3 Telegraph Office &
  Local Bus Stand
4 Local Bus Stand (Batmalu)
5 Museum, Library &
  Archaeological Office
6 Youth Hostel
7 Indian Coffee House &
  Hollywood Cafe
8 Ahdous Restaurant
9 Capri Restaurant
10 Broadway & Nedous Hotels
11 Lhasa Restaurant
12 Bathing Boats
13 Raghunath Temple
14 Pather Mosque
15 Shah Hamdam Mosque
16 Zain-ul-Abidin's Tomb
17 Bulbul Shah Mosque
18 Government Central Market
19 Green Acre Guest House
20 New Rigadoon Hotel
21 Hotel Hill Star

To send parcels you must go to the foreign post office in the Air Cargo Complex on Residency Rd (near the Tourist Reception Centre and across from the Cafe de Lintz). This is open Monday to Friday 10.30 am to 1 pm and 1.30 to 3.30 pm; Saturday 10.30 am to 2 pm and closed Sunday.

Telephone For telephone, telegram and telex facilities, the telegraph office is on Hotel or Manhara Azad Rd. Open 24 hours, it is notorious for lousy service, long and often unruly queues and difficulties in phoning long distance and overseas. It is cheaper and generally less crowded to make calls outside of day-time hours.

Banks & Money-changers By Indian standards Srinagar's banking facilities can be quite good, but with the large number of tourists queues to change money can be long.

The J&K Bank on the Boulevard is open later in the day than the competition and can be more convenient and less crowded. It's open Monday to Friday 10 am to 3 pm and 4 to 6 pm, Saturday 10 am to 2 pm and 3 to 4 pm, and closed Sunday.

Other banks include the State Bank of India in the Tourist Reception Centre and on Residency Rd. Grindley's (across from Polo View Rd with it's entrance on the Bund) and the Punjab National Bank are also on Residency Rd.

It is possible to change money on the black market but for many it is not worth the hassle or the risk of being cheated. The rates are usually less than in Delhi and only a little above the bank rate. The Boulevard by Dal Gate and, surprise, surprise, your houseboat are the places to go. It's always worthwhile bargaining over the rate.

The American Express office is at Kai Travels, on the Boulevard by the entrance to the driveway of the Oberoi Palace Hotel. They provide the standard services except the replacement of lost/stolen travellers cheques. For that you have to go to Delhi.

It's open Monday to Friday 9.30 am to 1 pm and 2 to 6 pm, Saturday 9.30 am to 1 pm, and closed Sunday.

Bookstores The best bookshops in Srinagar are the Kashmir Bookshop and the Hind Bookshop, across from each other on Sharmani Rd (the continuation of Residency Rd downtown). For the best available selection of newspapers and magazines, including *Time* and *Newsweek*, check the kiosk at the side of the India Coffee House nearby.

Choomti Trekkers, opposite the main post office on the Bund, carry a small stock of good books and operate a book exchange, buying and selling used books at reasonable prices.

Libraries Travellers are permitted to use Srinagar's various libraries for reference purposes. The main public library is in the same building as the Shri Pratap Singh Museum, on the south bank of the Jhelum River. In the adjacent building there is a reading room with most of the day's Indian newspapers and current editions of various magazines, including *Time* and *Newsweek*. Walking past the museum entrance, the library is at the back of the building and the reading room is to the right. It's open Monday to Saturday 10 am to 4 pm, and closed Sunday.

Another reading room with the day's Indian newspapers only is at the Sher-i-Kashmir Gardens library on Residency Rd.

The Kai Travels/American Express office has a great collection of books about Kashmir, Ladakh and Zanskar. Many are rarely found elsewhere. Managing director Mr Kai Suri is happy to let interested visitors benefit from browsing through his collection.

Foreigners' Registration Office This is the place to renew your visas. The staff have earned mixed reports about their helpfulness. While some visitor's say they are OK, others say that they charge a fee when they shouldn't and are generally not as good to deal with as other offices. The building is next to the park with the Government Handicrafts Emporium, near the Bund. It can also be reached from Residency Rd by taking the side road past the Air Cargo Complex.

Airlines The Indian Airlines Office is in the Tourist Reception Centre. Open daily from 10 am to 5 pm, it's usually very busy.

The Air India office is in front of the Broadway Hotel. You can reserve and confirm their international flights from here, as well as their flights within India.

Dal Lake

Initially, Dal Lake is one of the most confusing parts of Srinagar because it's not really one lake, but three.

Also it's hardly what you would expect a lake to be like as it's a maze of intricate waterways and channels, floating islands of vegetation, houseboats that look so firmly moored they could almost be islands and hotels on islands which look like they could simply float away.

Dal Lake lies immediately to the east and north of Srinagar and stretches over five km. The lake is divided by a series of causeways into Gagribal, Lokut Dal and Bod Dal. Nagin Lake, which is usually thought of as a separate lake, is also only divided from Dal Lake by a causeway. The causeways are mostly suitable for walkers and cyclists only so they make a very pleasant way of seeing the lake without worrying about traffic or shikaras.

The main causeway across the lake carries the water pipeline for Srinagar's mains water supply. Dal Gate, at the city end of Dal Lake, controls the flow of the lake into the Jhelum River canal. It's the steady flow of water through the lake, combined with its relatively cold temperature, which keeps it so clear looking.

This is remarkable considering what gets poured into it everyday, not only from the houseboats but from the city and outlying areas too. There is no real sewage disposal system, although houseboatmen and officials are good at telling stories to cover this up. You will see notices urging people to keep the lake clean and modern machines collecting the weeds, but the fact remains that the flush toilets, on even the most luxurious houseboats, empty straight into the lake. I have been told superb lies by locals explaining how every houseboat has a cesspool that is emptied each week.

Another unpleasant truth regularly hushed up is that water from the taps and shower heads on the houseboats sometimes comes straight from the lake. While this is not the case on most houseboats, it happens a lot more than the locals would have you believe. If you can see that the houseboat's water is being piped from land, you can be sure that you are not being expected to wash in dirty lake water. However, old habits die hard and you should always look out for a water tank on the houseboat roof. This has a hand pump that one of the family may operate each day to pull water up from the lake.

You will see the locals take advantage of the water not only by swimming, but by bathing, doing the laundry (including yours) and using the lakes and waterways as a toilet and waste disposal unit.

In the deeper parts of Dal and Nagin, bathing boats are popular, mainly with Indian tourists. Despite the way hygiene standards are neglected, the water in these areas does not seem so unpleasant and many of you will probably feel like taking a refreshing dip on a warm day.

The largest group of houseboats lies along the western edge of the Dal Lake near the lakeside Boulevard, towards Dal Gate. They are lined in looping rows and around small islands. Several hotels can also be found on flat islands in the lake. Beyond the houseboats to the north-west are the floating gardens.

The lake is at its most colourful when the lotus flowers bloom in July and August. The floating gardens, known as *rad* in Kashmiri, are one of the stranger aspects of Dal Lake. They're composed of matted vegetation and earth which are cut away from the lake bottom and towed to a convenient location where they are moored. Tomatoes, cucumbers and melons grow amazingly well in these gardens. If you look underneath you can see that they do literally float on the lake. Of course one problem with a floating garden is that a lazy and dishonest gardener can steal it!

You will often see weeds being pulled up out of the lake. This serves a double purpose – the lake waterways are kept clear and the weeds are rotted until they form an excellent compost for the gardens.

The shallowness of the lake and it's heavy growth of waterweeds is probably the main reason why there are so very few powered boats on the water. Dal Lake would be nowhere near as pleasant if there were powerboats rushing back and forth across its tranquil surface.

Around the lake are many of Srinagar's most interesting sights, particularly the pleasant Moghul gardens. It's also flanked by hills, mainly along its east bank. The Shankaracharya Hill provides a very fine view over the lake.

The two best ways to enjoy the lake are by shikara and by bicycle – see the Getting Around section.

Islands

There are three main islands in the lake, each popular excursion points. Silver Island (Sona Lank) is at the northern end of Dal Lake and is also known as Char Chinar after the four (*char*) chinar trees which grow on it. There's a small snack bar on the island as there is also on Gold Island (Rupa Lank) at the south end of the lake. It is also known as Char Chinar for it too has four chinar trees.

The third island is Nehru Park, at the end of the main stretch of the Boulevard and only a short distance from the shore. A favourite spot for Indian tourists, it has a restaurant, children's playground and, during the summer season, evening shows, dances and festivals.

North of Nehru Island a long causeway leads out into the lake from the Boulevard. At its end is Kotar Khana, the 'house of pigeons', which was once a royal summer house.

The Bund

From above Zero Bridge to below Badshah Bridge you can walk along the banks of the Jhelum River on the popular footpath known as the Bund. It's a pleasant relaxing place to stroll along and many *doonga* houseboats can be seen beside it.

The main post office, the Government Handicrafts Emporium (in the old British Residency) and a string of handicraft shops are all close to the Bund.

During the Raj period of the 19th century when the British first came to Kashmir in large numbers, the Bund was the most popular place to stay on a houseboat. This was because the British loved to be able to stroll along the river bank after breakfast and go to the post office, bank and shops without the inconvenience of relying on transportation. These days the houseboat owners on the Bund have a harder time attracting guests as Dal and Nagin Lakes are far more popular (see the Places to Stay section).

Jhelum River & Bridges

The Jhelum (Vetasta in Hindi) flows from Verinag, 80 km south of Srinagar, to the Wular Lake in the north. Passing through Srinagar, it's a wide, swiftly flowing, muddy-looking river which draws water from the lakes around the city as well as the many canals and rivers which meander through the area.

The Jhelum is famed for its nine old bridges, although some of them are being replaced by more modern structures. The stretch north of the city is especially beautiful with many fine views of Srinagar's old buildings on the riverbanks. You'll also find Srinagar's most interesting old

Top: Hazratbal Mosque by Dal Lake (TW)
Bottom: Houseboats on Dal Lake (NT)

Top: Kashmiri house, typical of those along Srinagar's waterways (RK)
Left: Srinagar houses (TW)
Right: Jami Masjid Mosque, Srinagar (TW)

mosques along this stretch and since the roads are too narrow and winding for most vehicles it's a great area to explore on foot or bicycle. You can also take a shikara along the river from Dal Gate or Zero Bridge.

Starting from Dal Gate in a boat, go south along the canal connecting Dal Lake to the river. On the right is the golf course and on the left the Srinagar Club where tourist visitors are welcome. Just beyond the club the canal enters the first Jhelum bridge, called Zero Bridge, which is close to the Tourist Reception Centre.

The next bridge is commonly known as the first bridge as it's the first of the 'old' bridges. Built by Amir Khan it's called the Amira Kadal. Between Zero Bridge and the Amira Kadal you drift along beside the Bund, past the Government Handicrafts Emporium and the Government Silk Weaving Factory on the opposite bank. Beyond that is the Shri Pratap Singh Museum.

The next bridge is the heavily trafficked modern Badshah Bridge and the Habba Kadal in the old part of town. On the left bank of the river, between the Badshah Bridge and the Habba Kadal, is the royal palace where the previous Maharaja used to live. Set back some distance from the riverbank, it's now a government building. Nearby is the secretariat building and the Mahatma Gandhi Memorial Park.

On the right side the Tsont-i-Kul or 'apple canal' joins the Jhelum. This canal starts from the Dal Gate and with a loop of the Jhelum makes part of Srinagar into an island. The busiest part of the old city is near the Habba Kadal bridge in an area where the national hospital and the Raghunath Mandir, Kashmir's biggest temple and the twin of the golden-spired temple in Jammu, also stand.

The third old bridge, the Fateh Kadal, is just before the Shah Hamdan Mosque and a new bridge has recently been built just upstream from it. The Zaina Kadal is the fourth bridge and crosses the river close to the tomb of its builder in the 15th

century, the famous Kashmiri Muslim ruler Zain-ul-Abidin, also known as Badshah.

The fifth bridge, the Ali Kadal, is named after his son. Lesser mosques close to the river include the Mosque of Bulbul Shah, close to the Ali Kadal. Bulbul Shah was a Kashmiri mystic and the first Muslim *fakir* to visit the valley. The ruined Badshah Mosque, close to the tomb of Zain-ul-Abidin, is enclosed by an old stone wall and there is a belief that the bricks of this mosque could cure smallpox. The Maharaja Ranbir Gang Bazaar, an important trade centre, is also here.

Just below the sixth bridge, the Nawa Kadal, you can see the Kota canal enter the river. This diverts the river's flow at times of flood and leaves the Jhelum between the Amira Kadal and the Habba Kadal.

Next by the seventh bridge, the Saffa Kadal, is the old Yarkand Sarai, a travellers' resting place. The Jhelum weir is just past this bridge and on the left bank are the graineries of the Kashmir Valley Food Control Department. Also close by is the large open ground known as *Idgah* where prayers are held during the Muslim Id festival.

Lastly, at the Taski Kadal you can again leave the river on the Tsont-i-Kul canal and pass under the floodgate back to the Dal Gate.

The options available for taking a shikara cruise on the Jhelum vary according to the water level, with some canals being allowed to dry up and the water diverted elsewhere.

Museum

The Shri Pratap Singh Museum is in Lal Mandi, just south of the river between Zero Bridge and Amira Kadal. It has an interesting collection of exhibits relevant to Kashmir, including illustrated tiles excavated near Harwan.

The museum is open from 10.30 am to 4.30 pm except on Mondays when it's closed all day, and Friday when it is closed for

Muslim prayers between 1 and 2.30 pm. Admission is free but the fast-talking guides will expect a tip if you allow them to escort you.

Moghul Gardens

From Tehran to Agra the Moghul emperors built gardens, or *baghs*, but it was in Kashmir, complemented by the lake and the mountains, that they reached their perfection. Indeed, along with the houseboats and the mountains, these gardens are Kashmir's feature attraction.

The gardens all follow the same rectangular layout with a series of terraces rising one above the other up the hillside. Down the centre flows a stone channel carrying water through a series of pools and cascades.

This system of carrying running water through the artificial cascades, and the layout of the fountains, was introduced to India in the 16th century by the artisans employed by Emperor Akbar.

Combine a visit to one or more of these gardens with a shikara cruise on the lake or a bicycle ride around the shore.

Chasma Shahi (9 km from Srinagar) The smallest of the Srinagar Moghul gardens, measuring just 108 metres by 38 metres, the Chasma Shahi or 'royal spring' gardens are well up the hillside, above the Nehru Memorial Park.

The freshwater spring in these pleasant, quieter gardens is reputed to have medicinal properties. The gardens were laid out in 1632 by Ali Mardan Khan and include three terraces, an aqueduct, waterfalls and fountains. The water from the spring supplies the fountains then goes through the floor of the pavilion and falls to the lower terrace in a fine cascade of five metres, over a polished black stone chute.

Some extensions have been made to the gardens. Like all the gardens the Chasma Shahi is open from sunrise to sunset but unlike the other gardens this is the only one which charges admission. There is a small shrine, the Chasma Sahibi, near the gardens which also has a freshwater spring.

Pari Mahal (10 km) The old Sufi college of Pari Mahal, the 'palace of the fairies', is only a short distance above the Chasma Shahi gardens. You can easily walk from the gardens up to the Pari Mahal then follow a footpath directly down the hill to the road that runs by the Oberoi Palace Hotel.

The Pari Mahal consists of a series of ruined, arched terraces and had, over the years, become considerably overgrown and neglected. Recently it has been turned into a very pleasant and well-kept garden with fine views over Dal Lake. It's attractively sited on a spur of the Zabarwan mountains.

The college was built in the 17th century by Prince Dara Shikah, the eldest son of Emperor Shah Jahan. The prince had a keen interest in Sufiism and Hindu philosophy and his right to the throne was usurped by his younger brother who became the Emperor Aurangzeb and was noted for his fanatical Muslim beliefs.

A shrine to the Goddess Parvati near the foot of the Pari Mahal hill is popular on Thursdays in May-June, the Kashmiri month of Jeth. Near the spring at the shrine is a large chinar with groves of fruit trees, poplars and willows all around.

Nishat Bagh (11 km) Sandwiched between the lake and the mountains, the Nishat gardens or 'gardens of pleasure' have a particularly fine view across the lake to the Pir Panjal mountain range in the west.

The gardens were designed in 1633 by Asaf Khan, Emperor Jehangir's brother-in-law, and follow the same pattern as the Shalimar gardens with a polished stone channel running down the centre and a series of terraces.

It's the largest of the Moghul gardens, measuring 548 metres by 338 metres, and often the most crowded. The walks beside the channel are bordered with lines of cypresses and chinars. The garden has 10 terraces and the remains of some Moghul period buildings including a double-storey pavilion enclosed on two sides by latticed windows.

Directly behind the garden is the Gopi Tirth, a small spring gushing forth crystal-clear water which feeds the garden water channel.

Shalimar Bagh (15 km) Set some distance back from the lake, but reached by a small canal, the Shalimar gardens were built by Emperor Jehangir for his wife Nur Jahan 'light of the world' in 1616. Although it is known now as the 'garden of love' it was originally named the *Farah Bakhsh* or 'delightful garden'.

The gardens, built in four terraces with the traditional water channel running down the middle, measure 540 metres by 183 metres. During the Moghul period the top terrace, the most magnificent, was reserved for the emperor and the ladies of the court. It included a pavilion made of black stone, supported by black marble fluted pillars. The pavilion was used as a banquet hall.

The gardens are beautifully kept and a *son et lumiere* (sound and light) show is performed every evening during the May to October tourist season. The English performance takes place at 9 pm and tickets cost Rs 10 or Rs 15. The gardens tend to be very crowded on Sundays.

Nasim Bagh (8 km) Only a short distance beyond the Hazratbal Mosque, the Nasim gardens, the 'garden of tepid airs' or 'garden of the morning breeze', were built by the Moghul Emperor Akbar after his conquest of Kashmir in 1586. He had 1200 chinar trees planted here – the oldest of Kashmir's Moghul gardens. Now it's used by an engineering college and is not kept up for the public like the other Moghul gardens in Srinagar. It is possible to camp in this garden, but permission has to be obtained from the Tourist Reception Centre.

Shah Hamdan Mosque
One of the oldest mosques in Srinagar, the wooden Shah Hamdan Mosque stands beside the Jhelum, three km from Srinagar, and is noted for the papier mache work on its walls and ceilings. No nails or screws were used in its construction. Originally built in 1395 it was destroyed by fire in 1479 and again in 1731.

Shaped like a cube with a pyramidal roof rising to a 38-metre high spire, the roof is also covered with turf in which flowers are planted in spring. Arcades, verandahs and porticos surround the large, central wooden hall. Non-believers are not allowed inside.

Nearby is a market which includes curios, wood carving, papier mache, embroidery, silverwork and precious and semi-precious stones.

Pather Masjid
Almost directly opposite the Shah Hamdan Mosque, on the other bank of the Jhelum, the Pather Masjid is a fine stone mosque built by Nur Jahan in 1623. It is no longer in everyday use and is consequently rather run down. You can reach it by crossing Zaina Kadal, the fourth bridge.

Tomb of Zain-ul-Abidin
On the east (right) bank of the river, between the Zaina Kadal and the Ali Kadal, is the slightly decrepit tomb of King Zain-ul-Abidin, the highly regarded son of Sultan Sikander, who built the Jami Masjid.

The tomb, four km from Srinagar, was built on the foundations of an earlier temple and shows a clear Persian influence in its domed construction and glazed tiles. Moulded bricks can also be found at intervals in the exterior walls. In the enclosures are fragments of inscriptions, the oldest in Kashmir in Pali characters. Over the posterior gate is an inscription in Persian.

Jami Masjid

Srinagar's most important mosque is an impressive wooden structure, five km from the city. Jami Masjid is notable for its soaring pillars, more than 300, which support the roof. Each is made of a single deodar tree trunk.

The main gate is to the south and the outer cloisters surround a spacious, green and peaceful inner courtyard. The roughly square building is 117 metres on each side, topped by four minars in the centre of each side and three pagoda-shaped minarets from which the faithful are called to prayer.

The mosque has a chequered history. First constructed by Sultan Sikander in 1385, it was enlarged in 1402 by his son Zain-ul-Abidin but was destroyed by fire in 1479. The mosque was rebuilt by 1503 but was destroyed in another fire during the reign of the Moghul Emperor Jehangir. It was rebuilt by the Kashmiri architect and historian Malik Haider Chaudara but burnt down yet again in 1674 during the reign of Emperor Aurangzeb. The present mosque dates from that time but was rebuilt, on the last occasion, to the original Indo-Saracenic design.

Shankaracharya Hill

Rising up behind the Boulevard beside Dal Lake, the hill was once known as *Takht-i-Sulaiman*, the Throne of Solomon. It is thought that a temple was originally built on top of the hill by Jaluka, Emperor Ashoka's son, around 200 BC. The present Hindu temple was built during the reign of Emperor Jehangir, but its enclosing wall and plinth is thought to date from the earlier temple.

A road runs up the hill to the television transmitting station just below the temple, and it's a very pleasant stroll to the top. Go up early when the sky is clear and you'll be rewarded with fine views over the houseboats on the lake directly below and out across Srinagar to the mountains in the distance.

Paths lead up from the Nehru Park end of the Boulevard (look for the small pavilion halfway up the hill) and from behind the bazaar just south of Dal Gate. This is the easiest route on foot. Leave the main street and enter the main bazaar, bear left and uphill where you pass the church and hospital on your right. On your left is the Muslim cemetery and the path to the temple starts beyond here. There's also a steep trail to the top from directly behind the hotels and bazaar at Dal Gate.

Hazratbal Mosque

If you were doing a clockwise tour of the lake by shikara, after winding your way through the floating gardens and the channels and waterways you'd eventually come out on the open lake and find yourself at the Hazratbal Mosque (Majestic Palace), seven km from Srinagar.

The fairly new and shiny mosque enshrines a hair of the prophet but is probably more interesting, to non-Muslims, for its simply stunning location on the banks of the beautiful lake with the mountains unfolding as a backdrop. The mosque bazaar is very busy on Fridays.

The sacred hair was brought to India in 1634 by Syyid Abdullah and acquired by a Kashmiri trader, Noor-ud-Din, in 1692. It eventually made its way to Kashmir in 1700. The mosque is a blend of Moghul and Kashmiri architecture with a three-tiered roof topping walls and porticos of brick masonry on a base of dressed stone.

The Kashmir University campus stands just 200 metres from the mosque. The campus was a grant from Dr Karan Singh, the present heir to the Dogra title.

Nagin Lake

Known as the 'jewel in the ring', Nagin is generally held to be the most beautiful of the Dal Lakes. Its name comes from the many trees which encircle the small, deep blue lake. Nagin is only separated from the larger Dal Lakes by a narrow causeway and it also has many houseboats moored around its perimeter. If you want to really get away from it all then Nagin (eight km from Srinagar) can be a good place to find a houseboat and do it.

Nagin Lake is deeper and less polluted than the others and the bathing boats at the northern end are, perhaps, more inviting. Mind you, the noisy and smelly motor boats don't help, nor do they provide very good water skiing. With the absence of any real emergency services, be extra wary of the boats and skiers when swimming or paddling a shikara, and vice versa.

The Nagin Club, on the bank of the lake, has a bar and a tea pavilion. It is a branch of the Srinagar Club and temporary membership is available to visitors.

Hari Parbat Fort

The 18th century fort tops the Sharika hill which is clearly visible rising to the west of Dal Lake. At night the fort is floodlit and can appear to be hovering above the lakeside.

Construction was begun by Atta Mohammed Khan in 1776, but the surrounding wall was built between 1592 and 1598 during the rule of Emperor Akbar. The wall stretches for five km and is 10 metres high and has two gates, the Kathi and Sangin Darwaza. The Kathi is the main entrance with Persian commemorative inscriptions surrounding it. The Sangin, however, is more ornate with sculptured windows on either side.

Visits to the fort, now used as an arsenal, are only possible with written permission from the Archaeology Department at an office next to the library reading room behind the Shri Pratap Singh Museum in Srinagar.

The fort (five km from Srinagar) contains a temple revered for its image of the Goddess Sharika. Outside the fort's southern gate is a shrine to the sixth Sikh Guru, known as the Chati Pad Shaki. The hill, which rises 122 metres from the valley floor, is surrounded by orchards of almond

trees where many Kashmiris come for picnics in spring and summer.

Pandrethan Temple

A small, beautifully proportioned Shiva temple built around 900 AD, the Pandrethan temple is in the military cantonment area on the Jammu road, five km out of Srinagar.

Shadaharwan

About 22 km from Srinagar and five km beyond the Shalimar gardens, this place is said to have been the site of a monastery in which the Fourth International Council of Buddhism was held in 300 AD.

At this time Kashmir was part of the Kushan Empire under the rule of the Buddhist Emperor Kanishka. The monastery is said to have contained a stupa, some chapels and other buildings. Recent excavations in the area uncovered some illustrated tiles on the hillside south of the nearby village of Harwan. You can see examples of the tiles, with their Central Asian influence in the people's dress and ornaments, in the museum in Srinagar.

Close by is the Harwan Lake at the foot of the 4267-metre Mahadev peak, a popular climb for hikers during summer. The lake is actually the reservoir which provides the water supply for Srinagar, and is supplied by the run-off from Marsar Lake. There is also a garden and trout hatchery at the site.

Burzahom

In the opposite direction to the Shalimar gardens, about five km to the north-west, are the even older excavations of Burzahom. This archaeological dig has provided evidence of people living in the vale up to 5000 years ago. The oldest excavations have revealed implements, pots, animal skeletons, arrowheads and tools from the neolithic age. Much of the material taken from this site is now in the museum in Srinagar, 24 km away.

Jesus in Kashmir

Search out the Rauzabal or 'prophet's tomb' in the oldest part of the city while you're in Srinagar. You'll have found the final resting place of Jesus Christ, or so the legend goes.

Following his reappearance after the crucifixion (not so much rising from the dead as a narrow survival) Jesus fled from Palestine, the Kashmir story relates, accompanied by his mother Mary and the disciple Thomas. They paused in Damascus but eventually made their way east to the sub-continent where Mary died in Murree, near Rawalpindi in present-day Pakistan. Supposedly you can locate her tomb there too.

Jesus and Thomas continued on to Kashmir where Jesus settled in Yusmarg while Thomas went to the south of India. Jesus is, of course, also one of the great prophets of the Islamic faith and in Kashmir his name translates as Yus Asaf. So Yusmarg is the 'meadow of Jesus'.

After marrying a Kashmiri girl from Pahalgam Jesus lived out his life in Kashmir, eventually dying aged 85 or more. There are numerous texts and clues pointing, according to interested Kashmiris, to his life in Kashmir. Even the Hemis Gompa in Ladakh is said to have evidence of a visit.

To reach Rauzabal, which is not signposted, cycle or take an auto-rickshaw past the green and white Dastgir Mosque. The tomb is off the main road to the right, beyond the open area and behind a gated fence. If you ask a few locals for Rauzabal you should eventually be directed to the right place. Admission is free, with signs explaining how donations can be made. Remove shoes before entering and dress accordingly, eg no shorts or bare shoulders.

If you are curious and interested in learning more about the belief that Jesus preceded your visit to Kashmir, there are some books on the subject. The best one that I have seen is German titled *Jesus Lebte in Indian* by Holger Kershen. Unfortunately, I have no details of the publisher but, as far as I know, there is a hard-to-find English translation. The two local books I came across are hopeless by comparison. Usually stocked by the Srinagar bookshops, these are *Christ in Kashmir* by Aziz Kashmiri, and *Mysteries of Kashmir – Kashmir the Promised Land* by Mohammad Yasin.

Legend has it that some Kashmiris are descendants of the Jews. Members of a missing tribe of Israel are believed to have settled here. Moses too is said to be buried in Kashmir near Bandipur, by Wular Lake.

Places to Stay

While renowned for its houseboats, Srinagar also has many hotels and although most foreigners are attracted to the floating hostelries, most Indian tourists prefer to stay on dry land. There is often bitter rivalry between the houseboat owners and hoteliers, with the competition for trade fiercely fought.

Houseboats

Briefly, Kashmir's houseboats originated in the Victorian era as a superbly British solution to a tricky political problem. The British Raj loved to escape from the heat and dust of summer on the plains. However, the Maharajah wouldn't allow them to own property. Boats of various types had been a regular part of life in Kashmir for centuries, and to get around their dilemma, the Brits took to the water themselves.

In 1888 Mr T Kehard had the first houseboat built and the concept soon caught on. They're a great escape from the noise and hassle which Indian cities seem to have an over-supply of. As soon as you get out on the water the traffic and confusion fades away.

Houseboats simply offer great entertainment – just sit on the verandah of your boat or laze on the roof and life passes by in front of you. A flock of ducks, children barely old enough to walk (but quite adept at paddling), hookah smoking shikara wallahs, fat ladies in saris, and travellers (who are usually paddling themselves in circles) – they all pass by. You don't have to go to the shops as the shops come to you by shikara. Jewellers, papier mache dealers, incredibly persuasive tailors, even the local supermarket will turn up – 'you want beer, soap, cold drinks, toilet paper?' And if none of those appeal – 'hashish?'

In the early morning you can see ravens and hawks swooping on the lake to catch insects and fish. Late in the afternoon the garden boats, laden with produce from the floating gardens, will glide by, or the weed collector, with his boat that seems always ready to sink, laden with the heavy and wet weeds of the lake to be used as fertiliser.

Although the view changes with the seasons the magnificent mountains of the Pir Panjal, with glimpses of the great Himalaya, are a constant backdrop. In winter this whole scene is covered with snow, with the exception of the clear waters of the lake itself. In exceptionally cold winters, however, even the lake freezes over.

Officially houseboats rest in five categories with official prices (singles/doubles) for each category (full board with meals or lodging only):

	full board	lodging only
Deluxe or 5-star	Rs 275/405	Rs 190/270
A class	Rs 172/253	Rs 120/175
B class	Rs 120/204	Rs 80/140
C class	Rs 78/138	Rs 30/60
D class*	Rs 54/72	Rs 20/40

*doonga boats

There are different costs for children or for sole occupancy of an entire boat.

Firstly, what is a houseboat and what do you get for your money? Basically it's a flat-bottomed, very stationary boat, between 20 metres and 40 metres long and between three metres and six metres wide. Construction is of pine, lined with cedar.

They follow a very standard pattern in their design. You board the boat by a small verandah, furnished with padded seats, then enter the living room/lounge area which is invariably furnished in a style you could describe as English 1930s chintz. From the lounge you enter the dining room followed by the small kitchen area, although food is generally prepared in a nearby kitchen boat. Stairs lead up from here to the rooftop sundeck. Finally a corridor leads back along one side of the boat to two or three bedrooms, each with its own bathroom and toilet.

The all-inclusive price will include your room, all meals (breakfast, lunch and dinner), tea at least a couple of times a day and transport back and forth between your boat and the shore in the houseboat's shikara. Of course getting back is only possible if your shikara man happens to be waiting at the landing. Generally you'll have to take, and pay for, one of the shikaras waiting there. Houseboats are usually owned in groups of two, three or more with one shikara to serve them all and also one kitchen boat (or land-based equivalent) to feed them all.

The top five-star boats are very luxurious with new furniture and fittings, chandeliers in the dining room, radio or even television, running hot water and so on. This technological luxury can be a little too much of a good thing, especially when the electrical goodies blow the fuses with regularity or when a neighbour plays the television too loud!

Moving down the scale the drop in standards is usually a matter of age rather than facilities for houseboats all look remarkably alike, just younger or older. Doonga boats are, however, usually much smaller, often just one-roomed and with primitive sanitation facilities. The working doonga boats, which are usually inhabited by locals all year round, are usually found along the banks of the Jhelum River.

The tourist office official prices are actually nowhere near as rigid as their neat categorisation might indicate. For a start the boats vary within their categories – there's five-star and FIVE-STAR! Similarly, some run-down A-class boats are no better than some well-kept C-class boats. Also there's competition, so even at the height of the season there are a lot more houseboat berths than visitors and out of season the competition is intense to try and lure you aboard. The end result is prices are generally subject to negotiation. At the worst you should be able to get away with paying the level that applies to the category one step down.

Warning The Hanjits (boatmen) are the class with whom Englishmen who visit Kashmir come most into contact, and from whom they are apt to form their opinion of the whole nation. They have indeed some of the best and some of the worst qualities of the Kashmiris intensified. They are men of active imagination, which is shown in their ready tales and in the lying legends they are always prompt to invent to amuse one. They are excessively greedy, never being satisfied as long as they think there is the least chance of getting more. The cowardice which is proverbially a characteristic of the Kashmiris is shown by the Hanjits whenever they are overtaken on one of the lakes by a storm of wind. They have much of good spirits and of humour, and in energy and versatility they are behind none of their nation.

– Frederic Drew, 1865
Jummoo & Kashmir Territories

Good old Fred didn't mince his words, and he didn't miss much either. His observations are basically just as accurate more than one hundred years later. Staying on a houseboat can be one of the best travel experiences to be enjoyed anywhere, but you need to be extremely wary of the various scams that you are likely to come up against.

Touts With about 870 registered houseboats, the competition between the individual houseboat owners is ferocious. An increase in hotel numbers has only added to the glut of accommodation which means that many boats remain unoccupied, even during the peak summer season. This has resulted in an anarchistic system of touting that is as ingenious and energetic as it is unscrupulous. You will even be approached by touts in Delhi and Jammu trying to talk you into making an advance reservation for their houseboat.

The first golden rule is never to pay in advance or make a commitment to a houseboat until you have seen it. Each year countless travellers end up paying in advance for a houseboat and find, on arrival, that either the boat doesn't exist or is nothing like as marvellous as described. It's often in a poor location, is

grubby or has lousy food. The touts can sound very convincing with stories of everything being booked solid and of their boats being the only good ones. Don't fall for any of it.

If you manage to avoid the touts en route, you will definitely meet them in Srinagar. A few haunt the airport but they mostly wait outside the Tourist Reception Centre, where the tourist buses arrive, and by the lakeside. Although most countries have touts trying to persuade travellers to stay at their place, in Srinagar they operate with a relentless energy and zeal that knows no moral boundaries.

Shikaras Equally as persistent and troublesome as the houseboat touts are the shikara wallahs. These men, and often young boys too, earn their living from paddling locals and visitors alike between the houseboats and the lakeside, and from longer cruises around the lake. They can be extremely irritating with their constant touting, particularly as you walk along the Boulevard by Dal Lake's ghats.

New arrivals need to make a note of the current fare structure to avoid being grossly overcharged. Also insist that you be paddled to the boats that you want to see, not simply those that pay commission to the shikara wallah. Once you know about these ploys, you can relax and enjoy the ride.

Finding a Houseboat Due to the nature of the houseboat concept, finding a boat on your own is not as simple as wandering down a few streets of a strange town to select a room for the night. Most houseboats can only be reached by shikara and, as described, you need to deal with the attentions of the touts and shikara-wallahs.

Apparently in an effort to reduce the number of touts who harass visitors, the tourist department recommends that travellers book houseboat accommodation through their counters at the airport or the

Tourist Reception Centre. Each day the Houseboat Owners Association prepares a list of some of the available boats in each category. However, most travellers find that this system is far from satisfactory.

This is because the official prices are charged when you can bargain for much less by dealing directly with the boats themselves. Also, you don't get to see the boats or have a true picture of their location and it is widely believed that the choice of boats is probably restricted to those of friends of the man behind the counter.

Instead, most travellers either let a tout grab them or they check out a few boats on their own. Do not feel obliged to stay on a houseboat if you don't like it, regardless of what a tout or boatman tells you, even if you did get a free ride from the airport or Tourist Reception Centre.

Because of the annoying attention that new arrivals attract from the touts and shikara wallahs, more and more travellers avoid the hassle and check into a hotel for the first night. This way they can dump their gear and take a shikara to look at some boats without appearing obvious as new arrivals.

Check List When looking to choose a houseboat, remember that this is Kashmir and that it's necessary to pin them down on every little detail before you decide to stay. Otherwise be prepared for arguments later.

Find out exactly what you can expect for each meal – be sure that you won't be getting the same dishes all the time, and ensure that if you opt to miss out on any meals during your stay, a suitable reduction will be made.

Check the water supply by looking for a connection to the mains supply, otherwise decide if you want to wash in lake water. Also ensure that there is running hot water. Doonga boats should provide buckets of hot water for washing.

Houseboats usually have a shikara to get you ashore when you want and this

should be included in the tariff. If not, bear in mind that this can mean delays while you wait for one to pass by.

Often an enjoyable stay on a houseboat depends on ensuring that you are not constantly being bothered by any of the boat's family, the crew or the shikara salesmen who continually paddle by, hassling you to spend, spend, spend on excursions, handicrafts, etc.

If you don't want to waste a lot of your time discussing water treks and mountain treks, and going through everything from woodcarvings to carpets, embroidery to papier mache, it's necessary to be very firm and decisive.

The houseboat owners rake off a handy commission from virtually everything that their guests buy, both on board and at many shops and factories ashore. It is widely accepted that for many houseboat owners this is their main source of income, not the revenue earned from accommodation.

All of them carry business cards proclaiming them to be experts in trekking, camping, shooting, fishing, sightseeing, Ladakh tours and handicrafts. Experience has shown that they are often guilty of overstating their capabilities, and that they are only really experts in salesmanship and dealing.

Location There are three areas to consider when choosing your houseboat – Dal Lake, Nagin Lake and the Jhelum River. Like deciding on the boat itself, the choice of location is a personal one.

Nagin enjoys the best reputation for quiet beauty and isolation. The east bank is perhaps the best area for views of the fort and sunsets. It also has more sun during the day with the opposite side in the shade most of the afternoon. However, Nagin's isolation does mean a longer trip into Srinagar as it's too far to walk, so this means cycling, taking the bus, or an auto-rickshaw/taxi.

Dal Lake is often overlooked in the beauty stakes, mainly because of the unattractive area opposite the Boulevard that is crowded with houseboats. The front row is within earshot of the noisy road and for many visitors this is the only part of the lake they get to see.

However Dal covers a large area and there are many places that easily match the attractions of Nagin. For example, continue towards and beyond Nehru Park where the boats are moored further back from the road. There you'll find lovely views of the open lake and the mountains. North of Nehru Park are boats with sunset views, moored amongst the floating gardens.

The Jhelum River attracts fewer travellers due to the popularity of the lakes. As a result you can usually bargain with the boat owners and get a cheaper price. The Jhelum is actually enjoying a small revival. It's a bit quieter than the lakes and, as the boats are moored alongside the riverbank, you don't need a shikara to get on board so there are hardly any shikaras or salesmen to bother you. It is quite attractive in parts and remember, it was here that the Raj preferred to stay when houseboats first caught on.

Payment Having chosen a houseboat, don't make the mistake of paying in advance, even if you are sure that you will stay for several nights. Many travellers have done so only to find the standard of food and service on board go overboard once they have paid up. Also, you may change your plans, meet other travellers and decide to move to their boat or join them on a trekking trip. Houseboat owners are generally unwilling to refund money, no matter the circumstances. Many will insist that you pay for two or three nights in advance when you arrive. Tell them that you want to see how nice the food and service are before deciding whether or not to stay.

All of these factors make it impossible to recommend individual houseboats. Also, experience has shown that listed boats are swamped by trusting travellers who often find that standards have fallen

dramatically when the owners have secured a steady supply of business. While this is often a problem when researching guides, in this case our decision is easy.

Over the years certain boats have regularly been the subject of complaints from travellers. Hopefully the tourist police's new interest in con-men will reduce these incidents. Meanwhile, these houseboats have earned themselves a dubious reputation for their dishonest practices and should be avoided: Lake Placid Group of Houseboats (Nagin), H B Lagoo Palace and Top Erin (Dal), H B New Montreal (Dal), and H B Young Bombay (Dal).

Hotels

With more and more travellers becoming disenchanted with the ways of the house-boat mafia, Srinagar's hotels have been getting more business. Their prices are higher than in most parts of India but, like the tribes of merchants they truly are, the Kashmiri hoteliers will usually bargain with you, especially if business is slow.

Hotels - bottom end Cheap hotels are scattered all around Srinagar. Those in Lal Chowk tend to be very noisy and grubby. The best of the cheapies are found in three main areas: amongst the houseboats around Dal Gate; along Buchwara Chowk which runs parallel with the Boulevard; and in the Raj Bagh area across the Jhelum River.

There are several hotels, surrounded by houseboats, on small islands on Dal Lake. Most of these are pretty spartan and cater mainly to Indian tourists. Popular with shoestring travellers, though, are the *Hotel Sundowna* and the *Hotel Savoy* next door which you can find by taking a shikara from the first ghat by Dal Gate. The cost is from Rs 10 for a dorm bed and Rs 30/40 for singles/doubles.

The *Hotel New Rigadoon* is a real step up. Clean and pleasant, its comfortable singles/doubles go for Rs 70/100, but it also has dorm beds for Rs 15. To find it, continue over Dal Gate and it's on the right after the bridge.

The *Hotel Hill Star* in Buchwara Rd has a lovely garden, pleasant management and staff, is fairly clean and does a good breakfast for Rs 40/80 singles/doubles. To find it from Dal Gate, head east along the Boulevard, turn south (right) by the John Trading Corp sign, and at the end of the block you come to Buchwara Rd.

Follow the signs to the nearby *Rubina Guest House*, *Hotel Sultan*, *Hotel Raj* and *Hotel Heevan*. Owned and operated by Bengalis, these are also above average by local standards. Continue eastwards along Buchwara Rd and you come to the *Tibetan Guest House* on the left. Another favourite, it's hidden behind a high wall and gate, so look out for it. No food or drinks are served here.

Rah Bahg, a quiet residential neighbourhood, stands on the south bank of the Jhelum, opposite the Bund. The *Bhat Guest House* is one of the cheapest places in Srinagar and suprisingly clean and comfortable with singles/doubles for Rs 26/30. There are several other choices in this part of the city too.

Elsewhere, the J&K tourist office operates four accommodation units in Srinagar and the Tourist Reception Centre has retiring rooms, normal rooms and suites ranging from Rs 80 for doubles and Rs 100 for suites. These are generally full during the tourist season. The two J&K operated hotels are the *Lalla Rukh Hotel* (tel 76590) in Lal Chowk and the *Badshah Hotel* (tel 76063 and 76599) in Badshah Chowk.

Also, there are tourist huts near the Chasma Shahi gardens which come complete with kitchen, but you really need to have your own transport. These cost around Rs 300 for a double and are booked through the Tourist Reception Centre.

Across the river from the city centre on the Wazir Bagh, Srinagar's *Youth Hostel* is rather out of the way. Foreigners need to be YHA members to use it, but it is very cheap with dorm beds for Rs 3 and doubles from Rs 15.

Hotels - middle The *Green Acre Guest House* (tel 73349), a large private house converted into a hotel in Raj Bagh, is a delightful haven from the hustle and bustle of Srinagar and the houseboat scene. Proprietors Mr and Mrs Wazir are genuinely nice people. There is a lovely spacious garden, a wide choice of decent rooms (all with bath) at different prices and consistently good food. The place is understandably very popular. Singles are Rs 120, standard doubles Rs 150, deluxe Rs 200, luxury Rs 300 and suites Rs 400. There is also a small lodge in the grounds with three double bedrooms sharing a kitchenette and dining room at Rs 90 per room. Tricky to find at first, cross Zero Bridge, turn right then left by the Snow Hut Cafe and it's on the left at the foot of the slope. From the Tourist Reception Centre it's better to take an auto-rickshaw if arriving with luggage, otherwise it's a 15-minute walk.

On Buchwara Rd, adjacent to the Lhasa Restaurant, the fairly new *Pinegrove Hotel* (tel 72405/73156) has singles/doubles at Rs 130/210 with bed and breakfast. These clean and well-furnished rooms and the smart public areas of the hotel provide a better deal than most of the competition.

On the Boulevard facing Dal Lake, the *Hotel Mazda* (tel 72842/75534) stands out from the many choices here. Next to the more prominent and expensive *Shah Abbas Hotel*, the *Mazda's* best rooms are in the main building at the rear as those in the front section are rather dingy. Singles/doubles cost Rs 95/145. Elsewhere along the Boulevard similarly priced places include the *Boulevard* itself, friendly and spacious but musty and dusty, and the strangely popular *Hotel Paradise*.

The *Lake Isle Resort* (tel 78446) is beautifully located on an island in the middle of Dal Lake. Singles/doubles cost Rs 175/200 for bed and breakfast.

Hotels – top end Srinagar's top establishment is the *Oberoi Palace Hotel* (75641-3), the one-time palace of Maharajah Hari Singh. It's off the Boulevard, several km around the lake from Dal Gate. The actual building is rather uninspired, but the gardens in front provide superb views over the lake. It has 110 rooms with singles/doubles for Rs 625/725 and suites at Rs 900/2500. Most people would agree that the hotel is worth a visit for dinner or a drink in the garden, but that the rooms are disappointing.

A good, modern alternative is the *Hotel Broadway* (tel 79001-2). More conveniently located across from the polo field on Mandana Azad Rd, it has singles/doubles for Rs 500/680, a good restaurant and a lovely outdoor swimming pool.

Out past the *Oberoi Palace* by Chasma Shahi, the *Centaur Lake View* (tel 77601) is the latest addition to the five-star line-up. Since opening it has not enjoyed the best reputation either for service or comfort.

In the days of the Raj, the only place in town was *Nedous Hotel*, near the Hotel Broadway. Today it is in a rather decrepit state with singles/doubles for Rs 200/260 that are not even worth half that amount.

The Boulevard is home to several hotels, the best of which are probably the *Welcome*, singles/doubles for Rs 250/350, the *Asia Brown Palace* behind the *Boulevard Hotel* at Rs 200 for singles and Rs 290 to Rs 390 for doubles and the *Shah Abbas* at Rs 325 to Rs 425 for singles and Rs 425 to Rs 525 for doubles.

The only hotel by Nagin Lake, the *Hotel Dar-es-Salan* (tel 77803), is elegant and reasonably priced with singles/doubles at Rs 225/350, suites at Rs 500 and good food available. It is beautifully located on the lakeside with gardens and views of the fort and the sunset.

Places to Eat

Probably because so many people eat on their houseboats Srinagar is not a very exciting place for eating out. Surprisingly, there has not yet been a successful floating restaurant, a logical follow-on to all those houseboats.

The Rs 90 buffet dinner at the *Oberoi Palace Hotel* is the ultimate splurge in town, but it's a shame that getting there and back (especially) is such a hassle. Even if you can afford the taxi, finding one late at night is not easy.

The *Hotel Broadway* also has a buffet some nights. At Rs 65 it's understandably less elaborate but still provides a respite from your standard Indian fare. Ordering à la carte on non-buffet nights can mean better food. Dishes average at about Rs 35 to Rs 45.

Alka Salka on Residency Rd across from Polo View Rd serves very good Chinese and Indian cuisine. A tiny place, it is usually packed and dishes are about Rs 20.

Ahdoo's in new premises on Residency Rd has long been one of Srinagar's best places for Kashmiri food and regular Indian specialities.

Mughal Darbar is another of Srinagar's better places for Kashmiri and Indian food. This is despite its often filthy appearance, its scruffy and inefficient waiters and the loud and overbearing locals. It's adjacent to the Suffering Moses store and across from the polo field on Residency Rd.

With the generally low standard of food that is available in the town's restaurants, the *Lhasa Restaurant* is often over-rated for its Chinese-Tibetan style cuisine. However, with its convenient location near Dal Lake, just off the Boulevard, its candlelight ambience and above average food are very popular with travellers.

Along Polo View Rd the dark and seedy nightclub-like *Capri* is another top-end restaurant. Its bar facility seems to attract more custom than the food though.

Moving down a little, the *Tao Cafe* on Residency Rd, by the turn-off to the main post office, has a lovely garden and is a nice place to sit and chat over tea or a cold drink. The food is OK and nothing special, but the slow service can involve a lot of postcard writing while you wait.

Further downtown, the dingy *India Coffee House* is the place for the local literary set to hang out in the mornings to talk politics and philosophy. The balcony is for women and families only, and the menu is limited to hot or cold coffee and a few snacks, all pretty good. The waiters' uniforms are the best thing about the place. The *Hollywood Cafe* opposite is equally unimpressive to look at but the extensive menu provides fairly decent food by local standards.

Dimples, in the same area, serves good milkshakes (I recommend the banana), and if you like Indian sweets *Shakti Sweets* (also near the Hollywood), has a good selection.

Near Dal Gate a couple of bakeries do a roaring trade with travellers. *Sultan Bakery* is my personal favourite, particularly for gingernuts, apple pie and cheesecake. Around the corner, just off the Boulevard, the *Glocken Bakery* seems to be everyone else's first choice, if only because it has tables and serves hot and cold drinks. You should stock up with bread and other goodies at either of these places before heading up to Leh by road or starting a trek.

For really cheap food, there are some South Indian cafes near Dal Gate and off the Boulevard. The *Ramble Restaurant* has been highly recommended for its large portions of vegetarian food and rice and for its frothy milk tea. Urgh!

Getting There & Away
Air Indian Airlines fly to Srinagar from New Delhi (Rs 715), Chandigarh (Rs 610), Amritsar (Rs 415), Jammu (Rs 240) and Leh (Rs 360). Flights are more frequent during the summer tourist season when there are usually several flights a day

between Delhi and Srinagar using 737s and Airbuses. Some will be direct while others will operate via Chandigarh, Amritsar or Jammu. Flight time from Delhi on the direct flights is about one hour and 10 minutes. As usual in India you should book your flight as early as possible.

At Srinagar airport, 13 km from the city, there is often a fairly chaotic scene as the tourist office tries to register every incoming foreigner and insists that you book accommodation through the Tourist Reception Centre. They're generally happy if they get the names and passport numbers of a dozen or so travellers, and in any case it's a harmless procedure although you'll get better prices for houseboats if you negotiate yourself with the boat owners.

In Srinagar the Indian Airlines office is at the Tourist Reception Centre (tel 73538 & 73270) and is open from 10 am to 5 pm. It's usually very busy and a lot of waiting can be involved in trying to purchase or alter tickets. It's also at the Tourist Reception Centre in Jammu (tel 2735 & 7088).

Bus See the Jammu chapter for details about bus services to Srinagar. When planning to leave, it is best to book a seat as soon as possible as buses are often fully booked the day before departure. Buses also go from here to Leh (see the Ladakh chapter).

Nearly all buses arrive at and depart from the Tourist Reception Centre's bus compound. The only exceptions are some B-class buses which stop at Lal Chowk.

It's about a 15-minute walk from the Tourist Reception Centre to Dal Gate and the first of the shikara ghats for the Dal Lake houseboats. A bus might take on auto-rickshaw drivers, houseboat touts and various other salesmen every step of the way.

Train To book trains from Jammu while in

Srinagar, enquire at the railways office in the Tourist Reception Centre.

Taxis & Jeeps If you can afford them, taxis and jeeps are available for long distance trips and those within the vale. To Jammu costs Rs 194 per seat or Rs 776 per vehicle. For Leh see the Ladakh chapter.

Getting Around

There is a wide choice of transport available either on the lake or out and around it, plus a variety of tours. The tour buses are generally much more comfortable than the usual run of over-crowded buses and, since many of them offer one-way fares, they can be used for getting to hill stations in the valley.

Srinagar lends itself to human-powered transport – by feet, bicycle or shikara. Many of the interesting parts of town are in easy walking distance of most of the hotels and houseboats, though for me renting a bicycle is the best thing for getting around the town.

Walking along the Boulevard into the area of Residency Rd, the Tourist Reception Centre, the polo ground and the Bund will provide plenty of sightseeing and shopping opportunities.

Airport Transport Taxi drivers and houseboat touts are not allowed into the airport arrival area so this is an opportunity for a little peace and privacy. An airport bus to the Tourist Reception Centre in Srinagar costs Rs 12.50 and you can ask to get off before the centre. Buses leave the centre for all outgoing flights.

Taxi fares for most of the main destinations are clearly posted outside the arrival terminal. As you walk outside you will normally be besieged by a horde of drivers and touts trying to entice you their way. You will often get a cheap or free ride if you agree to go direct to a houseboat with a tout. If you are thick-skinned enough you should not feel obliged to stay if you don't want to. Taking the bus is a lot cheaper and delays having to decide

where to stay a bit longer. Ignore demands for extra money by unofficial baggage handlers who put luggage on the roof-rack as your ticket allows for that.

Shikaras The best known Kashmiri transport is, of course, the shikara. These are the graceful, long gondola-like boats which crowd the Srinagar lakes. They're used for getting back and forth from the houseboats or for longer tours.

There is an official standard fare for every trip around the lake and these prices are prominently posted at the main *ghats* (landings). In practice the fares can be quite variable. To be shuttled across to your houseboat should cost Rs 2 in a covered ('full spring seats') shikara but the kids who are always out for a little pocket money will happily paddle you across to the closer houseboats for 50 paise in a basic, open shikara.

Of course late at night, particularly if it is raining, the tables are turned and getting back to your houseboat at a reasonable price may require a little ingenuity! Try paddling a shikara yourself sometime and discover that it's nowhere near as easy as it looks. You'll spend lots of time going round in circles trying to master that single, heart-shaped paddle. Even if you do start to travel in a straight line you'll find it requires a good amount of stamina to maintain the pace.

Bus The Jammu & Kashmir Road Transport Corporation buses go from the Tourist Reception Centre while private buses operate from a variety of stands in Srinagar. Taxi and auto-rickshaw drivers will usually know which stand you need.

Some main long-distance routes are reserved for the J&K buses (Jammu, Leh, etc) but others are open for competition which means that there will be many buses operating. Fares are set for all routes and the drivers or conductors are usually very helpful. Take a No 12 bus to Nagin Lake or the Hazratbal Mosque.

Taxis & Auto-rickshaws Stands for these are at the Tourist Reception Centre and other strategic locations in town. Srinagar's taxi-wallahs are extremely reluctant to use their meters so you'll have to bargain hard. Count on about Rs 10 to Rs 15 for a taxi from the Tourist Reception Centre to Dal Gate or the houseboat ghats (Rs 5 to Rs 10 by auto-rickshaw) and Rs 40 to the airport. Large items of baggage may cost extra. For longer trips the official fares (one-way/return) are posted by the stands.

Bicycle Seeing Srinagar by bicycle is an extremely pleasant way of getting around. Although the mountains soar up all around the valley, Srinagar itself is surprisingly flat. Bicycles are economical too. You can hire bikes for Rs 10 per day and there are several bicycle stores along the Boulevard close to Dal Gate. Be careful of the traffic as like all Asian drivers the Kashmiris rely on their horns more than their brakes. Following are some suggested trips.

Around Dal Lake – an all-day trip going by the Moghul gardens which is particularly pleasant around the north of the lake where the villages are still relatively untouched; across the lake – ride across the lake on the causeway, a nice trip since there are no problems with vehicle traffic and there is plenty of opportunity to observe the lake life without being in a boat; Nagin Lake – ride out to the Hazratbal Mosque via Nagin Lake and then make a complete loop around the lake on the way back. This trip can easily be combined with a trip along the Jhelum, taking in the various mosques close to the river. The streets here are very narrow so vehicles keep away and bike riding is pleasant.

Tours The J&K Road Transport Corporation operate several daily tours from the Tourist Reception Centre. Private bus companies, particularly the KMDA (Kashmir Motor Drivers' Association) also have tours.

The one-way and some return fares for J&K RTC tours from Srinagar are:

Pahalgam	daily	Rs 33/56
Daksum	daily	Rs 33/56
Gulmarg	daily	Rs 33/56
Aharbal	Tues,Thur,Sun	Rs 33
Verinag	Wed,Sun	Rs 30
Wular Lake	Mon,Wed,Fri	Rs 30
Yusmarg	Tues,Thur,Sun	Rs 30/48
Sonamarg	daily	Rs 30/48
Moghul Gardens	twice daily	Rs 33

Places to Shop

There are a string of Government Handicraft Emporiums scattered around Srinagar but the main one of these is housed in the fine old British residency buildings by the Bund. Here you'll find a representative selection of fairly good quality items at reasonable prices. Even if you don't buy and take advantage of the Government's quality guarantee, it's a good idea to familiarise yourself with what's available.

Other good shopping areas include the Boulevard by Dal Lake and the Bund. Despite its rude owner, Suffering Moses is worth a visit for its high quality items. The Government Central Market, across Badshah Bridge, has a variety of stalls and again some government quality and price control is exercised. Hari Singh St, near the Amira Kadal Bridge, is a popular older shopping area, as are Polo View Rd and Lambert Lane in the centre.

There are literally hundreds of other shops scattered all over Srinagar and if you don't fall prey to those persuasive salesmen they'll pursue you to your houseboat as countless shikaras patrol Dal Lake like shoals of sharks, loaded down with the same items you'll find in the shops.

Rest assured that your houseboatman will do his utmost to talk you into spending money in his direction. He will invite you to visit his brother's/uncle's or cousin's/friend's shop/factory or showroom/house or, by coincidence, one of the aforementioned will happen to be passing by and you will suddenly be confronted with a display of goods of unbelievable quality at unbeatable prices.

Water Trekking

Chances are your houseboatman will suggest that you go on a water trek. Properly organised and with good company, such a venture can be a very enjoyable experience.

A Kashmir water trek involves being paddled by shikaras along the various lakes, rivers and canals. You can relax as you drift along and observe the bird life – eadwells, pintails, red-headed pocherds, mallards, bulbels and the ever-present kingfisher, amongst others. At night you camp out.

A typical trek would be for three days, although some last five or more. For example, you could leave from your houseboat, cross Dal and Nagin and follow the Nalla Amirkhan, a narrow scenic canal connecting with Anchar Lake. Surrounded by a huge swamp rich in aquatic birds, this used to be a bird sanctuary. The next day follow a channel into the Jhelum River which you later leave to follow a canal that leads into Mansabal Lake. On the final day you continue to Wular Lake, India's largest, from where you are driven back to Srinagar. Returning by shikara naturally makes for a longer trek.

Normally you would be accompanied by a shikara wallah or two, a cook and perhaps a guide. There are no set prices for the various water trek options so travellers are easy targets for the houseboatmen and their dubious reputation for overcharging. Choomti Trekkers in their houseboat on the Bund opposite the main post office regularly arrange water treks and are a good source for free information with no obligations. Check prices with them before agreeing to anything with your houseboat or shikara man.

The Kashmir Valley

There are many interesting places around the Kashmir Valley. Some of these make good day trips, others are pleasant to stay at in their own right or make good bases for day walks or longer trekking trips.

The J&K Road Transport Corporation operates a variety of day tours around the valley, backed up by privately operated bus company tours. You can also get out and about in local buses or taxis.

The two main valley resorts are Pahalgam and Gulmarg. Other places of interest are covered in the sections along the route to Pahalgam, the Sindh Valley and South of Srinagar.

TO PAHALGAM

The road to Pahalgam starts out towards Jammu but later branches off to the east at Anantnag. There are several points of interest along this route including Moghul gardens. Indeed, if you take a bus tour to Pahalgam you'll be thoroughly saturated with Moghul gardens by the time you arrive.

Pampore

About 16 km out of Srinagar on the main highway south, Pampore is the centre of Kashmir's saffron industry. Highly prized for its flavouring and colouring properties, and rather expensive, saffron is gathered from flowers which are harvested in October.

Avantipur

This popular stop on Pahalgam excursions has two ruined Hindu temples, both constructed by King Avantivarman, after whom this ancient centre was named, between 855 AD and 883 AD.

The larger temple is dedicated to Vishnu and is known as the Avantiswami temple. The central shrine is enclosed by a huge wall with four smaller shrines around the centre. The courtyard is paved and enclosed and measures 52 metres by

Top: Gangabal Sar, one of two glacial lakes at the foot of Mt Harmukh, Kashmir (BP)
Bottom: Gulmarg (TW)

Top: Cave and crowds, Amarnath Yatra (RK)
Left: Pilgrims en route to cave, Amarnath Yatra (RK)
Right: A well-earned rest

45 metres. The entrance still bears some fine relief sculptures and the columns, richly covered in carvings and sculptures, give the temple an almost Grecian appearance.

The other temple, dedicated to Shiva and known as the Avantishvara, is about a km before the Vishnu temple, but also close to the main road. It is in a courtyard, enclosed by a massive stone wall with a gateway on the western side.

The nearby village of Bijbihara has a huge chinar tree, claimed to be the largest in Kashmir. Avantipur is 29 km from Srinagar.

Sangam

About six km further down the road, Sangam is interesting for its strong local industry of (believe it or not) cricket bat manufacturing! You'll see thousands of cricket bats displayed by the roadside and thousands more roughly cut lengths of wood being seasoned.

Anantnag

At this point, 56 km from Srinagar, the road forks with one route turning north-east to Pahalgam and two others south-east to Achabal, Kokarnag and Daksum or Vering. The Jammu road leaves this route at Khanabal just before Anantnag.

Anantnag has sulphur springs, esteemed for their curative properties. The largest spring is believed to be the home of Ananta, the serpent on which Vishnu reclines and from which the town takes its name – Abode of Ananta. Ananta means 'endless' and the water issues from the base of a small hillock and rushes into another spring in the middle of which is a natural mineral deposit column which the locals revere as a lingam.

On the 14th day of a full moon fortnight in September/October a festival is held and the people fast and pour a mixture of rice and milk into the spring to feed the goldfish that live there.

At one time Anantnag was known as Islamabad but this name is no longer used, due to the confusion it would cause with the not-too distant capital of Pakistan.

Achabal

The Moghul gardens in this small town (58 km from Srinagar) were begun by Nur Jahan, Emperor Jehangir's wife, and completed by Jahanara, daughter of Emperor Shah Jahan, in 1640. It's one of the most carefully designed of the Kashmir gardens and was said to be a favourite retreat of Nur Jahan.

Water from a copious spring flows from the garden in three stone-lined canals, over three terraces and three cascades, with several fountains in the main canal. There are three pavilions on the upper terrace, shaded by chinar trees.

There's a tourist bungalow, tourist huts and a camping ground at Achabal.

Kokarnag

You may be suffering garden overload by the time you get here, but Kokarnag has yet another one, noted for its roses. Like Achabal there is a tourist bungalow, tourist huts and a camping ground.

Daksum

Above Kokarnag along the Bring River Valley, 90 km from Srinagar, is the small hill resort of Daksum at 2438 metres. It's on the trekking route to Kishtwar and has a rest house, tourist bungalow and plenty of camping spots. From Daksum the trail rises fairly steeply to the Sinthan Pass at 3748 metres which is open from April to September. See the Trekking in Kashmir chapter or the Lonely Planet *Trekking in the Indian Himalaya* travel guide.

Mattan & Martand

Only a few km north-east of Anantnag (and 61 km from Srinagar) on the Pahalgam road, Mattan is an important Hindu pilgrimage point due to its fish-filled springs.

A complicated legend relates that the springs were created when Shiva broke open an egg which had been thrown there, the egg being the reincarnated form of a forgetful boy who had been cursed by a wandering sage ... and that's only half the story!

On a plateau above Mattan and three km to the south stands the huge ruined temple of Martand. Built by Lalitaditya Mukhtapida (699 AD to 736 AD) it is the most impressive ancient ruin in Kashmir. The ruins are 67 metres by 43 metres and consist of a portico with a small detached shrine on either side and a quadrangular courtyard. The courtyard was surrounded by 84 columns – the multiple of the number of days in the week by the number of signs in the zodiac.

The road from here to Pahalgam follows the course of the Lidder River past some good trout fishing stretches.

Verinag

Close to the foot of the Pir Panjal Range, the spring at Verinag is said to be the source of the Jhelum River, which flows north through Srinagar. Emperor Jehangir built an octagonal stone basin at the spring in 1612 and in 1620 his son, Shah Jahan, laid out a garden around it. The spring is said to be more than 15 metres deep and is reputed never to dry up or overflow. There is a tourist bungalow at Verinag, which is 80 km from Srinagar.

PAHALGAM

Pahalgam (altitude 2130 metres) is probably the most popular hill resort in the Kashmir Valley and is 95 km from Srinagar. Not as high as Gulmarg, the night temperatures do not drop so low and it has the added advantage of the beautiful Lidder River running right through the town.

Pahalgam is at the junction of the Aru (or West Lidder) and Sheshnag (or East Lidder) rivers and is surrounded by soaring, fir-covered mountains with bare, snow-capped peaks rising behind them. The Aru flows down from the Kolahoi Glacier beyond Lidderwat while the

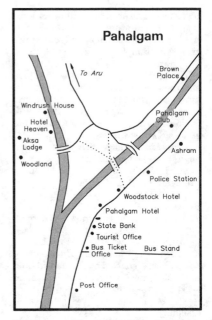

Sheshnag originates from glaciers along the Great Himalaya.

There are many short walks from Pahalgam and it is an excellent base for longer treks such as those to the Kolahoi Glacier or to the Amarnath Cave. Pahalgam can also be used as a starting point for treks out of the region – see the Trekking in Kashmir chapter and Lonely Planet's book *Trekking in the Indian Himalaya*. Pahalgam is particularly famed for its many shepherds and they're a common sight, driving their flocks of sheep along the paths around the town.

Information

The tourist office (tel 24) is just around the corner from the bus halt on the main road. The office staff may be able to help with hiring porters or ponies but otherwise are not much use. Fishing permits have to be obtained in Srinagar.

There is a bank in Pahalgam and a post office during the tourist season. If you're planning on trekking from Pahalgam there are plenty of shops selling food supplies although it's cheaper and more plentiful in Srinagar. If trekking is altogether too strenuous, Pahalgam also offers the Pahalgam Club with tennis and badminton courts, a mini-golf course, ping-pong, a library and card evenings!

Pahalgam Walks

Mamaleswara Only a km or so downstream from Pahalgam and on the opposite side of the Lidder is this small Shiva temple with its square, stone tank. It is thought to date from the reign of King Jayasima in the 12th century, although it is possibly even older.

Baisaran This meadow, about five km from Pahalgam and 150 metres higher, provides excellent views over the town and the Lidder Valley. The grassy glen is surrounded by pine forests and snow-clad mountains. You can hire ponies for this trek from near the centre of town.

Tulian Lake If you continue 11 km on beyond Baisaran you reach the Tulian Lake at 3353 metres, 1200 metres higher up. It is covered in ice for much of the year and surrounded by mountain peaks which rise more than 300 metres above its shores. It also can be reached by pony trek.

Aru The pleasant little village of Aru is actually the first stage from Pahalgam on the trek to Lidderwat and the Kolahoi Glacier. It makes an interesting day walk from Pahalgam, following the Lidder River for 11 km upstream. The main track, which also unfortunately takes cars, is on the left bank of the river. There is a less used and much more difficult path on the right bank.

At Aru you will often find the Gujars, living in their log huts with their flocks of sheep and goats, en route to the higher pastures for summer. Aru has a government tourist hut, several small tea houses which will offer you the floor for the night,

and the Green View Guest House near the river just before you reach the town.

Fishing

Pahalgam is one of Kashmir's popular trout fishing beats. Kashmir is famous for its trout although they tend to be rather small. Also, fishing licences are hard to get and expensive. They only allow a set number of rods on each stretch of the river so there is often a queue for licences. The cost in Pahalgam is Rs 50 per day for the licence. Add to that Rs 20 for rod and equipment rental and Rs 20 for the compulsory guide and you've spent Rs 90 before you start which is rather a lot for the six fish which is the daily limit. It's not surprising that trout rarely feature on Kashmiri menus!

Places to Stay

Accommodation in Pahalgam varies between the uninspiring hotels, popular with Indian tourists, that line the main street, a few top-end establishments and the Alpine-style lodges, popular with travellers, that stand on the far side of the West Lidder Valley, a few km walk away from the bus stand.

Places to Stay - bottom end The various hotels along the main street are not particularly brilliant and charge a lot for the little they provide. Most travellers head across the river to one of the lodges on the western bank. From the bus stand head north (right) along the main street and bear left where you see signs pointing to the lodges.

The most popular of these is *Aksa Lodge* (tel 59) nicely positioned in well-kept grounds with views of the valley. Although the rooms can be a bit basic, the overall set-up is very comfortable and generally well-run. Rooms vary in size with singles at Rs 30 to Rs 120 and doubles at Rs 50 to Rs 200. Unlike his less impressive competition owner Mohammad Yasin will not bargain, except off-season.

As well as the lovely garden with tables and chairs for great alfresco breakfasts in fine weather, there is a pleasant lounge with a good stock of magazines and newspapers and taped music. Be sure to ask for a screening of one of Mohammad's documentary videos which include subjects such as Ladakh and the Amarnath Pilgrimage. Hot water is always available and the food is good.

The other lodges tend to pale by comparison, but although they charge about the same, you can bargain with them to save money. The best of these is probably the *Brown Palace*. However, it is a long way from town and although they usually pick up arrivals at the bus stand in their jeep, it is a nuisance having to walk all that way the rest of your stay. The owner has tried to match the marketing approach of the *Aksa Lodge* with identical signs and brochures but the place itself is rather dingy by comparison, although the owner is nice enough. Another option is *Windrush House*. To get there, continue past the path leading up to *Aksa Lodge* and go down to the right, on the riverbank.

The *Hotel Kolahoi Kabin*, between the two rivers, is under new management and could be worth checking out – singles/doubles at Rs 50/150. The other lodges are a lot more decrepit. These include the *White House*, *Woodland*, *Bentes Lodge* and the *Highland Palace* (about which we've heard complaints of unwanted homosexual advances).

The *Government Tourist Bungalow* has doubles for Rs 35 while the adjacent *Tourist Huts* have one to two-bedroom versions at Rs 90/150.

Just up the road from the *bungalow* the Rishikesh *Yoga Niketan* ashram operates in summer only and offers free hatha yoga and meditation lessons. You can rent a large tent for Rs 110 for two weeks or Rs 195 per month. They ask for a two-week minimum although they are flexible. You can stay there with your own tent for just Rs 30 per month.

Places to Stay – top end The *Pahalgam Hotel* (tel 26/52) is the top establishment here with singles/doubles at Rs 525/700 and suites for Rs 900, all full board. Facilities include central heating, television, bar, heated swimming pool and a health club with sauna, steam bath, massage and gym. Not bad at all for the price. The adjacent *Woodstock Hotel* (tel 27) has singles/doubles at Rs 350/450 without the extras.

Below *Aksa Lodge* by the river the *Hotel Heevan* (tel 17) has singles at Rs 275 to Rs 350 and doubles at Rs 350 to Rs 425.

Places to Eat

Most travellers who stay at the west bank lodges tend to eat there as walking into town is a bit far and not worth the trip anyway. The food in the lodges can be a bit hit and miss, but in those I've recommended you get to eat quite well.

The *Lhasa Restaurant* on the main street is not as good as its namesake in Srinagar. The *Pahalgam Hotel* does a pretty good set lunch/dinner for Rs 65. The nearby *Khalsa Janta* and *Tabela* restaurants are also among the best available.

Getting There & Away

Local buses from Srinagar cost Rs 10 and take 2½ to four hours. There are six to 10 departures a day. J&K Road Transport have tour buses which cost Rs 33 one-way or Rs 56 return. They leave the Srinagar Tourist Reception Centre around 7 am and by the time you arrive in Pahalgam around 1 pm you'll have had a thorough surfeit of Moghul gardens.

Taxis cost more than Rs 431 return although you can sometimes find a taxi going back from Pahalgam empty and willing to bargain. If you are in Pahalgam and want to get a return ticket on one of the more comfortable J&K tour buses you have to catch them when they come in around noon. Get someone from your hotel to do it for you. You can get buses direct from Pahalgam to Jammu.

Ponies can easily be hired in Pahalgam for trekking trips. The fixed costs to popular destinations are all clearly posted but they're basically bargaining guidelines. When your bus/taxi pulls into Pahalgam you will usually be besieged by ponymen insisting you go on a pony trek with them.

GULMARG

Gulmarg is not a town like Pahalgam, but simply a large meadow about three square km in area dotted with new hotels, dilapidated huts and dominated by a golf course and ski slopes. Standing at 2730 metres, 52 km from Srinagar, the name means 'meadow of flowers'. In spring it's just that, a rolling meadow dotted with countless colourful bluebells, daisies, forget-me-nots and buttercups.

It's still a popular day trip from Srinagar although many people extend their stay or use it as a base for trekking. The road from Srinagar rises gently towards the lower slopes of the Pir Panjal Range, passing through rice and maize fields. From Tangmarg, at the foot of the range, there are two paths to Gulmarg – a steep footpath (also suitable for ponies) and a winding sealed road.

In winter Gulmarg is the skiing centre of India. There are four ski lifts on the slopes – a two km long aerial ropeway from Gulmarg to Khilanmarg, a rope tow on the training slope and two other ski lifts on the higher slopes.

A cable car is under construction and due for completion by 1990. The skiing season is November to March. Equipment hire is about Rs 50, lessons are Rs 40 and lift passes are Rs 30, all daily. Contact SDSingh, Hut 209A for more information. Westerners working in the Gulf, Hong Kong, Singapore, etc regularly ski here, along with a few Aussies.

In summer Gulmarg boasts one of the highest altitude golf courses in the world – the Gulmarg Golf Club stands at 2652 metres. Spring and autumn tournaments are held in June and September and there are many huts and hotels scattered around the flower-covered fields.

Notable for the absence of bunkers, the golf course was designed by Australian golfer Peter Thompson. Green fees are Rs 130 which includes caddy, clubs and balls. Lessons on the driving range cost Rs 50 per hour. Gulam Din, a Gujar, is the pro here, spending the winter months at the Delhi Oberoi course.

Like Pahalgam, pony trekking is a main attraction and the ponymen can be very irritating with their determined efforts to persuade you to go riding. Prices are posted.

Skiing in Kashmir

We had a ski-bearer for the first day – he was very helpful in finding accommodation, ski-hire places, lifts, etc. It almost broke his heart when we told him we didn't need him the second day. He charged Rs 30 a day for the two of us, a bit out of our budget. The standard was from nursery to easy intermediate but the ski slopes were deserted. You can also walk up to

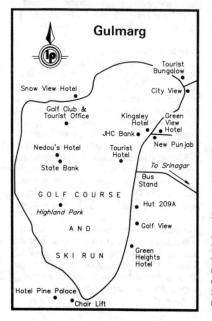

Gulmarg

Tourist Bungalow

Snow View Hotel

City View

Golf Club & Tourist Office

Kingsley Hotel

Green View Hotel

JHC Bank

Nedou's Hotel

Tourist Hotel

New Punjab

State Bank

To Srinagar

Bus Stand

GOLF COURSE

Hut 209A

Highland Park

AND

Golf View

SKI RUN

Green Heights Hotel

Hotel Pine Palace

Chair Lift

14,000 ft and ski down to 9000 ft, if you're good. Some Aussies staying in our place would mess about on the slopes and the local instructors would go away and hide, 'cos they couldn't compete! Lessons weren't really recommended. The equipment was reasonable, perhaps two or three years older than stuff one would find in Europe. Skis, boots and poles cost Rs 160 for five days and you can also hire parkas. Lift passes were Rs 20 for a half day on four drag lifts or Rs 55 for 20 goes on the chain lift. There was no queueing for lifts; often they would stop the chair lift when we got to the top and wait for us to ski down. The snow was excellent for us, but the day we left some of the slopes were wearing a bit thin.

– M L Bridge

Information

The tourist office is the blue-green building complex on the other side of the golf course from the bus stand. It's open daily from 9.30 am to 6 pm.

Unless you are a keen skier, golfer or pony rider, Gulmarg's day walks are the resort's saving grace in a sad atmosphere of neglect. Those of you who saw the movie *Heat and Dust* will recognise the gorgeous scenery.

Gulmarg can get pretty cold, even compared to Pahalgam, so come prepared with plenty of warm clothes. Sleeping bags are essential. Gulmarg has a bank but service can be a bit hit and miss – they obviously aren't used to changing money!

Gulmarg Walks

Outer Circular Walk An 11 km circular road runs around Gulmarg through pleasant pine forests with excellent views over the Kashmir Valley. Nanga Parbat is clearly visible 137 km to the north, Haramukh 60 km to the east, while to the south you can see the Ferozpore and Sunset peaks (Romesh Thong) and the Apharwat Ridge. Nanga Parbat, the 'lord of the mountains', is the fourth highest peak on earth at 8500 metres.

Khilanmarg This smaller valley is about a six km walk from the Gulmarg bus stop and car park. The meadow, carpeted with flowers in spring, is the site of Gulmarg's winter ski-runs and offers a fine view of the surrounding peaks and over the Kashmir Valley.

It's a 600-metre ascent from Gulmarg to Khilanmarg. In early spring, as the snow melts, it can be a very muddy hour's climb up the hill. The effort is rewarded, if it's clear, by a sweeping view of the great Himalaya from Nanga Parbat to the twin 7100-metre peaks of Nun and Kun to the south-east.

Alpather Beyond Khilanmarg, 13 km from Gulmarg at the foot of the twin 4511-metre Apharwat Peaks, this lake is frozen until mid-June. Even later in the year you can see lumps of ice floating in its cold waters. The walk from Gulmarg follows a well-graded pony track over the 3810-metre Apharwat Ridge, separating it from Khilanmarg, and then up the valley to the lake at 3843 metres. The more adventurous trekkers can climb straight up the boulder-strewn slope of the ridge and descend the other side to the path.

Ningle Nallah Flowing from the melting snow and ice on Apharwat and the Alpather Lake, this pretty mountain stream is 10 km from Gulmarg. The stream continues down into the valley below and joins the Jhelum River near Sopur. This long, grassy valley is a popular picnic spot and the walking path carries on, crossing the Ningle Nallah by a bridge and continues on to the Lienmarg, another grassy meadow and a good spot for camping. In early summer you will probably share the camp sites with Gujars moving their herds to the high meadows.

Ferozpore Nallah Reached from the Tangmarg road or from the outer circular walk, this mountain stream meets the Bahan River at a popular picnic spot known as 'waters meet'. The stream is reputed to be particularly good for trout fishing. It's about five km down the valley from Gulmarg but quite close to Tangmarg. The river can be reached by walking three km down the path from the gap near Tangmarg and then heading south through the forest, down a slope towards the stream.

Near here is a bridge which leads to the small 'waters meet' picnic spot on the right bank. Looking south from Tangmarg the river can be traced up to its source, close to the rugged peak known as Ferozpore or Shinmahinyu. On the right bank the stream branches, the left path leading to Tosamaidan, while the right bends away towards the Gogaldara road at a second bridge, about 32 km upstream, and then leads away to the Ferozpore Pass, Poonch and Kantar Nag.

You can continue from here to Tosamaidan, a three-day 50 km walk to one of Kashmir's most beautiful margs, crossing the Basmai Gali Pass at about 4000 metres (one of the easiest and safest routes into the Punjab). The track is very close to the ceasefire line with Pakistan and on the right you will pass the Jamainwali Gali.

Ziarat of Baba Reshi This Muslim shrine is on the slopes below Gulmarg and can be reached from either Gulmarg or Tangmarg. The Ziarat, or tomb, is of a well-known Muslim saint who died here in 1480. Before renouncing worldly ways he was a courtier of the Kashmir King Zain-ul-Abidin.

Places to Stay – bottom end
Accommodation in Gulmarg is very basic with hot water hard to find, yet prices are not very low which discourages most travellers from staying overnight. Prices usually apply to a room, regardless of whether one or two people use it.

On arrival you will notice the *Tourists Hotel* (tel 53) opposite the bus stand. A remarkably baroque and weathered fantasy in wood, like something out of *Lord of the Rings*, it is however rather dirty and grubby inside with rooms for around Rs 30 to Rs 50.

Follow the ring road to the right and you will be heading towards the *City View* which appears after the large modern hotels on the right slope. Its superb views and friendly owner help make the basic facilities more bearable. A double room costs around Rs 30. The nearby *Tourist Bungalow* (tel 41) is probably the most comfortable place in this category with singles/doubles at Rs 45.

On the way to these last two places you pass through a collection of shabby old buildings housing various stores, eating places and hotels. The *Kingsley Hotel* (tel 55) asks a ridiculous Rs 150 for its rooms, while the old *New Punjab* asks Rs 30. The pleasant *Green View* is a nice contrast at Rs 120 per room.

Turn left from the bus stand and after a few minutes walk you come to the *Golf View*, up the slope to your left. Nothing special, it has rooms for Rs 50.

Places to Stay – top end
The *Hotel Highlands Park* (tel 7/30/91) is Gulmarg's over-rated premier hotel. Singles/doubles cost Rs 525/725 and suites cost Rs 1200, full board. A complex of bungalows set amongst gardens, it fails to deliver the goods as a top-grade establishment ought to. The rooms, whilst nothing special, are OK but the food is very poor for this level. A new *Ashok* hotel is under construction nearby so the threat of competition will hopefully improve the standards here. The pleasant bar is the hotel's saving grace and sitting out on one of the terraces with a drink can be a nice way to enjoy Gulmarg.

Nedou's Hotel (tel 23) down on the other side of the hill is still operating. This was Gulmarg's premier hotel many years ago. Singles/doubles cost Rs 400/500.

Places to Eat
The choice is extremely limited and not very good. At the bottom end are the South Indian cafes by the bus stand. Elsewhere, prices are considerably higher except in the cheaper places to stay. At

the top end, the *Highland Park* puts on a dreary but plentiful set lunch/dinner for Rs 80. *Ahdoo's* restaurant, next door to the bus stand, probably serves up the best food in Gulmarg.

Getting There & Away

There are a variety of buses running from Srinagar to Gulmarg, many on day tours. On these tours you have only a few hours at the hill resort, just long enough for one of the shorter day walks or some pony trekking. The deluxe tour buses cost Rs 56 return or Rs 33 one-way and leave at 9 am from the Tourist Reception Centre. Ordinary buses leave hourly and cost Rs 15 return or Rs 10 one-way.

Until recently the road from Srinagar only ran as far as Tangmarg, which is seven km from and 500 metres below Gulmarg. The last stretch had to be completed on foot or by pony. The road has now been completed all the way to Gulmarg, although there are still buses that terminate at Tangmarg. The winding road from Tangmarg is 13 km, nearly twice as far as the more direct pony track.

SOUTH OF SRINAGAR

There are several other interesting places south of Srinagar, principally to the south-west of the valley.

Chari Sharif

On the road to Yusmarg, 30 km from Srinagar, this is the site of the shrine or *ziarat* of Sheik Noor-ud-Din, the patron saint of Kashmir. The valley also has the ziarats of a number of his followers.

Yusmarg

Standing in the Pir Panjal hills, beyond the airport at an altitude of 2700 metres, the meadow of Yusmarg is reputed to have the best spring flowers in Kashmir. The beautiful valley is at the foot of the Sangisafaid Valley on the northern slopes of the Pir Panjal Range.

Yusmarg, which is only 40 km from Srinagar, has tourist huts and is a good base for treks into the surrounding hills. One path leads to the nearby picturesque Nila Nag Lake where there's a forest rest house.

There's a road from Yusmarg to Yus, where a track leads off towards Sangam and Sunset Peak, up the valley of the Khanchi Kol. Sunset Peak, at 4746 metres, is the highest mountain in the Pir Panjal Range.

Other popular treks include those to Sangisafaid (Chitta Pathar) and Dodha Patri.

Shupian

Lying in the crook of a bend of the Pir Panjal Range, at the foot of several passes which lead out on to the plains, this fairly large town is an important trade centre for the valley's wool industry, and is famous for its apples. It lies on the Rembiara River 50 km from Srinagar and has several rest houses and a couple of guest houses. It is also the base for treks to Konsarnag, Yusmarg and the Aharbal Falls. The first stage on the trek to Konsarnag is the drive to Kongwatan.

Aharbal

This was another popular resting place for the Moghul emperors when they made the long trip north from Delhi to Kashmir. It's in an area famed for its apples and its interesting waterfall.

The Aharbal Falls, said to be the best in Kashmir, are about 10 km from Aharbal from where there is a motorable road and a trekkers route leading through dense pine forest. The road leads over a high bridge from where a magnificent view of the awesome gorge created by the Vishav River can be seen. Less than two km further on are the foot of the falls, where the river drops more than 15 metres over a distance of three km.

The road continues on a further three km to the top of the falls, where from a rock outcrop you can look down around 60 metres to the river rushing below, and another six km to the village of Sedau.

Aharabal, which is about three to four hours by road from Srinagar, is also the start of the popular trek to the Konsarnag Lake via the upland meadow of Kongwatan – see the Trekking in Kashmir chapter.

Kongwatan

This is a charming meadow just a short distance from the Vishav River. Among the pines near the river bank is a small sulphur spring and a forest rest hut.

The place is inhabited by nomadic Gujar shepherds, said to be descendants of the biblical Abraham and Isaac, or Gujar Rajputs, who come each summer from the plains with their flocks of cattle and buffalo to spend July and August in the high meadows. They wear black clothes and a small cap, embroidered and set with kari shells. The caps of the women project over the neck to protect them from sunburn. The women are very agile and seem to do all the work as well as taking care of the children.

SINDH VALLEY

North of Srinagar the Sindh Valley is an area of mountains, lakes, rivers and glaciers. The Sindh River flows down from the Amarnath and Haramukh glaciers into the Anchar Lake. The Leh road from Srinagar follows this river to beyond Sonamarg. The Zoji La Pass marks the boundary from the Sindh Valley into Ladakh.

Dachigam

This wildlife reserve was once the royal game reserve but animals within its boundaries are now completely protected. There are said to be panther, bear, deer and smaller animals in the reserve and there is a good chance of seeing the endangered Hangul (or Kashmir stag) and Langur monkeys. It's very quiet and uncrowded.

Permits to enter the reserve cost Rs 20 and are simply and quickly obtained from the wildlife warden at the Tourist Reception Centre. The reserve is quite close to Shadaharwan – see the Srinagar chapter. Camping is not generally possible at the reserve and overnight trips are only allowed by special arrangement for studying snow leopard or bear which exist in the remoter regions of the park. It's closed Sunday.

Dachigam is a good starting point for the climb to the top of the 4267-metre Mahadev Peak. The walk begins from the upper end of the reservoir.

Getting There Dachigam is 21 km northeast of Srinagar. Take a bus to Harwan (Rs 1) from the local bus stand. The trip takes nearly an hour. From the Harwan bus terminal it's five minutes to the park gates where, for a tip, a guide will show you around.

Anchar Lake

Although this large lake (5½ km by four km) is only 11 kms from Srinagar and easily reached by bus, it is rarely visited. In winter it is home for a wide variety of water birds including mallard, pochard, gadwall, snipe and teal. A daily bus leaves Srinagar for the lake at 8.30 am and returns late in the afternoon.

Gandarbal

Just beyond the Wular and Manasbal lakes turn-off from the Leh road, 19 km from Srinagar, this pleasant little town marks the point where the icy Sindh River leaves the mountains and enters the plains. Gandarbal is the official headquarters of the Sindh Valley and was originally called Doderhom. It has a bazaar, a post office and two hospitals.

About five km from Gandarbal in the village of Tullamulla is the shrine of Khirbhawani, the goddess Ragni, the Hindu guardian goddess of Kashmir. The marble temple, built by Maharaja Pratap Singh, stands in a small spring. It is an irregular, seven-sided structure and is said to be surrounded by 360 springs, most of which have run dry or been silted up.

The village is a floating garden

surrounded by swamps. Its many islands are covered with willows, poplars and wildflowers, while the island on which the spring stands is covered with chinar, mulberry and elm trees. The nearby village named after Khirbhawani has almond groves where the best quality almonds in Kashmir are said to grow.

Gandarbal can be reached from Srinagar by road or by boat along the Mar Canal, or by a six-hour round trip via the Jhelum River and Anchar Lake. There are many excellent camping places along these routes.

Manasbal Lake

This secluded, crystal-clear sheet of green water was named after the sacred lake of Mansarowar that skirts the equally sacred Mt Kailas. Manasbal Lake, which averages 12 metres deep, is covered with lotus flowers and in winter it is a bird watchers' paradise as it is one of the largest natural haunts of aquatic birds in Kashmir.

Mt Baladar overlooks the lake's eastern bank while on its northern bank are the ruins of Darogabagh. A Moghul garden with a good view over the lake was built by Queen Nur Jahan and is called *Garoka*, or 'bay window'.

A grove of chinar trees at the nearby village of Safapur is known as Badshah Boni (Royal Chinar), and was planted in imitation of the Nasim Bagh in Srinagar. Safapur is irrigated by a canal taken from the Sindh River, constructed by Badshah in the 15th century. Nearby is a cave dug by a mystic, with his grave lying next to a small shrine. Near this is a tourist hut.

Camping is possible at another lakeside chinar grove known as Qoz Bagh. There is also a government rest house by the lake.

Manasbal Lake is in the Jhelum Valley, 28 km from Srinagar, on the route to the Wular Lake via Safapur. The lake can be reached from Srinagar via Shadipur or via Nasim and Gandarbal.

Wular Lake

Claimed to be the largest freshwater lake in India, the Wular Lake can spread over almost 200 square km but its actual surface area tends to vary. The Jhelum River flows into the lake, 40 km downstream from Srinagar, and then out again.

The lake, calm though it may appear, is noted for the fierce winds that sometimes blow up. The deepest part of the lake is known as *Mota Khon*, the 'gulf of corpses', since the bodies of people drowned in the lake were all supposed to be washed to this place.

At one time there was an artificial island on the lake, where boatmen could shelter if the weather turned bad, but silting on that side of the lake has joined the island to the lakeside. It's now a popular picnic spot.

Wular is 50 km from Srinagar and there are several large towns and other places of interest around the lake shore. Sopur, at the south end of the lake where the Jhelum leaves it, is noted for fruit growing, particularly apples and walnuts.

The main resort town for the lake is Ningal Nullah, five km from Sopur. From there you can hire sailing boats to cruise on the lake or for fishing.

Beyond Sopur is the Lolab Valley, reached either by road from Sopur or by following the bridal path from Kiuhnus. To the west of the Lolab Valley is an extensive flat meadow called Bungas which is 2896 metres above sea level and 114 km from Srinagar. It's like an undeveloped Gulmarg.

Kiuhnus Bay is a small valley 20 km from Sopur and 12 km from Bandipur. Further up this valley of the Madumati River are several waterfalls.

The important town of Bandipur, famous for its woven blankets, is on the eastern shore of the lake, at the foot of the 3355-metre Tragbal Pass. On the north-west side of the lake, near Ashtiung, is a ziarat or shrine to Baba Shukur-ud-Din, a disciple of the saint Nur-ud-Din.

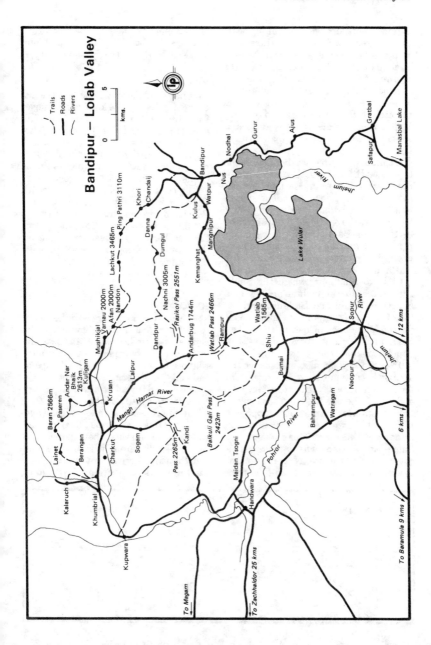

Houseboats, doongas and sailing boats can be hired on the lake. The three main mooring places are at Ningal Nullah, Kiuhnus Bay and at Ajus Spur on the south-east side. Around the lake are various canals which lead through the silt at the river mouths up into the rivers themselves. One of the best is to the Erin Valley which starts from Nodhal and winds 6½ km up to two high-altitude lakes.

Baramula, to the south-west of the lake, is on the main route to Rawalpindi, the chief route from Kashmir to the Indian plains prior to independence. Roads also run from here to Gilgit and Hunza, into the restricted zone controlled by Pakistan. Baramula is the legendary place from which Vishnu is said to have drained the waters which once filled the Kashmir Valley.

Close to Shadipur, where the Sindh River flows into the Jhelum, are the ruins of several Hindu and Buddhist shrines. Shadipur has a camping site and is noted for the abundance of fish in the waters around it. Narmarg, above the lake, is a popular trekking centre.

To get to Wular Lake, buses leave the Tourist Reception Centre in Srinagar in the morning for a day trip around the lake and back. The bus first stops at Anchar Lake, then on to Safapur, next stopping at Manasbal Lake before travelling to Bandipur 56 km away. This is followed by lunch at Watlab where there is a government rest house. Next is a tour of the mosque of Baba Sakar-ud-Din, then on to Sopur. The lake can be reached by river as well as road. See the Water Trekking section in the Srinagar chapter.

Baltal

This beautiful meadow is right at the foot of the Zoji La Pass 98 km from Srinagar. The river at the foot of the Amarnath Glacier meets the Indus River near Baltal (2743 metres) and during the Amarnath pilgrimage there are tents set up at Baltal, costing around Rs 6. Food is also available at that time but it's not very good.

It is possible to walk to the Amarnath Cave, more usually approached from Pahalgam, in one day. Check about conditions before departing, though, as the weather can be treacherous and at other times melting snow and ice make the route very dangerous. There is one major snow bridge to cross.

SONAMARG

At 2740 metres, Sonamarg is the last main point in the Kashmir Valley before the Zoji La Pass into Ladakh. At the pass, the green, lush Kashmiri landscape abruptly switches to the barren, dry landscape of Ladakh. Thus Sonamarg is not only a good base for treks but also a departure point for trips into Ladakh.

The name means 'meadow of gold' and although this could be due to the profusion of flowers that carpet the meadow in the spring it is also possible that the name derives from Sonamarg's strategic trading position in the days

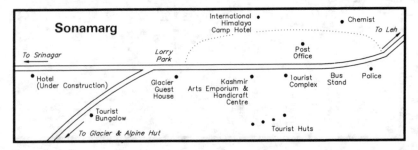

when this was a major route into Central Asia.

Legend has it that there is a well here and that its water has mystical qualities which turn everything into gold.

Sonamarg is not much to look at as it's simply a tatty collection of huts lining the road. These include a small selection of cheap restaurants, souvenir shops and dirty hotels that cater for the heavy traffic en route to and from Ladakh.

The surrounding scenery, however, is more pleasant and Sonamarg is a popular day-trip with Indian tourists staying in Srinagar. Most western travellers are less impressed by the attractions of pony rides and short walks.

A standard activity is to walk or ride the four km trip to the Thajiwas Glacier. A path leads up to the Shakhdar Hill, overlooking the glacier from the north-east. It is dangerous to climb the steep slope leading up to the glacier. Often in early summer you will meet groups of Gujar passing through Sonamarg on their way to the alpine meadows for summer. See the Trekking in Kashmir chapter.

Places to Stay

Sonamarg closes down in winter, only fully functional when the road to Leh is open. Only those starting or finishing treks or waiting to hitch a ride will normally want to stay here overnight.

The *Glacier* and *International* guest houses on the main street are as basic and dirty as you will find, without being particularly cheap. The best places are run by the Government.

The *Rest House* in the tourist office complex has doubles for Rs 35, and up the hill behind it are some *Tourist Huts* which with two double rooms, a kitchenette and dining room cost Rs 105. It is usually best to make reservations for these at the Tourist Reception Centre in Srinagar.

En route to the Thajiwas Glacier and about a 25-minute walk from the main street is a *Tourist Bungalow* with doubles for Rs 45. Close to the glacier the *Alpine Hut* has dorm beds for Rs 7 and doubles for Rs 105.

Behind the main street, the *International Himalaya Camp Hotel* has about 30 tents and charges Rs 30 per person or Rs 140 for full board and caters mostly to trekking groups.

The top-end *Sonamarg Glacier Hotel* under construction on the approach from Srinagar should be open now in the singles/doubles for Rs 200/350 price range.

Places to Eat

The various restaurants do a good trade feeding the large number of truck drivers, soldiers and passengers who pass through. The general rule of thumb is to patronise the ones that look the busiest. Prices are low and the food is basic but usually tasty. Those who do not enjoy such standards of dining should be prepared and bring food from Srinagar or Leh.

Getting There & Away

Buses leave the Tourist Reception Centre in Srinagar in the morning and cost Rs 58 return or Rs 30 one-way for the 83 km trip. For most travellers, it will be enough to stop here en route to/from Ladakh. The taxi fare from Srinagar is about Rs 431 return or Rs 360 one-way.

Trekking in Kashmir

There are many beautiful treks in and around the Kashmir Valley. These vary from short day walks from valley hill stations and longer walks in the valley and across the surrounding ranges, to hard treks out of the Kashmir region to Zanskar or Ladakh. Many of these routes follow the trails used by the Gujar shepherds to take their flocks to high altitude pastures during summer.

SONAMARG-WANGAT

This 81 km trek can take up to six days, or longer in early June or late October when there may be snow or heavy thunderstorms. It reaches a maximum altitude of 4191 metres. For the first few days the route follows the Sogput Dhar, a ridge of the western Himalaya, crossing and recrossing it at convenient points. The first part of the trek as far as Nichinai is straight forward, but from here there are several routes to Narannag and Wangat. There is also a route beyond Wangat for the longer trek to Erin and Bandipur.

Day 1: Srinagar-Sonamarg

The 84 km journey from Srinagar to Sonamarg takes three to four hours by bus or car. The route goes through the villages of Gandarbal, Kangan, Gund and Kulan en route to Sonamarg, which is the last large village in the Kashmir Valley on the way to Leh. Kangan is the point at which you will rejoin the Srinagar road if you come down through Wangat.

Kangan is also the best (and last) town at which to buy supplies – good vegetables and fruit, biscuits and bread, matches, etc – or get your stove repaired or buy a second cooking pot.

Sonamarg is at an altitude of 2740 metres and has tourist huts as well as wood and water if you are camping. Ponies can be rented here.

Day 2: Sonamarg-Nichinai

Half a km past the Shitkari Bridge and over the Sindh River on the road toward the Zoji La and Ladakh, the trail leaves the bank of the Sindh and climbs towards the stone water mill up the left side of the mountain. If you have started late in the day you can stay the night at the small village of Lashimarg where there are good camping sites.

From here it's a steep climb up the Galwanbal, a forest-covered mountain, to the top at an altitude of 3109 metres. From here the trail climbs gently through the Hirampathri meadows, to an altitude of 3658 metres, and the Nichinai Nar stream. The trail then follows the narrow, steep valley of the Nichinai to the Nichinai Bar Pass at 4080 metres. There is a glacier on either side of the valley here, and to the east lies the Bushkapathri Range, while to the west lies the Sahnai Range, covered in glaciers and snow beds.

Nichinai is at 3620 metres, 900 metres above Sonamarg and 15 km distant. Wood and water are on hand in the camp.

Day 3: Nichinai-Krishansar

The 13-km trek starts by crossing the 4080-metre Nichinai Ridge then follows the river before crossing it at Hirampathri. You pass the Vishansar Lake at 3680 metres and reach the camp at Krishansar at 3819 metres. The lake lies in the widest part of the valley at the foot of the glacier. The slopes on the south-eastern side of the mountain are ideal for camping.

The lake is just over a km long and about half a km wide. It's stocked with trout, but as it is within a national park, fishing permits are required. There is a good site for camping with water available, and if there are Gujars herding their sheep, they may sell you wood, but at high prices.

Day 4: Krishansar-Dubta Pani

Cross the stream that flows out of Vishansar and the path climbs another 150 metres to the tarn of Krishansar at 3818 metres. Huddled within the small, narrow valley, Krishansar usually has icebergs floating in it even as late as August.

From here the trek to Gadsar is about 23 km and begins with a steep climb to the Razbal Gali, at 4191 metres, followed by a rapid descent over snow to Yemsar, the 'lake of death', about 200 metres below. During the descent there is a string of tarns, which in spring and early summer are surrounded by blossoming wildflowers.

Around a bend in the trail the beautiful Gadsar Lake at 3900 metres suddenly appears. Glaciers from the surrounding peaks come almost down to the lake, which is circular and surrounded by mountains on three sides. The fourth side is a grassy slope, covered with flowers; a good spot for camping. From here the track descends gradually along the bank of the Gadsar to the mouth of the gorge at the foot of Mt Kasturgand, the home of the Kastura or musk deer.

The path through the gorge leads on to a three-day trek to Gurai, a beautiful series of rolling valleys. The route to Gangabal avoids the gorge, but crosses the stream and zig-zags up the flowery mountain slopes of Kasturgand, a steep climb through clumps of birch and pine. The path follows the mountain ridge until it reaches Dubta Pani, where the stream goes underground to reappear at the foot of a gorge about a km below. There is no wood at Dubta Pani, so you should collect fuel on the final ascent to the camp at 3280 metres.

Day 5: Dubta Pani-Gangabal Lake

The day's 17 km trek starts with a short walk to the Satsarsan Lake (3600 metres), another place with good camp sites. The path continues across the rocky valley floor and ascends to the Satsaran Bar Gali Pass at 3680 metres where you have a fine

view of the lake. The pass is open from June to October only. From the pass the route descends for about 100 metres and then begins a steep 500-metre climb on the right to the 4081-metre Zajibal Gali Pass, also open only from June to October. From here you can see the Nund Kol Lake at 3501 metres.

You can camp at Mengandub, near the top of the pass, or continue to Gangabal Lake. A sharp ascent of about a km brings you to the spot where the Gangabal Valley comes into view. The pass commands a magnificent view of Harmukh, opposite, with the Gangabal and Nund Kol lakes reflecting the glaciers and sky. The descent to the valley is about 600 metres down a gradual, grassy slope to the banks of the lakes. The camp site at Gangabal Lake (3570 metres) has wood, water and trout fishing. The lake is the site for a major pilgrimage each August.

Wardens patrol the national park here and fishing is totally controlled. The warden will more than likely confiscate your fishing gear and any fish you may have caught. However, if you arrive early in June and can stand the pain of the freezing glacial lake, the trout lie dormant just below the surface waiting for the water to warm and a rod and line are hardly necessary. The lake is fed by melt from the glacier which splits in two on one of the flanks of Harmukh.

Day 6: Gangabal Lake-Wangat

The 19 km trek descends 1500 metres to Wangat at 2050 metres. Leaving Nund Kol, there is a primitive stone and wood bridge which crosses the swiftly flowing and painfully cold Mungshungun Nullah. Thoughtless trekkers have, from time to time, broken off parts of the wooden planks of the bridge to use for firewood, as there is no wood at the camp site. As a result the bridge is becoming less and less reliable. It is possible to ford the river here very early in the morning before it rises with the melting snow of the day.

The trail then follows the river valley

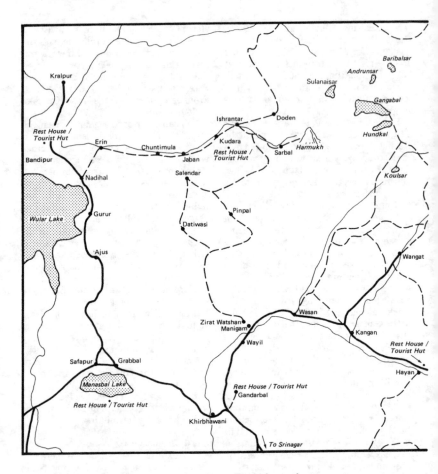

before climbing to the right, crossing a small ridge and coming out at Trunkul, or 'field of grass', a beautiful meadow which is usually crowded with the Gujar and their herds. There are two forest huts at Trunkul, both of which have suffered again from thoughtless trekkers using the timber for cooking fires. Although the tree line begins here, most of the wood lying on the ground has been scavenged by Gujars and it is difficult to find wood for a camp fire.

From here there are two routes to Narannag, each about 17 km – one is a steep and sometimes slippery descent following the river while the second is a more interesting trek across the ridges above the river, followed by a sharp descent to Narannag through a pine and deodar forest. This second path leads to Poshi Matun where there is a spring near the top of the peak. This small meadow looks down into the valley of the Sindh. From here there is a steep descent of

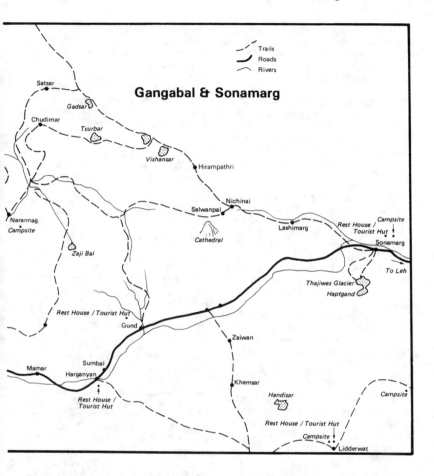

Gangabal & Sonamarg

almost 1200 metres over sedimentary slate. Some of the path is rocky and slippery, but it also winds through the fragrant fir and pine forests down towards the green valley of the Kranki Nadi.

At the foot of this descent is the small village of Narannag, 10 km from Kangan. Here there are the ruins of Buddhist temples built by Jaluka, a son of Emperor Ashoka, and King Lalitaditya. The ruins are composed of massive and tightly fitted stone blocks, formed into a large temple complex. There is a huge bath about five metres long and two metres broad and almost two metres deep, carved from a single block of stone.

Nearby, a spring said to have magical healing powers issues from a large pool beneath the mountain slope.

There is a well-maintained forest hut at Narannag with a six-bed dormitory, a kitchen and hot water for showers and washing.

From here it is five km along the sealed

road to Wangat at 2050 metres where there is a rest house and camping facilities, with wood and water. The bus leaves Wangat for Srinagar at 1.30 pm and the trip takes 2½ hours.

Day 6 (alternative): Gangabal-Wular Lake

An alternative to turning south from Gangabal to Kangan is to continue west to Wular Lake. From Gangabal take the track towards the Loolgul Gali Pass (4052 metres) which is open from June to October.

The five km trek to the top passes, with short detours, the spectacular lakes of Andansar and Loolgul. The descent from the pass is over a boulder-scattered slope down a track which leads to Sulanaisar, a small lake in a small valley on the right. From here it is 10 km to the open meadows and two small lakes of the Sarbal Valley. For those wanting to climb Harmukh, the valley is an ideal place to set up base camp.

The path gradually descends from here through forests along the valley of the Chitrasur Nullah, to its junction with the Erin Nullah Valley, 13 km away, and the village of Kudor. This village is 24 km from Nadihal, a pleasant walk through rice and corn fields.

Nadihal is 50 km from Srinagar on the way to Bandipur. Ponies may be hired at either Bandipur or Nadihal. From here you can take a pleasant boat trip along the Wular Lake and up the Jhelum River to Srinagar.

WULAR-GANGABAL (via Poshpathri)

This is an alternative route on the reverse trek from around the Wular Lake to Gangabal and then either down to Wangat or on to Sonamarg.

Day 1: Srinagar-Erin

It's about 80 km from Srinagar to Erin via Bandipur. Get off the bus at the small village of Nadihal from where you walk to Erin (altitude 1983 metres). Here there is a rest house and riverbank camping sites.

Day 2: Erin-Chuntimula-Poshpathri

The 11 km trek starts by crossing the Erin River near the rest house. The first three or four km of the route, which ascends in stages, is in good condition as it is maintained by the forest smallholders. The route passes the village of Kudara, where there is a rest house, and reaches Poshpathri at 2440 metres.

Day 3: Poshpathri-Sarbal

A difficult 8½ km ascent takes you to Minimarg after which the rest of the 11 km route to Sarbal is not so difficult. There is a good camp site on the banks of the Sarbal Lake at the foot of Harmukh, but you will have to bring firewood. The Shirsar Lake stands above Sarbal.

Day 4: Sarbal-Kundsar Lake

The day's nine km trek starts from the left of the Gujar huts, follows a steep ascent for about 2½ km then climbs more gradually the rest of the way to the lake at 3800 metres.

Day 5: Kundsar Lake-Gangabal Lake

The 11 km trek first follows the bank of the Kundsar then, after about 1½ km, climbs over a glacier and dips into a depression for nearly three km. After another three km the route turns left and drops 150 metres then climbs about 150 metres to the top of a ridge before descending to the lake.

You will need rope, ice-axes and U-bolts for this trek because of the crevices in the glacier. You can camp at the lake (3572 metres) or at Nund Col about 1½ km away. There are many fish in the lake and there are two forest huts at Trunkul.

Day 6 onwards

From day six onwards you can either turn south to Wangat, as on day six of the Sonamarg-Wangat trek, or continue east to Sonamarg, as on day one-to-five of that same trek.

PAHALGAM-KOLAHOI GLACIER

This short trek from Pahalgam is one of the most popular in Kashmir, as from June through September the route can be quite crowded.

Day 1: Srinagar-Pahalgam

It's about 90 km from Srinagar to Pahalgam and only takes two hours by car, but rather longer by bus. The route follows the Jammu road out of Srinagar then turns up the Lidder Valley through several villages to Pahalgam. There are fine views of rice paddies and snow-capped peaks all along the road. The Lidder has many fish but a trout fishing licence is rather expensive. Pahalgam is at 2130 metres and has a wide variety of accommodation.

Day 2: Pahalgam-Aru

It's only about 12 km from Pahalgam, the 'village of shepherds', to Aru. Cars can follow this part of the route, which runs along the right bank of the Lidder River through pine forest. Riding and load-carrying ponies can easily be obtained in Pahalgam, either directly from the pony owners or through the tourist office.

Aru (also spelt Arau) is a picturesque village at the confluence of two smaller rivers. There are several places to stay – see the section on Pahalgam in the Kashmir Valley section.

Two routes lead from Aru to the Kolahoi Glacier. The first leads straight through the forest to Lidderwat, starting with a steep ascent then following the Lidder River for the rest of the way. The other route is much harder, particularly for ponies, and goes right to Armiun, past Soipathri, then over the 3880-metre Hari Gali Pass.

Day 3: Aru-Lidderwat

It is about 12 km from Aru to Lidderwat where there is a magnificent camping spot at the meeting point of the Kolahoi Glacier's stream and the stream from the Tarsar Lake. Lidderwat also has a two-room PWD Rest House and the pleasant Paradise Guest House.

Day 4: Lidderwat-Kolahoi Glacier-Lidderwat

It's a day trip from Lidderwat to the glacier (13 km) or to the Tarsar Lake. The stretch to the glacier leads east through a pine forest until Satlanjan where the landscape opens out. The glacier begins at 3400 metres and extends to over 4000 metres. To the north-west of Kolahoi, beneath the glacier, is the Dudh Nag Lake at 4267 metres. Mt Kolahoi, from which the glacier descends, is 5485 metres high.

Day 5: Lidderwat-Pahalgam

It's an easy walk back to Pahalgam or an extra day may be spent going to the Tarsar Lake (3962 metres). From the lake, you can climb over a 250-metre ridge which separates Tarsar from the Marsar Lake. It is also possible to continue on from Lidderwat to the Sindh Valley, meeting the road from Srinagar to Leh near Sonamarg, along the following route.

PAHALGAM-SONAMARG

Day 1-2: Pahalgam-Aru-Lidderwat

The first two days are as for the Kolahoi Glacier trek from Pahalgam. An additional day can be added to actually visit the glacier before continuing from Lidderwat.

Day 3: Lidderwat-Sekiwas

The 10 km walk ascends the Sekiwas Nullah to Sekiwas at 3430 metres.

Day 4: Sekiwas-Khemsar

The 11 km trek takes you over the 4115 metre Yemhar Pass to Khemsar at 3659 metres. The descent from the pass is fairly easy during July and August. There is no firewood at Khemsar.

Day 5: Khemsar-Kulan

The trail descends through forests to the Sindh River where you cross the Kulan Bridge at 2226 metres. Sonamarg is only 16 km from Kulan and can be reached

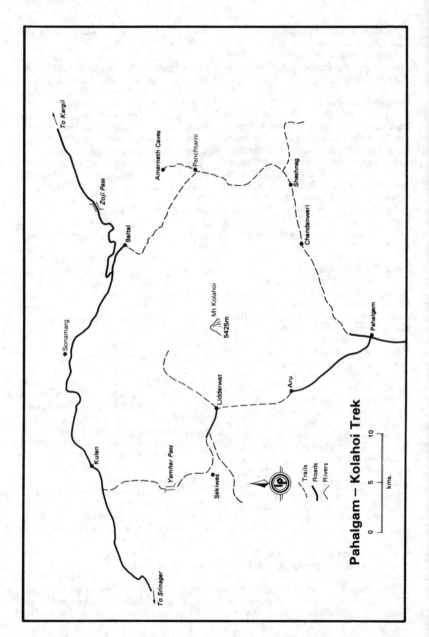

Pahalgam – Kolahoi Trek

either by a good track up the Sindh Valley or by bus.

SONAMARG-AMARNATH

Although the traditional *Yatra* pilgrimage trek to the Amarnath Cave is from Pahalgam, you can also walk there from Sonamarg.

Day 1: Sonamarg-Baltal

This 15 km trek takes about five hours and is an easy walk since there is little altitude change between Sonamarag and Baltal. You should be able to get a lift on a truck to the road block. From there it is better to walk as the road block is closed until noon or later, waiting for traffic to come across the Zoji La from Ladakh.

Walk along the pleasant river valley track, although during the Amarnath Yatra you can be pestered by begging nomad shepherds. The river valley track is also two to three km shorter than the vehicle road. A military camp is the first sign of Baltal, which can be reached in a day from Srinagar.

Day 2: Baltal-Amarnath

The 15 km trail to Amarnath climbs over a thousand metres from Baltal at 2743 metres to the Amarnath Cave at 4175 metres and takes about 10 hours. The route crosses one major snow bridge over a river and climbs steadily up, crossing the Satsing Pass, 3½ km before Amarnath at 4115 metres, dropping down and then climbing up again to the cave. There are tea stalls at the river and after the junction with the main trail.

From Amarnath, follow the traditional Yatra trail down to Pahalgam.

PAHALGAM-AMARNATH CAVE

At the time of the full moon in the month of Shravan (July-August) thousands of Hindu pilgrims make the annual Yatra to the Shri Amarnath Cave. At 4175 metres, 45 km from Pahalgam, the cave contains a natural ice lingam, the symbol of Lord Shiva.

During the Yatra it is possible to obtain wood, kerosene and other necessities at Chandanwari, Sheshnag and Panchtarni, but at other times these must be brought from Pahalgam. Also during the Yatra there are tea stalls and restaurants all along the trail and tent hotels about every five km. Food is, of course, cheaper the closer you are to Pahalgam and it tends to be very simple so you'll probably appreciate some snacks like chocolate bars, so bring some.

Although the tourist office may tell you that you need tents, ponies, a guide, a cook, porters, 'and everything but a harem of dancing girls and a brass band' all you really need is a porter to carry your pack as the air gets pretty thin at 3000 metres and the high point of the trek, Mahagunas Peak, is nearly 4500 metres.

If you're in good trekking shape you don't even need a porter. The trail is clearly defined so there's no problem with getting lost, although a sharp-pointed stick is necessary for crossing the many ice and snowfields. Bring warm clothing. At Amarnath the temperature at night will be below freezing.

There are different opinions on whether to go to Amarnath at the Yatra time or not, as two trekkers relate:

It's really more fun to trek at other than the Yatra time when the trail becomes a real mob scene. At that time prices escalate in the rest stops as well. A few weeks before the Yatra an entire village of tents springs up at each rest stop, offering food and lodging. So a week or two before or after the Yatra these facilities will be set up and the Sikhs (usually) who run them will be hungry for customers. This way you don't have to carry food or bedding. The ice lingam is not likely to be much of an attraction, except for Shiva freaks, but the terrain is spectacular. Once you get over Mahagunas Peak it's a real moonscape and you'll run into old snowfields as you approach the cave.

This has to be one of my favourite experiences in nine months in India. Everybody, from all Hindu castes, was there; from the sadhus smoking chillums, naked and walking barefoot

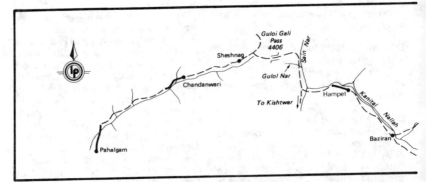

through the snow, to the rich and fat decadents being carried along by coolies. Kashmiris were there for the business, renting horses and tents, putting up tea stalls all along the 100 km trek. The police, well organised and friendly, were walking as well – taking care of the most hysterical pilgrims or those nearest to death! In other words, the atmosphere and the scenery together make this not so much a hard trek as a mass migration by a happy band of nomads. In fact it was sad to see it end after a week and we stayed in Pahalgam for a good week afterwards, saying goodbye to friends we made along the way. The organisation of the Yatra is amazingly well done and it's an experience highly recommended, giving you a glimpse of a wide variety of Indian characters and a better understanding of their culture.

Day 1: Pahalgam-Chandanwari
The route follows a jeepable road for 13 km to Chandanwari (2900 metres) where the Sheshnag and Astanmarg rivers meet. Although famous for its snow bridge, this is a colourful place during the Yatra with many *sadhus*. Since it is the first stop from Pahalgam there is a wider variety of food available and at lower prices than further along the trek. There is also a PWD Rest House.

Day 2: Chandanwari-Sheshnag
There is a choice of routes for this 14 km trek. One route goes past the Pisu hill while the other goes via the Pisu Gali (the pilgrim route on which, during the Yatra,

there are beggars). The walk climbs steadily from Chandanwari, with one particularly steep ascent near a waterfall.

The Sheshnag Lake is at 3700 metres and there are camping facilities at Zojipal, while at Wavjan, just above Sheshnag, there is a PWD Rest House with doubles for Rs 20. The view down to the lake is superb and in season there are tent hotels for pilgrims.

Day 3: Sheshnag-Panchtarni
The 11 km from Wavjan (3950 metres) to Panchtarni (3500 metres) is the hardest day on the trek because you have to cross many snowfields and the snowbound Mahagunas Pass at nearly 4500 metres.

From there it is eight km down to beautiful Panchtarni ('five streams'), the meeting point of five small rivers. The simple but pleasant PWD Rest House has doubles for Rs 20. It is possible to walk from Chandanwari to Panchtarni in one day.

Day 4: Panchtarni-Amarnath Cave
The final stretch to the cave is just eight km, climbing from 3500 metres at Panchtarni to 4175 metres at the cave. The tent accommodation here is rather bad and there are only a few places to camp. Outside the peak of the Yatra season you can sleep in the cave although it's very cold. A km before the cave there

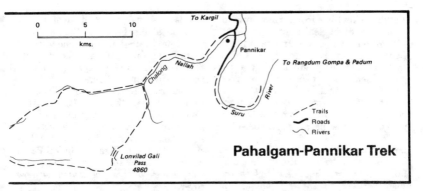

Pahalgam-Pannikar Trek

are good camping grounds and concrete shelters.

It is possible to continue from the Amarnath Cave to Baltal, on the Srinagar-Leh road about 15 km from Sonamarg. This is an alternative to returning from the cave to Pahalgam. See the Sonamarg-Amarnath trek report.

PAHALGAM-PANNIKAR (Suru Valley)

This trek is quite hard and is best made between June and September. Porters can be hired in Pahalgam but you must expect to pay Rs 40 or more per day. You should carry a tent and all necessities must be brought from Pahalgam, including food and kerosene for cooking. The only places with lodging available are Chandanwari and Sheshnag, as on the Amarnath Cave trek. After that you're on your own and for some stretches it's necessary to carry water. Places marked on the map along this route are often just meadows.

Day 1 & 2: Pahalgam-Chandanwari-Sheshnag

The same as the Amarnath Cave trek.

Day 3: Sheshnag-Rangmarg

The route ascends the 4406-metre Gulol Gali Pass then descends on the left bank of the Gulol Nar down to the mouth of the Sain Nar. Here you take the right bank (definitely not the left!) and complete the 7½ km walk to Rangmarg.

Day 4: Rangmarg-Hampet

The trail follows the Sain Nar until it joins the Kanital Nullah on the left then follows on the left bank to Hampet, a distance of 5½ km.

Day 5 & 6: Hampet-foot of the Lonvilad Gali

From Hampet the track continues on the left bank of the Kanital Nullah to Baziran. Here the trail divides with a long route leading straight ahead to Pannikar. Follow the Kanital on its right bank to the foot of the Lonvilad Gali, a distance of 22 km over the two days.

Day 7: Lonvilad Gali-Chalong Glacier

The route ascends the 4660-metre Lonvilad Gali then descends over a glacier which comes from the Chalong Nullah. The overnight halt is made at the foot of the glacier.

Day 8: Chalong Glacier-Pannikar

The 15 km walk starts with the descent into the valley of the Chalong Nullah, which leads to Pannikar. From Pannikar a road leads north to Kargil or east to the Zanskar Valley.

KONSARNAG TREK

This four-to-five day trek in the Pir Panjal Range reaches a maximum altitude of 3700 metres.

Day 1: Srinagar-Aharbal From Srinagar to

Aharbal takes three to four hours by road, a journey which leads through several picturesque villages standing in rice paddies. On the last part of this stretch the road ascends gradually. There is a government rest house and a good camping site, with water and wood, at Aharbal (2460 metres). Take a look at the waterfall, about 10 km from Aharbal, and the conifer forest past the rest house.

Day 2: Aharbal-Kongwatan

The nine km trek to Kongwatan only takes about three hours and follows the Vishav River to the 1½ square km Kongwatan meadow at 2559 metres, where there is a rest house with two rooms. With an early start from Srinagar you can reach Kongwatan on the first day.

Day 3: Kongwatan-Mahinag

The day's walk starts through thick forest then climbs slowly beside the Vishav River. The ascent from Kongwatan to the Yechini is a distance of 16 km. The path, which is in good condition, goes along the right bank to Mahinag and after some time crosses to the other bank and becomes rougher. The plateau of Mahinag is surrounded by lovely mountains and has a group of glass-clear, ice-cold springs.

Mountaineers can find numerous climbing opportunities in this area. It is possible to continue straight on to the mountain lake of Konsarnag in the same day but it is better to camp for the night at Mahinag (2989 metres).

Day 4: Mahinag-Konsarnag-Kongwatan

The ascent to the pass overlooking Konsarnag Lake is 305 metres, the last 60 to 70 metres of which is very steep and covered with snow. A slip could mean a fall to the snowfield below. From the top of the pass you can see that the stream flowing from the lake has dug a deep gorge about 12 km long.

The way down to the lake is not difficult and can be accomplished by sliding over the snow. Across the lake and over to the left is a snowfield at the foot of the Brahma Shakri Peaks, at the head of a snowbound valley. It is possible to climb to the lake (altitude 4419 metres) and return to camp in Mahinag after rounding the lake in about 12 hours.

Konsarnag Lake is below the three towering peaks of the Panjal Range, 25 km from Shupian, and is said to be shaped exactly like a right foot with five toes and a heel – hence its name of Vishnu Pad. It is surrounded by the Bharma Shakri Peaks which are up to 4800 metres high with steep slopes which are permanently snow covered.

Lying from north-east to south-west, the lake is about three km long and up to a km wide, with an estimated depth of 50 metres. The deep, dark blue waters are excellent for swimming. The lake is fed by streams on the north-eastern shore and becomes progressively narrower until it ends in a point towards the south-west. On the northern side is a subterranean passage through which water is seen and heard, gurgling down towards Kashmir.

Day 5: Kongwatan-Srinagar

From Kongwatan, return to Aharbal and then by road to Srinagar.

SRINAGAR-DAKSUM-KISHTWAR

This five-day trek out of the Kashmir Valley into the Jammu region reaches a maximum altitude of 3700 metres and is best made between June and September.

Day 1: Srinagar-Daksum

The 100 km trip can be made by bus or taxi and takes about three hours. There are camping facilities with wood and water in Daksum and ponies can be hired there or in Wagil. Overnight accommodation in Daksum must be booked in Srinagar.

Day 2: Daksum-Sinthan Pass

This 16 km trek takes about five to six hours and reaches the maximum altitude of the trek. There are wooden huts in Sinthan and wood and water are on hand.

Daksum – Kishtwar

Trails
Roads
Rivers

Day 3: Sinthan-Chhatru
This eight km trek takes two or three hours. Wood and water are at the camping area and there is a small shop in the village for replenishing provisions.

Day 4: Chhatru-Mughal Maidan
There are some shops in the village which is reached after a nine km trek.

Day 5: Mughal Maidan-Dadhpeth
It's an eight km trek to Dadhpeth from where there are daily buses at 10 am and 4 pm to Kishtwar.

Kishtwar has a Dak Bungalow and other accommodation or camping possibilities. It has some notable waterfalls and is a centre of saffron cultivation. Kishtwar is also a popular departure point for other treks (including one into Zanskar) and mountain climbing. From Kishtwar you can reach either Jammu or Srinagar by bus in one day.

Srinagar to Leh

The road between the Kashmir Valley and Ladakh is surfaced most of the way. It winds its way from the Sindh Valley, through the Drass Valley into the Indus Valley.

The road goes through rice and maize fields and crosses the Sindh River over partly submerged bridges – old wooden bridges over which the military have built pioneer bridges. It passes through the villages of Gandarbal, Kangan and Gund before reaching Sonamarg, the last sizeable settlement in the Kashmir Valley. The road was built after the 1962 Indo-Chinese conflict and must be one of the most fascinating, terrifying and yet exhilarating trips in the world.

Sonamarg is less a place to stay than a departure point for trekking tours and riding trips in the mountains. Popular trekking routes include Sonamarg-Amarnath Cave, Sonamarg-Thajiwas Glacier and Sonamarg-Wangat.

Beyond Sonamarg is the border to the Ladakh region. As you climb the Great Himalaya out of Sonamarg you leave behind one world and enter a place which has for many become a sort of Shangri La. The world beyond the Himalaya has always been remote and inaccessible, as soaring mountain ranges, snow-covered passes and impossible altitudes have always protected this region from invasion by conquerors and tourists.

Srinagar to Kargil

ZOJI LA

The first pass is the Zoji La (3529 metres), 110 km from Srinagar. After rainfall or during the spring snow-melt beware of rock slides on this 1000-metre ascent. The Zoji La Pass is not sealed and its condition depends on how severe the past winter has been. The road up to the pass is exhilarating, but there are times when you'll wonder if you were sane to make this trip.

Travelling in early spring is particularly hazardous when the Beacon Road Patrol crews are still working to shore up vast landslides, avalanches and ice slips that have eaten away huge chunks of the road.

twice its height, cut by the snow ploughs and bulldozers. Melting snow flows from underneath this ice which could, at any moment, break off and crush the bus. On other stretches, the narrow track, gouged out by bulldozers and compounded by the trucks and the picks of the labourers is barely wide enough to accommodate the wheels of the bus. If you have a window seat looking down into nothingness, reaching the Gates of India will be a great relief.

The actual pass is a low flat plain and beyond it the country seems bereft of life. The mountains are bare rock and rubble while the river valleys are simply gravel and mud. However, the clean, clear air and unique countryside compels one to look closely for signs of life. You will most likely see goats tended by herders in black robes, yaks and *dzos* (common cattle cross-bred with yaks) plodding steadily towards the high passes.

the road moves through the source of the Drass River and along the river's valley. The first settlement after the pass is the town of Matayan on the Gumbar River, inhabited by Kashmiris, Dards and Baltis. The people speak Urdu, Dardi, Kashmiri and Balti. The farther settlements are mostly on the mountain sides above the road, which passes through the villages of Prandrass and Murad Bagh before reaching Drass in a 15 square km valley.

DRASS

This is a small village 147 km from Srinagar with a TCP and a large military camp on the Drass River, en route to Kargil. The Public Works Department (rest house) has a tourist officer and stands on the right-hand side of the road from Srinagar. It can't be missed as it is directly opposite the Rahi Tea Stall where there is 'Hot tea available anytime'. All the buses stop here and tourists are asked to register their names and passport numbers.

Drass is famed for its freezing temperatures and heavy winter snowfalls. In fact, it is the second coldest inhabited place in the world after Siberia, with a minimum recorded winter temperature of –40°C. In this area the dialect spoken, *Hambabs*, is named after the weather and means snowfall.

From Drass to Kargil the road follows the river, at times running less than five km from the ceasefire line with Pakistan. At a lefthand curve outside of Drass, four 7th century Buddhist bas-reliefs stand next to the road; they are the Maitriya Buddha, Avalokitesvera, an equestrian figure and a lotus.

The road runs to Kharbu (10 km), to Channigund (14 km) and then Kargil (10 km). The villages along the route are all hundreds of metres above the road, on small plateaux.

Beyond Tashgam the valley narrows and the mountains on both sides of the river reach between 5000 and 5500 metres. The road runs over steep passes and narrow gorges with the river rushing alongside. Shortly before the road from the Drass Valley turns off into the Suru Valley a bridge, passable by jeep but barred to foreigners, crosses the Drass River into a restricted military area.

For trekking from Drass to Sanku (Suru Valley), see the Zanskar chapter.

Zoji La Pass

The final hours on the bus from Drass to Kargil may seem never-ending, but the scenery offers log and rope bridges stretched across the Drass and Kanji Nallah rivers, and trails in the rocks leading upwards.

KARGIL

Kargil is the second largest town in Ladakh and has a predominantly Muslim population of just over 5000. At 2650 metres, it is at the confluence of the Suru River and the Wakha Brook in the Lower Suru Basin and is 204 km from Srinagar.

Kargil is striking for its unique, irrigated fields. Since irrigation is so important in this region, the distribution of water requires great care. Every village is divided into groups called *Gowar*, of from five to 10 families, to ensure an equitable arrangement. Willows and poplars grow beside the irrigation ditches which lead to the terraced fields and line the road for much of its length in this region. These trees furnish building materials for the construction of houses in this nearly treeless land.

The Kargil region actually gets more rainfall than the rest of Ladakh and the area grows plentiful wheat, barley, vegetables and, of course, the apricots for which it is famous. The town was once an important trading post due to its strategic location at the intersection of trade routes from Russia to India and from China to the west. Over the past 30 years political changes have considerably reduced its importance. Now it is simply a village at the junction of the Drass and Suru rivers, 20 km from the Indus; a stopping point with hotels, camping facilities and a service station on the road to Leh. The buses to and from Leh stop for the night here and leave between 3 and 5 am.

The recent construction of the Zanskar road to Padum has once again added to Kargil's importance. The bazaar is now bustling and it is possible to purchase everything you might need for a trek – even kerosene stoves. If you are considering trekking in Zanskar or Ladakh remember

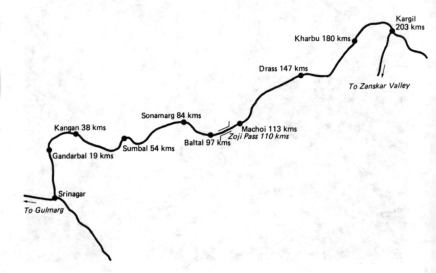

that until reaching Padum travellers must virtually live off their supplies. Anything forgotten in Srinagar should, therefore, be bought here. Due to the strong religious beliefs of the local population great difficulties accompany the purchase of alcohol!

The dialect spoken is called *Purig* which is a long-drawn synthesis between Balti and Ladakhi with an emphasis on pronouncing each and every syllable. In addition to learning Urdu and English, the children also study Arabic. They are basically taught this to read rather than to speak or write, the primary aim being to recite the Koran, a religious requirement for Muslims.

In contrast, the Buddhist children elsewhere in Ladakh are taught to recite the Tibetan lamaist scriptures, for which they must learn the Tibetan language. Neither Kargil's Muslim children, nor Leh's Buddhist children become fluent in spoken Arabic or Tibetan with this training.

Kargil's Muslims are predominantly Shi'ite (as in Iran) – noted for their extreme orthodoxy, with women conspicuously absent from the streets and general forms of entertainment frowned upon. Visitors are not made to feel unwelcome, far from it, but you should act and dress accordingly.

Information

Tourist Office Kargil's new Tourist Reception Centre, adjacent to the taxi stand on the main street, should be in operation by now. It replaces the original tourist office up the hill behind the school and the hospital, off Hospital Road.

It was planned that some trekking equipment would be stocked for hire. The tourist officer and his staff are knowledgeable and helpful, so see them for assistance with any queries about trekking, the road to Zanskar, etc.

Post & Telegraph Also on the main street, this office offers limited and unreliable telecommunication services, but a standard postal service. For poste restante, have envelopes marked with a plea such as

Srinagar-Leh Route
Kilometres from Srinagar

Shergol 237 kms
Mulbekh 244 kms
Bodh Kharbu 274 kms
Namika Pass 259 kms
Khalsi 337 kms
Nurla 348 kms
Fatu Pass 295 kms
Lamayuru 310 kms
Rizong 363 kms
Saspul 372 kms
Alchi 370 kms
Lekir 382 kms
Basgo 392 kms
Nimmu 398 kms
Leh 434 kms
Spitok 421 kms

To Manali

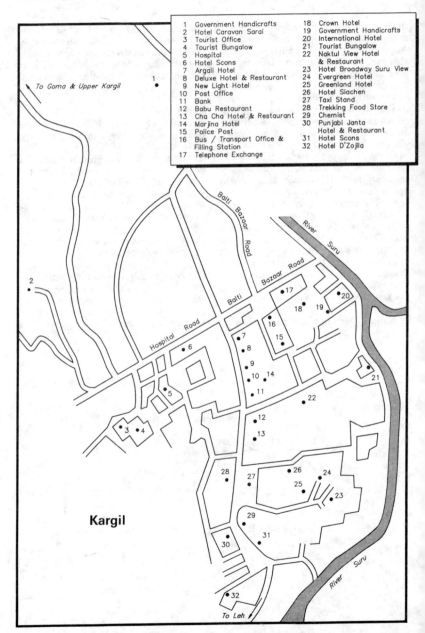

1 Government Handicrafts
2 Hotel Caravan Sarai
3 Tourist Office
4 Tourist Bungalow
5 Hospital
6 Hotel Scons
7 Argali Hotel
8 Deluxe Hotel & Restaurant
9 New Light Hotel
10 Post Office
11 Bank
12 Babu Restaurant
13 Cha Cha Hotel & Restaurant
14 Marjina Hotel
15 Police Post
16 Bus / Transport Office &
   Filling Station
17 Telephone Exchange
18 Crown Hotel
19 Government Handicrafts
20 International Hotel
21 Tourist Bungalow
22 Naktul View Hotel
   & Restaurant
23 Hotel Broadway Suru View
24 Evergreen Hotel
25 Greenland Hotel
26 Hotel Siachen
27 Taxi Stand
28 Trekking Food Store
29 Chemist
30 Punjabi Janta
   Hotel & Restaurant
31 Hotel Scons
32 Hotel D'Zojila

To Goma & Upper Kargil

Balti Bazaar Road

River Suru

Bazaar Road

Balti

Hospital Road

Kargil

River Suru

To Leh

'hold for six weeks' (give generous dates) or you risk having your mail returned or dumped after only two weeks.

Banks There are branches of the State Bank and the J&K Bank which are open Monday to Friday, 10 am to 2 pm (winter 10.30 am to 2.30 pm), Saturday from 10 am to noon (winter 10.30 am to 12.30 pm), and closed Sunday.

Things to See
Kargil has a lousy reputation among travellers who generally arrive late in the day after hours on the road from Srinagar or Leh, and leave at an irritatingly early hour the next morning. The low standard of its cheap accommodation and eating places seal Kargil's fate, which is known as 'that awful place where we had to stop overnight on the way to and from Leh'. There is little of real interest to point out, but if you do find yourself with a few hours to kill then you should know the following.

Kargil's generally uninteresting architecture includes the Imambaras which are Shi'ite mourning houses. Shi'ites congregate at these every year for the first 10 days of the first month (*Muharram*) of the Islamic calendar to mourn the martyrdom of Mohammad's two grandsons, Hassan and Hussein, in the Battle of Karbala (Iraq). This was fought for the rights of succession to the position of Caliph, between the grandson's and their forces on one side, and the numerically superior Yazid and his forces on the other.

Basically like a mosque in appearance, the Imambaras are manned by the *Aghas*, often referred to as Muslim mystics. These gents are learned holy men who lead the faithful in the interpretation of Islamic beliefs and law. They have great legal powers with all issues short of manslaughter being decided by them. They have studied Islamic theology at university in Baghdad and are accomplished scholars in Arabic and Persian, as well as speaking the local dialect, in which they give their religious guidance.

The main bazaar in Kargil has many Kashmiri products including embroidery, turquoises, tobacco, raw sugar and exotic spices. You will also find cloth woven from the finest wool of the long-fleeced mountain goats, brass bowls, flower vases, wine cups and tall jugs (used for coffee, tea or other liquors), leather shoes embroidered with silk or gold, silver chains, rings, bracelets and charms, paintings, pashmina shawls, brightly coloured rugs and other more Chinese-looking items.

Goma Kargil (Upper Kargil) offers pleasant panoramic views and some typical local villages within about an hour's walk each way. A rough road (see the map for directions) goes up near a brook and a thick plantation of poplars, willows and wild roses. Further up the hill beyond Goma Kargil is a hot spring popular with locals for its curative powers. There is also the ancient shrine of the early Muslim missionaries that attracts a regular stream of devotees.

It is a short walk to nearby Poyen, perhaps the oldest of Kargil's villages. To get there, cross the wooden bridge near the main bazaar in Kargil. Another possibility is to take a local bus to Mulbek (see Kargil to Leh section).

Nearby Tsaluskot is the grainery of the region, attracting people from Zanskar and Leh who come to buy grain. The houses have stone foundations and a superstructure of unbaked, heavy clay bricks.

Kargil is also the departure point for trips and treks to the Suru Valley and Zanskar.

People of the Kargil Region
The Kargil region is mainly populated by a people known as *Purig Pa*, a contraction of the more descriptive term *Pod-Rigs-Pa* meaning 'of Tibetan race'. The region's local name has always been *Purig* and the local population still calls it this, with Kargil being used after the Dogra administration made the town their garrison HQ in 1846. The Purig-Pa people are a

mixture of Darad immigrants and Tibetan nomadic tribes, and more recently Tibetan invaders.

The *Brokpas* or *Drokpas* are the remaining descendants of Ladakh's Darad immigrants. Unlike their Drass cousins who became Muslims after the mid-15th century, these Brokpas have neither accepted Islam nor assimilated into the mainstream of Ladakh's Tibetanised population.

The remote locality of their lower Indus villages and the custom of marrying mostly amongst themselves have helped preserve their identity. They continue to follow a faith that is a strange mixture of animism and shamanistic rites and ceremonies. Among these are several ancient ceremonies which illustrate traditions of ancestor worship, goat worship and nature worship. Goats are still ritually slaughtered at the altar of their exclusive dieties on many occasions. An example of this is their most popular festival, *Bonona*. Celebrated every three years at Garkon and Dah alternately – their two principal villages – it primarily involves the ritual slaughtering of goats at the altars of their Goddess of Wealth and Goddess of Fertility.

The Brokpas features are distinctly Aryan – tall, well-built, fair complexion with straight and occasionally blond hair.

The women are renowned for their regal beauty, although the custom of rarely bathing must be mentioned. Both men and women are very fond of flowers and ornaments – even the men wear flowers in their hats, as well as earrings, necklaces, bracelets and strings of imitation pearls. Their traditional costume, worn regularly, is distinct from other Ladakhis – tight trousers of undyed coarse wool with a short upper garment decorated with geometric designs along the borders. This strange ensemble is topped off by a colourful cap invariably adorned with a bouquet of dried flowers.

The Brokpas currently number around 1000 and live in four villages in a part of Ladakh that is off-limits to foreign visitors due to the border dispute with Pakistan. However, some of them may be seen occasionally in Kargil's bazaar.

– GM Kakpori of Kargil

Places to Stay – bottom end

I was told, in all seriousness, that someone actually visited Kargil to study bed bugs! After visiting some of the places offering

accommodation you will understand why. The prices quoted here are extremely variable and what you end up paying will depend considerably on your ability to bargain.

On the main street, the *Popular Chacha, De Lux, New Light, Purik, Punjab Janta* and *Argalia* provide the rock-bottom standard at around Rs 20 a bed. For a little more, things get a little better at the *Naktul View*, between the main street and the truck park, and the *Crown* and *International*, on the other side of the truck park.

The best deals in town by far are the two *Tourist Bungalows* with clean doubles for Rs 35 and Rs 50. Unlike the previous options where hot water is unheard of, buckets of hot water are available upon request. The rooms are very comfortable for the price.

With these being the exception, there is a significant jump in the price between the basic/bedbug and the basic/bearable category. The *Greenland Hotel* has running hot water and acceptable singles/doubles at Rs 115/150. The *Marjina Tourist Hotel* has singles at Rs 80 to Rs 120 and doubles at Rs 130 to Rs 175, while the newer and nicer *Hotel Scons* has singles/doubles at Rs 175/250.

Places to Stay – top end

With singles/doubles in the Rs 220/350 range, Kargil's top choices are expensive for what they provide. The *Caravan Sarai* has views across the town and stands on the hillside off Hospital Rd. The *Siachen* is adjacent to the taxi stand with the *Broadway Suru View* around the other side. The *D'Zojila* stands on the outskirts of town and you can call them (tel 28) to send a jeep when you get off the bus.

Places to Stay – around Kargil

Drass has a *Tourist Bungalow* with six double rooms and there are bungalows at Mulbekh, Pannikar, Juldo and Gulmatongo for about Rs 35 to Rs 50 for doubles. There are *PWD Rest Houses* at Sanku and

Top: Lamayuru Gompa (GW)
Left: Traversing the Great Himalaya at Zoji La before the road is open to traffic (BP)
Right: A tanka in Lamayuru Gompa (TW)

Top: In the back streets of Leh (TW)
Left: Monk in Spitok Gompa (RS)
Right: Stupas on the Srinagar to Leh road (NT)

Rangdum on the route to Zanskar and at Bodh Kharbu. Reservations for these must be made with the executive officer in Kargil and *Tourist Bungalow* reservations can be made with the tourist officer in Kargil.

Places to Eat

Kargil's food is little better than its accommodation. One exception to the generally low standard was the *Naktul*, next to the hotel of the same name – easily the best place in town with its Chinese dishes. Elsewhere, the *Marjina Tourist Hotel* leads the pack, with the *Babu*, *Popular Chacha* and *New Light* taking the overflow and those fooled by the rash promises of French, Italian, German, Chinese and Tibetan cuisine.

Kargil is renowned for its apricots. You can buy the dried variety and good jam either on the main street or from the Fruit Growers Co-op.

Getting There & Away

In addition to the buses going to Leh and Srinagar, there are daily bus services to Mulbekh, Drass, Pannikar and twice daily services to Sauku and Trespone. Check with the Tourist Reception Centre for schedules.

To Zanskar The bus service to Zanskar is a lot less reliable. Basically a bus leaves Kargil for Padum twice a week (Rs 56). However, at the beginning and end of summer, when fewer locals make the trip, they leave less frequently. Check with the Tourist Reception Centre and consider hitching a ride with a private truck (about Rs 70 to Rs 100). Jeeps can be hired for a prohibitive Rs 4000.

The recently completed road through the Suru Valley, along which is the Rangdum Gompa, turns south from Kargil and crosses over the Pensi La Pass to Padum. At the best of times the road is very rough and negotiable only with difficulty. If the road is open all the way the fare on a truck from Kargil is about Rs 39, or a jeep can be hired for about Rs 2300.

See the Zanskar chapter for trekking information. Even during winter it is sometimes possible to reach Srinagar from Kargil via Kishtwar, following the Suru River and going over the Bhoktal Pass at a height of 4380 metres.

AROUND KARGIL

Mt Kala Pahad (4575 metres), near Kargil, was under Pakistani control until the 1971 India-Pakistan conflict. In that war the borders of India were pushed further to the west, but you still cannot travel directly to the Indus Valley and along the Indus to Leh. Instead, you must take the hard way over the Namika La and Fatu La passes and reach the Indus Valley by Khalsi. A road is being built around the Namika La Pass, 'which touches the sky', through the forbidden zone, west of the present road.

In this region are the interesting villages of Garkon, Dards, Dardchik and Dha Hanoo, the population of which (altogether about 700 people) is light skinned and speaks a language which sounds like Russian, although it also contains elements of Persian and Sanskrit, the languages of Aryan invaders. The remote locality and the custom of marrying only amongst themselves has preserved their distinctive identity. The government of a village is the responsibility of a seven-man council, chosen by all the men in the village. In July these villages celebrate a harvest festival which lasts for several days. Garkon is 80 km from Kargil.

Muta & Polyandry

The custom of *muta*, limited-duration marriages, is practised by some members of the Shi'ite Muslim sect. An ancient Islamic tradition, it originated when the men had to go to war for long periods of time, spending years away from home. In order to avoid them being tempted to use prostitutes, they were permitted to enter into temporary marriage contracts with widows or unmarried girls. Certain conditions prevailed, including an obligation to provide material support to the women involved. These days *muta* is not used except as an act of sympathy or charity towards a widow or woman of little means. A *muta* contract may be revoked within a few days but the 'husband's' liabilities towards his 'wife' continue for a minimum of 40 days. In the case of pregnancies, the husband is bound to support his child's upbringing. Female partners cannot enter into another *muta* contract before the 40 days have expired.

Polyandry is a Tibetan Buddhist custom prevalent in all areas of Tibetan cultural influence. Still practised in some of the most remote parts of Ladakh and Zanskar, it exists when a woman has more than one husband at the same time. The family property in a Tibetan Buddhist family is strictly indivisible and is inherited by the eldest son only. All younger sons must live as his dependents and as a result they cannot afford to marry and support their own families. Hence the solution of polyandry: the eldest son's wife marries her husband's younger brothers (except for any who may be monks). This fraternal form of polyandry is the most common here. Together with the great number of unmarried monks and nuns, the practice functions as a social form of birth control with Ladakh's population hardly altering since the mid-19th century.

– GM Kakpori of Kargil

Kargil To Leh

KARGIL-SHERGOL
The road starts to climb shortly after Kargil and leaves the Suru Valley at a small pass which leads into the Wakkha Valley. Here you cross the religious border and see the first smiling Ladakhis with their typical Tibetan headgear. As the river valley broadens, more and more irrigated barley and wheat fields appear. In early summer there are women ploughing and planting, in mid-summer women weeding and tending the irrigation canals, and in late summer women harvesting the crops.

SHERGOL
The small village of Shergol is 33 km from Kargil (237 km from Srinagar) and is the first true Ladakhi village you'll come across. The village, on the righthand side of the Wakkha River, is hard to see from the road as it lies in a ravine behind a mountain, on the opposite side of the river from the road.

The only visible evidence of the village (population 210) is a small gompa perched halfway up the eastern slope of this mountain, and appropriate to its size the gompa has only two monks who are tended by a single nun. Some of the rooms, such as the kitchen, are hewn from the rock and resemble holes more than rooms. The gompa has some beautiful wall paintings which are well worth seeing.

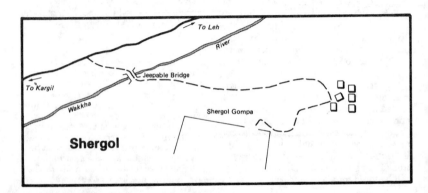

Monk at Mulbekh

At the foot of the mountain is a less important gompa.

MULBEKH

Seven km on brings you to this Wakkha Valley village (244 km from Srinagar). The palace of Raja Chalon of Mulbekh is on the lefthand side of the road and above the village on the slopes is a double monastery. It's a difficult ascent, particularly if you are not acclimatised to the altitude of Ladakh. Two paths lead to the gompas and the righthand path is the easier.

Here, as with all gompas in Ladakh, you should enquire in the village as to whether or not the monks are present. Often the gompas may be deserted and closed for days at a time as the monks are out in the fields or in other villages tending to their normal work. Only in the mornings and evenings can you be sure of encountering lamas who are not engaged in prayer. We were able to put two lamas into action by showing them pictures of

the Dalai Lama. These pictures of a holy person are, naturally, also holy and are handled accordingly – carefully touched, pressed on the forehead and reverently returned. With amazing speed the lamas then ascended the mountain and opened the gompas (the Serdung and Gandentse gompas) for us.

Choose the direct, steep path up to the gompas as it gives a better view of the Wakkha Valley.

A festive highpoint is the harvest thanksgiving festival (*Shuba*) which is celebrated at the same time in practically all larger Wakkha Valley villages. Mulbekh Shuba is a great attraction when the oracle of Mulbekh makes an appearance. In contrast to the oracle of Shey, this one is incarnated in a young farmer.

Chamba Statue A km beyond Mulbekh, beside the road on the righthand side, is a seven-metre figure of the *Maitriya* or future Buddha, cut into the rock. The

Chamba statue at Mulbekh

figure is thought to date from the Kushan period, about the time of the birth of Christ. Inscriptions on the side of the rock are in the Kharoshti script. A small temple which partly obscures the figure was built in 1975.

GEL

If you would like to lengthen your stay at Mulbekh and experience some of the local way of life, visit the village of Gel. Picturesque on a steep slope above the Wakkha River, it resides (like many Ladakhi villages) in a bygone era. Although it is only a few km from the surfaced road, Indian soldiers rarely come here.

When we visited Gel not only did the children cry when they saw us, but adults held the animals fast in their quarters, barricaded the doors and observed us suspiciously from the roofs of their houses. The ice was rapidly broken, however, when we wanted to buy an expensive *giri* (hand spindle with distaff).

With the construction of a new jeep road to the Namika La, the modern world is now encroaching on Gel.

MULBEKH-LAMAYURU
(via Namika La & Fatu La)
From Mulbekh the road climbs through a sandhill landscape to the 3718 metre Namika La. The descent from the Namika La, with its twisting and turning razorback road, is quite an adventure.

The first village beyond the pass is Kangral – a small collection of houses where it may be possible to obtain fuel. A dirt road branches to the left, leading to Stakchey, Samra, Chiktan (with old palace ruins), Sihakar, Sanjar and along the Indus to eventually meet the Kargil-Khalsi road.

The principal town in the valley of the Kanji Nallah is Bodh Kharbu, a large military camp which stretches out on the right and left sides of the road. The two travellers' rooms in the PWD Rest House, on the lefthand side of the road, can sometimes be used by tourists. There are many government projects underway during the beautiful summer months so your chances of finding a room free are not good.

The road follows the river for a short time and then winds its way up to the 4094 metre Fatu La Pass which is always cool and often windy. This is the highest pass

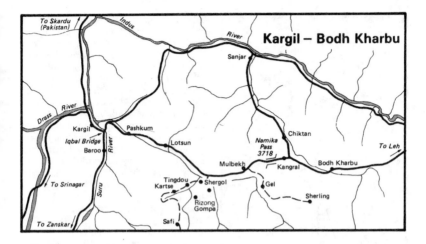

on the Srinagar-Leh road, and although you will think you are traversing the most logical point on the pass, you will see yak trains much higher up on the righthand slope, crossing in apparent isolation with their easy and slow gait. If your eyes are good you will be able to see their Ladakhi herders walking along perhaps several hundred metres away. From the top of the pass you get a good view down the river valley towards Kashmir, while ahead you are looking towards the Indus River Valley over several mountain ranges and towards Tibet.

The stretch of road from the pass to Khalsi is one of the most fascinating along the route. About 15 km from the top of the pass at Lamayuru is the old Tibetan monastery of Yungdrung below the road on a crumbling mountain. There is a village on the mountain side.

LAMAYURU

According to legend, in the Lamayuru Valley at the time of the Sakyamuni Buddha, there was a crystal-clear lake where the *nagas* lived. Arahat Madhyantaka prophesied that in later times a monastery would be built there and through a supernatural force he emptied the lake. In the 10th century, Naropa, one of the 80 wise men, visited the valley and spent many years meditating in a hut.

The first Lamayuru monastery was built under Rinchen Zangbo at the end of the 10th century, under orders from the King of Ladakh, who had 108 gompas built in west Tibet. Its five buildings were built on the broken mountain in the valley. Only the central building stands today, yet you can still see remains of the four corner buildings to the west. The gompa has an impressive 11-headed, 1000-eyed image of Chenrezig.

In the 16th century the monastery was declared a holy site in which even criminals could seek sanctuary. For that reason, even now it is known to Ladakhis as *Tharpa Ling*, Place of Freedom.

In its heyday, up to 400 monks lived in the monastery but now there are only 20 to 30 who belong to the yellow-hat sect. Many of the lamas go to other parts of Ladakh as teachers.

Although the monastery has some fields they are insufficient to feed all the monks. Therefore, like many Ladakhi monasteries, they are dependent upon the

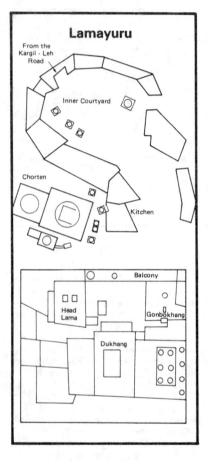

Lamayuru

From the Kargil - Leh Road

Inner Courtyard

Chorten

Kitchen

Balcony

Head Lama

Gonbokhang

Dukhang

Tibetan calendar (February-March) and in the fifth month (July). During the first festival, which attracts many people from the districts of Sham and Stod, the ritual of hurling a votive offering is observed.

The Drogpo Valley and Lamayuru Gompa (which is 310 km from Srinagar) come into sight 14 km beyond the Fatu La Pass. The road leads into the village of Lamayuru and on into the valley a short distance beyond. If you want to go to the monastery, continue a few km further along the main road towards Leh. A steep route to the right leads into the valley, for 4WD vehicles only, and ends at a low, small gateway into a small inner courtyard of the gompa. Before this gate there is nowhere for a vehicle to turn around. Admission costs Rs 5.

If you want to see more than the gompa, descend to the valley where, at the foot of the monastery mountain, the village (population 500) follows its medieval lifestyle.

You can also take a short walk into the fields to see the mani walls, take care to keep the wall on your right.

At Lamayuru it is interesting that the mani walls – piled up by devout pilgrims, stone by stone, often dragged there from many km away, and with the mantra 'om mani padme hum' carved on them – have more than a religious significance. These stone walls protect the fields in the valley bottom from the avalanches which can be loosened by snow and rain. Similar mani guard walls can be seen past Khalsi and at Hemis. Leh has the longest mani wall but it is no longer possible to walk the full pilgrim path of several km because it leads into military areas.

The basic but friendly *Dekung Labrong Hotel* is on the highway above the gompa. With an OK restaurant, doubles are Rs 25. The gompa itself has dorm beds at Rs 10 and there is another hotel nearby.

WANLA GOMPA

Slightly south-east of Lamayuru this gompa is reached by a climb of several km to the top of a pass. The old monastery was

donations of believers. In order to channel these donations small daughter gompas were erected in outlying villages, their superior lama being the head lama at Lamayuru. Similarly, the Sankar Gompa in Leh is an under-gompa of the Spitok Gompa.

Several times each year the monks from all the under-gompas come to Lamayuru for general prayers. These colourful occasions, with mask dancing for three days, fall in the second month of the

Lamayuru Gompa

Lamayuru Gompa

built about a thousand years ago during the time of Rinchen Zangbo. Its main image is of the 11-headed Mahakaruna or Avalokitesvera, which stands more than two-storeys high. The wall paintings are of the Buddhas, Bodhisattvas, mandalas and other religious icons. There is also a sacred image of Atisha.

Wanla is a point of pilgrimage for people from the districts of Sham, Stod and other parts of western Ladakh and Zanskar. It is on the trekking route from Lamayuru to Padum.

KHALSI

Beyond Lamayuru, the military road winds round many sharp curves (the so-called Langro Curves), on a slope in a side valley of the Indus, then crosses a barren rocky slope to the river banks. Beware of the speedbreakers before the last curve!

Near the ruins of old fortifications, with the remains of a hanging bridge, the road crosses a stable iron bridge on the right bank of the Indus. After some sharp bends it passes through a military camp close to where the Khalsi-Gurgurod road branches off to the left. This road will eventually lead directly to Kargil, avoiding the Fatu La and Namika La passes.

Khalsi today (Khalatse, 337 km from Srinagar) is a rest stop for buses and has many restaurants on the main road offering reasonably priced food – usually *dahl* and rice. It's a charming village with abundant dried apricots and there is a passport checkpoint just before you enter Khalsi.

RIZONG

The Rizong Gompa (363 km from Srinagar), and its associated nunnery Julichen (*Chulichen*), are two of the more interesting places in Ladakh and well worth a visit. Both are of the Gelugpa or yellow-hat sect of the Shas Rimpoche in Dharamsala.

Rizong is an active teaching gompa,

founded in 1829, and stands at 3450 metres. While up to 30 lamas live there, including young novices, more often than not many will be out in villages or other gompas. However, the resident manager Lobsang Tsundus is usually happy to show you around and offer butter tea, although he speaks only Ladakhi.

Try to get hold of a copy of *An English Buddhist in a Tibetan Monastery* (Routledge & Kegan Paul, London, 1962), which describes a stay in the Rizong Gompa. The book is out of print and hard to come by, but is an interesting account of life in a monastery.

The gompa is built on a sheer rock face and sprawls over seven levels. The approach, up a twisting, narrow gorge of dry, crumbling shale, is spectacular. The walk to the gompa takes about 1½ hours from the marked turn-off, and the last half hour is steep. Women are not allowed in the gompa after 4 pm, but this rule is flexible – if you arrive at 3.30 pm you will probably be allowed to stay for about an hour.

To find the nunnery, follow the road for about 45 minutes to its end at a low, stone wall which marks the boundary of the birch woods, apricot groves and barley fields maintained by the nuns at Julichen. The path rises steeply to the left, then flattens out and after about 10 minutes you come to the nunnery.

You can camp in the woods at the end of the road, and it's a good idea to set up camp and leave your packs here before tackling the more strenuous part of the walk. There is plenty of wood and fresh water for cooking. You can also leave your packs at Julichen before heading up to Rizong.

Inside the nunnery to the left is a large courtyard where nuns will be busy spinning wool, weaving and drying barley. Some of the nuns object to being photographed. Women may stay at the nunnery but not at the gompa; the opposite applies to men. If you do stay you will be expected to survive on tsampa and

Mandala in Rizong Gompa

butter tea unless you bring and prepare your own food.

To reach the Rizong Gompa from Julichen, the track winds through barley fields and apricot trees to a fork marked by a chorten, mani walls and blue prayer banners. Take the track to the left, away from the fields and up the dry gully. The track winds steeply upwards past new mani walls and inscriptions (and graffiti) on the slate and mudstone.

As you come across the first chorten the gompa comes into view, at once commanding and surrounded by the sheer, bare hillsides. Just past the gateway chorten is a sign telling visitors that smoking, drinking intoxicating liquor and eating meat are forbidden beyond this point. Behind and to the right of the tree on which this sign hangs are two very low-roofed huts, one surrounded by a wall. These huts house pools fed by the spring which is the sole source of water for Rizong. Legend has it that the founder of the monastery caused the spring to appear.

The path then winds steeply up the hillside to the gompa entrance, which is a small door on the left side of the third level, only visible from the short level path leading to it. The gompa is well maintained and has several large prayer halls, an impressive array of *thankas*, a large library of well cared for books stored behind glass, a small printing shop for preparing several of the texts from the hand-carved wooden blocks, and a fine array of statues.

The most striking aspect of the gompa, however, is the variety, colour and number of the wall paintings. Three stand out: the *Tsarchu* or 10 lives of the Buddha, which runs around three walls of the chamber with the statues of the *Chamba* and *Cho*; the colourful *Checkchik* to the left of the entrance to the *Chikhang*; and a very old Chinese painting of a scholar, in the chapel next to the quarters of the head lama. These latter two are kept covered.

You can also see the stone drum with which the Rizong monks beat out their prayers. The drum, made from a hollowed out tree stump which has been covered with a stone slab, is hit with a small stone hammer.

ALCHI

Although there are a great many temples, caves and *stupas* in Ladakh which were built by Rinchen Zangbo in the 11th century, Alchi Choskor is the largest and most famous, with a widely renowned collection of paintings and massive, lavishly carved and painted wooden statues, many of Buddha. Some of the artwork reminded one traveller of Eastern European folk art.

A road leads off the highway to a bridge over the Indus at a point 33 km beyond Khalsi and two km before Saspul. The old bridge, which could only be crossed in a small jeep, has been replaced by a new bridge which buses use. Travellers can now travel directly to Alchi along the new graded road.

In the village of Alchi (370 km from Srinagar) are many chortens, some of which possess gatelike openings and others have the bases of small towers at their four corners.

The Alchi gompa is unusual in that it is on lowland, not perched on a hill top like other Ladakhi gompas. The main structures include principally the *Rinchen Lhakhang*, then the *Lotsa Lhakhang* or Translator's Temple, the *Jamyang Lhakhang* or Manjushri Temple and the so-called *Sumtsag Lhakhang* or three-tiered temple.

There is a campground at Alchi with tents, simple rooms and a restaurant – run by Artou Travels of Leh. There is a row house with basic rooms from Rs 20 a single plus a far more interesting Tibetan-style dormitory with three beds. There's no electricity but candles are provided.

SASPUL

Cave dwellings and a small fort can be seen on the left side of the road at Saspul

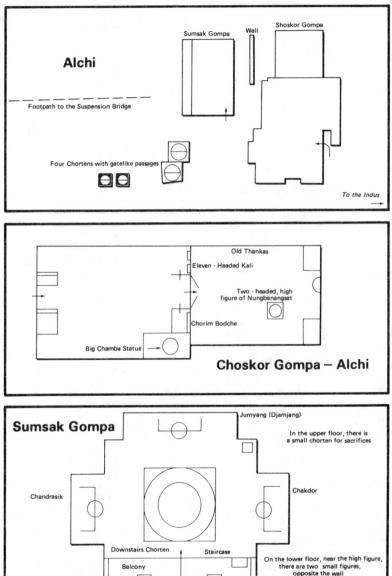

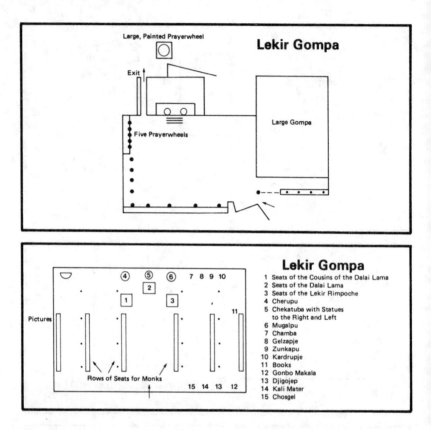

Lekir Gompa

Large, Painted Prayerwheel

Exit

Large Gompa

Five Prayerwheels

Lekir Gompa

1 Seats of the Cousins of the Dalai Lama
2 Seats of the Dalai Lama
3 Seats of the Lekir Rimpoche
4 Cherupu
5 Chekatuba with Statues
  to the Right and Left
6 Mugalpu
7 Chamba
8 Gelzapje
9 Zunkapu
10 Kardrupje
11 Books
12 Gonbo Makala
13 Djigojep
14 Kali Mater
15 Chosgel

Pictures

Rows of Seats for Monks

(372 km from Srinagar). There's a nice, fairly new hotel-restaurant run by a friendly family here. The area is beautiful, on a bluff above the Indus, and makes a good spot for a day or two stopover. From here you can reach Rizong, Alchi and Lekir by bus, jeep or on foot.

LEKIR

The turn-off to the Lekir Gompa, one of the most interesting monasteries in Ladakh, is 9.5 km from Saspul (382 km from Srinagar). The original monastery buildings were constructed about 900 years ago but there have been additions since, including a new Gonkhang which was built in 1983.

The steep road to the gompa has many hairpin bends but is now a good, all-weather road although the bridge over the Lekir River is not very stable. Both the approach to Lekir and the view from its roof are quite outstanding.

About 150 yellow-cap lamas belong to the gompa and the head lama is Tensing Chergal. The monks ring out their prayers by hitting a wooden beam which they use as a bell. There are three grades of lamas: Chunjung, Gyetsul and the highest grade, Gyelong.

The gompa school has 30 pupils who learn three other languages beside Ladakhi: Tibetan for religious purposes, Hindi and English. The pupils, who are prepared as recruits for the monastery, live part of the time with their parents and part of the time in the monastery.

The Indian Government has two elementary schools in Lekir village.

BASGO

Above the road at this small town (392 km from Srinagar) is the heavily devastated Basgo Fort.

Basgo Gompa is worth a visit on account of its Buddha figures, but unfortunately its wall paintings have been badly water damaged. The gompa has a two-storey golden *Chamba* statue in a

Monk school in Lekir

School for monks in Lekir Gompa

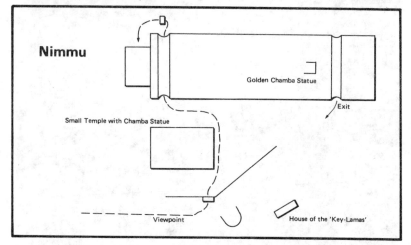

European sitting pose, and the second largest Buddha statue in Ladakh, also in a European sitting posture. Smaller Chamba statues stand in front of the figure of the white-clothed *Chamonada*. One of the three monks who live in a small house below the gompa will have the key.

NIMMU
In the green fields on the righthand side of the road at Nimmu (398 km from Srinagar) are four gate chortens. Just 2½ km beyond Nimmu the road leads to where the Zanskar River flows into the Indus through a large cleft rock known as the Nimmu Gateway (Nimmu *Gyasgo*). From here it is only 35 km to Leh.

Ladakh

Ladakh has been dubbed, somewhat romantically, the Last Shangri La, the Moonland, and even Little Tibet; yet all these descriptions hold some truth.

Ladakh is the most remote region of India. It is a barren, virtually rainless, high altitude area which lies north of the Himalaya on what is known, geographically, as the Tibetan Plateau. The Himalaya serve as a barrier to the clouds carrying rain from the south so virtually none of it gets across to fall on Ladakh. As a consequence the region has only a few cm of rain per year (as little as the Sahara), creating the 'moonland' effect – a barren, grey-brown, yellowy-white landscape utterly devoid of vegetation. Only where rivers carry water, from far-off glaciers or melting snow, to habitation do you find plant life.

Ladakh really does seem to be a miniature version of Tibet. Apart from the fact that Ladakh is on the Tibetan Plateau and the two regions have experienced a similar isolation from the rest of the world, the people of Ladakh and Tibet are also related and share a cultural and religious heritage that goes back centuries. Ladakh also has many refugees who fled Tibet with the invasion from China. In fact, Ladakh today is probably far more Tibetan than Tibet itself, which has been considerably changed by the Chinese.

Finally, Ladakh could well be the last Shangri La. Due to its strategic location – the area is disputed by the Indians, Pakistanis and Chinese – it was virtually closed to outsiders from the end of WW II until 1974. The daunting height of the Himalaya added to this isolation. Even now the main route into Ladakh is open for less than six months of each year. Also, until 1979 there was no regular civilian flight into Ladakh, so from October to June the region was completely cut off.

Ladakh is now open to outsiders, or at least as open as its geography and political boundaries permit. No special permission is needed to enter Ladakh and within the region you can travel with relative freedom.

Because of its fairly recent exposure to the outside world, and the rapid growth in tourism, it is especially important to treat Ladakh, its people and their culture with respect and care. It's a gentle, crime-free, peaceful and religious society and visitors have a duty to keep it that way.

Ladakh is full of amazing sights – strange *gompas* (monasteries) perched on soaring hilltops, dwarfed by snow-capped mountains; ancient palaces clinging to sheer rock walls; and all around, the barren shattered landscapes are splashed with small but brilliant patches of green. But most of all it is notable for its colourful delightful people who are so extraordinarily friendly. It's an amazing place.

Facts about the Region

HISTORY
The early history of Ladakh was succinctly summed up by Moorcroft, the English explorer who lived in Ladakh from 1820 to 1822:

The earlier history of Ladakh is that of Tibet in general, as it originally formed one of the provinces of that kingdom, governed as to temporal matters by an independent prince, and in spiritual affairs by the Guru Lama, or chief pontiff of Lhasa.

Earlier still, rock carvings scattered around the countryside indicate that the region has been used for thousands of years by nomadic tribes, blended from the Mons of north India, the Dards of Baltistan and the Mongols of Central Asia.

Over the centuries Ladakh has also had

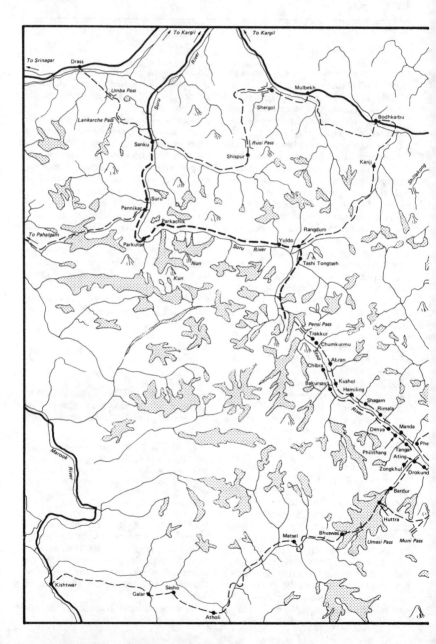

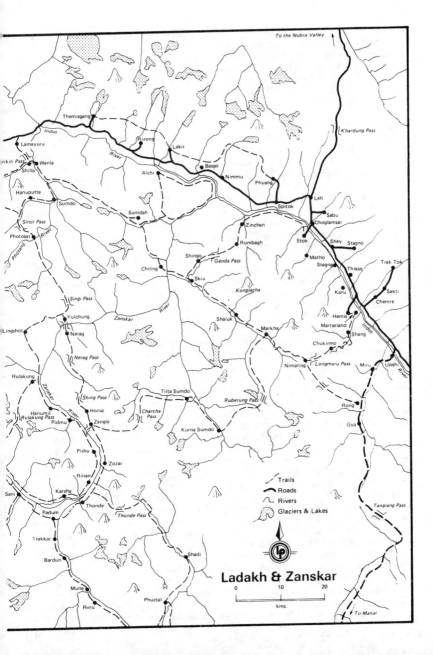

Ladakh & Zanskar

0   10   20

kms.

Trails
Roads
Rivers
Glaciers & Lakes

a variety of names. Hiuan Tsang, the 7th century Chinese traveller referred to it as *Ma-lo-pho*, the 'red land'. It has also been known as *Kachanpa*, the 'land of snow' and *Ripul*, the 'land of mountains'. Finally, *Ladwak*, the 'land under the passes' evolved into the current name Ladakh.

Early rulers of Ladakh were the Thi dynasty, followed by the Che-lik and Uto-ylde kings. In 842 AD, according to the written history of Ladakh, the Lha-chen dynasty was founded by Skyid-Lde-dyimagon. His grandson, Nima-gon, ruled from 975 to 990 and extended the kingdom far and wide by defeating invading tribes from Central Asia. The victorious king built a new capital at Shey, near Leh, as well as constructing many forts and reorganising the army.

In 1150 Naglug came to power and built many palaces. He was followed by Tishi-gon in 1230, who was a patron of Buddhism. In 1290 Norub-gon became king and was another promoter of religious activities. It was during his strong reign that the famous Buddhist scriptures, the 100-volume *Kandshur* of Ladakh, were compiled.

His son, Gyalpo Rinchen, extended his rule to Kashmir and at the same time accepted Islam. He ruled under the name Sultan Sadar-ud-Din from 1324 to 1327 and was Kashmir's first Muslim king.

In 1531 Ladakh was invaded by Mirza Haider Dughlat who marched through the Nubra Valley, defeating the local chief and his nobles. He took Leh without resistance and pressed on to Kashmir.

Ladakh's golden age started in 1533 when Soyang Namgyal united the region, established his capital at Leh and built a palace at Tsemo along with a grand temple decorated with numerous Buddhist images. A brave warrior, he had conquered Shigar, Kharko and other areas of Baltistan in his youth and had extended his domain to the outskirts of Lhasa in Tibet.

Namgyal did not depose the ruling monarchs of those areas but allowed them to remain and rule under his authority. He devoted his time to public works and was responsible for the roads and bridges in Baltistan and Ladakh before his death in 1555. The Namgyal dynasty of Ladakh exists today, as the Rani of Stok still occupies the Stok Palace and has been elected to the Indian Parliament.

Soyang Namgyal was succeeded by his brother Jamyang Namgyal, who immed-iately faced an invasion by the Muslim ruler of Skardu, Raja Ali Sher. Ali Sher's daughter, Khatoon, followed her father into battle and lost her heart to the Ladakhi king. Ali Sher too, was entranced by Namgyal's lovely daughter. There was a double wedding in Leh and the bleak capital overnight became a sparkling city for the splendid affair. The princess was crowned queen with the name Argiyal bestowed by a priest and Ali Sher went back to Skardu.

Their son Singe Namgyal assumed the throne in 1610 and defeated the King of Baltistan, who had attempted to invade Ladakh with the support of the Moghuls. Singe Namgyal was also interested in the construction of gompas and ordered the building of Hemis, Chemre, Themisgam and many chorten and mani walls.

Singe Namgyal divided the kingdom between his three sons. His descendant in Ladakh, Deldan Namgyal, ruled from 1645. He had the golden Buddha statue erected in Shey and his generals subjugated the Baltis and made them pay tribute.

Kashmiri troops, assisting the Baltis, were also beaten by the Ladakhis, but in the following years (around 1685) the Ladakhis were unable to repel invading Mongol forces. Ladakh once again came under Tibetan influence and in order to escape this domination the Ladakhis sought and received military support from their former enemies, the Kashmiris.

The Governor of Kashmir sent troops to help the King of Leh regain his throne, but in return for this help the King had to pay a regular tribute to Delhi and a mosque had to be erected in Leh. Some sources maintain that the King actually had to convert to Islam, but this is uncertain.

Delek Namgyal, who ruled from 1665, was succeeded by Ngeume Namgyal in 1695. He maintained the good relationship with Kashmir, introduced the art of paper making to Ladakh, wrote many books on Buddhism and constructed a large fort in the Nubra Valley. He died in 1750 and in the following years, until it was completely conquered by Kashmir, Ladakh was ruled by insignificant kings and became fragmented into small, weak states.

After the establishment of Sikh rule over Jammu and Kashmir, in an event known as the Dogra invasion of 1834, Ladakh was invaded by Zorawar Singh, the general of Maharaja Gulab Singh. Heading 5000 troops, Zorawar Singh was confronted at Mulbekh by King Dorje Namgyal. Singh retreated to Suru for four months and then negotiated a peace. He retreated further to Lamayuru and then invaded the Zanskar Valley. From there he marched over the Zanskar Range, reached Spitok on the Indus and fired on the Leh Palace, destroying one wing. The shell holes and other damage remain to this day.

King Dorje Namgyal surrendered and his place was taken by various town governors appointed by the Maharaja of Jammu, who was descended from Ladakhi nobility (*Chalons*). Thus only the military was comprised of Kashmiris, as the government was again in Ladakhi hands. The dethroned royal family were given Stok, the palace where they live today. The last king, Kunsang Namgyal, died in 1974 but is expected to be succeeded by his son when he reaches an appropriate age.

Since India's independence, and the resulting conflict between India and Pakistan over Kashmir, Ladakh, like Kashmir, has been divided between the two nations. Following the Chinese invasion of Tibet in 1959 there have been Indian and Chinese troops stationed on the eastern border and in 1962 there was another major conflict when the Chinese occupied part of Ladakh, including the Changchenmo Valley. Since then Ladakh has been divided into three parts.

Due to the strong military presence in Ladakh, India has considerably developed the region's infrastructure but the Chinese and Pakistanis have also been hard at work, building strategically important roads. There is now a road through the Chinese-held part of Ladakh, close to the ceasefire line. Another road from Kashgar in north-west China goes over the Karakoram Range into the Pakistani region to Hunza, Gilgit and the Indus Valley, west of Kargil.

GEOGRAPHY

Ladakh occupies the westernmost extension of the high and dry Tibetan Plateau in the extreme northern corner of India. Two of Asia's most eminent mountain ranges bound it on either side: the Himalaya in the south and the Karokoram in the north, both running roughly parallel in a generally south-east to north-west direction.

The main settlements in Ladakh are strung along the Indus River Valley, which runs in an approximately north-west to south-east direction.

In turn, the Zanskar Range parallels the Indus Valley to the south and separates Ladakh from the Zanskar Valley. To the north-east of Ladakh is the high Changtang Plateau, reached by several passes. This barren, sparsely populated area, with its high altitude salt lakes, is well into the restricted zone of Ladakh and much of it is under Chinese control.

Only about 40 km from Leh, but again deep into the restricted zone where foreigners may not enter, is the lovely Nubra Valley, noted for its apple, apricot, walnut and mulberry trees. The Shyok River flows through this small and comparatively warm valley and yak, sheep and goats graze in small forests. Also, the soda for Ladakhi tea comes from here. The valley is only accessible for a couple of

A young and an old Ladakhi in Leh

months each year since it is July before the snow melts from the passes. Entry to the Nubra Valley is either over the dangerous (due to avalanches) Khardung La Pass at over 5300 metres, or by the even higher Digar La Pass (5500 metres).

Ladakh is made up of the two administrative districts of Leh and Kargil. Mountain ranges partition the region into the following six areas.

Central Ladakh, around Phyang to Chemre, is relatively warm in summer, while the second area of Rong on the eastern side of central Ladakh, where the Indus Valley narrows up to its headwaters above 4000 metres, has a very cold climate.

The third area, Rupsho, is in an open plain south-east of the Indus and around the Leh-Manali road. It lies between 4000 metres and 5000 metres and is very cold and dry. The people are mainly sheep and goat herders.

Tangse, the fourth area, is a small valley surrounded by mountains over 4500 metres high, and is near the monasteries of Tikse and Karu, over the Changla. The fifth area is the Nubra Valley while the Kargil-Zanskar region around the Nun and Kun Range and the Suru River is the sixth.

There are three main routes into Leh. The Manali-Leh road and the Suru-Leh are not good for vehicles while the Srinagar-Leh road is closed from November to June each year. Special permission is needed to travel along the Manali-Leh road which is sparsely populated. The Indus or Sindh is the main river through Ladakh but others include, in the Kargil area, the Drass, Suru, Wakkha, Shigar, Shingo and Phoo.

PEOPLE

The Ladakhis are mostly Tibetan-Mongoloid in appearance – a healthy-looking people, deep brown in colouring due to the strong summer sun. Many Ladakhis are nomads and herd goats, noted for their fine pashmina wool, to high altitudes in summer.

Their economy is mainly a subsistence

one – woollen clothing, jewellery and religious objects are the main items they make. The Ladakhis have domesticated a range of animals including, of course, yaks and dzos. Horses, yaks, ponies and donkeys are used for transportation, the dzo for ploughing and horses for riding. Sheep and goats are kept for meat and wool while the short, stout and ferocious dogs keep invaders and wild bears at bay. Wild animals in the region include wolf, markhool, fox, hare, snow leopard, mountain mouse, marmot and bear.

Ladakhi houses were traditionally built on slabs made of stone and earth bricks with timber poles and twigs, roofed by grass topped with mud. Now, however, Ladakhis have taken to building in fields, so where the houses used to be three to four storeys high, they are now only one or two. Electricity is provided in the main towns by diesel generators. (A large hydro-electric scheme at Stagna was destroyed by floods in 1978 and the rebuilding of the channels and weirs is a very long and slow process.)

In the Ladakhi family boys have a higher status than girls. A woman's work is regarded as being in the house where she holds supreme power. The tradition of polyandry still continues in some valleys in Ladakh.

Ceremonies

When a child is born the family usually holds a festival for their relatives, neighbours and friends after the first 15 days, at age one month and after a year. All are invited to come to the house, to eat and drink all day, and are given *tsampa* cakes, butter and sugar, and tea.

When a marriage occurs festivities again continue all day with music and dancing. The first day is spent in feasting at the bride's house, the second at the groom's place. Boys are usually married or promised for marriage at about 16, girls at about 12. To make a proposal a relative of the boy goes to the house of the girl and gives a ring together with presents of butter, tea and *chang* (beer). If the gifts are accepted then the marriage follows some months later.

The boy offers a necklace and clothes to the girl. The parents of the girl give the couple clothes, animals and land if they are rich. These gifts are known as a *raqtqaq* or dowry.

When the father of the family dies his place is taken by the eldest brother. The other brothers must obey the eldest brother. All inheritance of the family goes to the eldest brother and then to the next brother when he dies.

If the family consists of all girls, then the father will bring the husband of the eldest daughter into the house and all land stays in the daughter's name and passes to her first son. Both sets of parents must accept the proposal of the boy for the girl. Usually the marriage is negotiated by both sets of parents, who will choose a suitable partner for their child on the basis of manner, health and ability to earn income and look after a house.

Ladakhi Dress

Men traditionally wear a thick woollen robe called a *goucha*, fastened at the neck and under the armpit and tied at the waist with a colourful sash known as a *skerag*. The skerag is about two metres long and 20 cm wide, is wound round and round and tucked in. In this sash men carry the small essentials of Ladakhi life such as flints, cap, tea cup, etc.

The women wear a similar robe called a *kuntop* but on their backs they add a colourful shawl, a *bok*, in which a baby or parcels can easily be carried. It used to be worn for warmth and as protection on the back against heavy loads of sticks and rocks. Traditionally it had a brightly coloured design on the outside, with yak or goat skin on the inside to keep the wearer warm. This has now been changed by fashion to a simple ornament of brightly coloured material, although in winter many women still wear the goat skin for warmth.

The women wear their hair in two long pigtails, a style also followed by some men. They top the ensemble with a top hat or *perak* which somehow remains firmly balanced, perched on top of their heads. The traditional perak has three, five, seven or nine lines of turquoise, according to the rank of the wearer. Only the very richest and royal of families could wear nine lines. When the woman dies the perak passes to the eldest child in her family. Shoes, known as *papu*, are made of woven yak hair or wool, often gaily decorated, with a sole of yak leather.

Although many men are abandoning their traditional dress for western clothing, the women still predominantly wear their colourful local dress.

BUDDHISM

Although the Islamic influence extends out of the Kashmir Valley as far as Kargil in Ladakh, the predominant religion is overwhelmingly the Tibetan, Lamaist form of Buddhism. As the Kashmiris look towards Mecca, so do the Ladakhis look towards Lhasa. This Lamaist influence extends to the use of Tibetan script for the holy books of *Kandshur* and to the clear Tibetan architectural influence, particularly evident in the design of the Leh Palace which bears so many similarities to the larger Potala in Lhasa.

Lamaism is a form of Buddhism heavily influenced by the pre-Buddhist Bon religion of Tibet. This is especially noticeable on the stones and banners which carry pictures and carvings of Bon demons and gods. At the pinnacle of the Lamaist pantheon is the divine trinity of Avalokitesvara, Manjushri and Vajrapani, but there are an extraordinary number of other gods and demons. Their pictures totally cover the walls of many gompas and to further complicate matters there are unique incarnations which are only recognised in certain gompas!

Lamaism is the monastic side of the religion and the discipline requires long hours of meditation and years of study by the monks. The monasticism of the Lamaists contrasts with the more visible Buddhist rituals which most Ladakhis observe, such as pilgrimages to gompas, chortens, mani walls, and holy tombs, or turning prayer wheels and chanting mantras. Their religious observances are a part of everyday life.

Lamaism probably came to Ladakh around the 10th century. It has been the religion of Tibet since 632 AD under the reign of King Songtsen-Gampo, but had additions made to it under the influence of the magician Padmasambhava.

Ladakhi monasteries belong to two main sects – the red-caps and the yellow-caps. The yellow-cap (or Gelugpa) sect are a reformed sect which follows the Dalai Lama as a reincarnation of the 14th century Bodhisattva Avalokitesvara. These sects are further divided with the Dukpa, Dekong, Saskin and Nyingma schools wearing red or maroon robes and caps, and the Gyaldon and Ludok schools wearing yellow caps.

An important element in Ladakhi Buddhist society is that *lamas* are not solely confined to the priesthood, their main profession, but also work as teachers, physicians, medics and astrologers.

Women are admitted to the order and are known as *tschomohs* and have their head shaved. Both lamas and tschomohs work in the fields of the gompa. The head lama of any monastery is known as *Khaushak*, and next to him is the *Loban*.

Tibetan Buddhism places great importance on the doctrine of reincarnation. When a person dies their spirit may be born again in another body. Both in Ladakh and Tibet it becomes impossible to thoughtlessly kill a fly or squash an insect. In winter the people break the ice in the pools to save the fish before they freeze to death. They believe that the more life one saves the happier is the lot of the soul. Incarnations are created involuntarily through the forces of *karma* or the law of cause and effect. Certain lamas are incarnations of Buddha and after years of study are entitled to be known as *Rimpoche*, or one who comes again and again to show the path to buddhahood.

Monks are not allowed to have private possessions except their butter lamps and bowls and perhaps an icon or amulet box.

Boys enter the monastery as students as young as three or four and don the red robe which they will wear for the rest of their lives. After 30 or 40 years of study and passing the final tests, they are then qualified for senior positions as lamas. Each must pass tests which are controlled by the Dalai Lama's own teachers.

The Dalai Lama always wears a yellow silk cap at receptions and ceremonies and all the objects in regular use by him are of the same colour. The use of yellow is a privilege he alone possesses. His robes, though, are always the red robe of a monk, once prescribed by Buddha, and differ in no way from that of monastic officials. The name Dalai Lama is not used in Tibet at all. This is a Mongolian expression meaning 'broad ocean'. Normally the Dalai Lama is referred to as *Gyalpo Rimpoche*, which means 'precious king'. He represents the return to earth of Chenrezig, one of the thousand living buddhas who have renounced *nirvana* in order to help mankind. Chenrezig is the patron god of Tibet and his reincarnations are always the Kings of Bo – as the Tibetans call their land.

In Leh it is possible to find some families whose members are Muslims, Christians and Buddhists since the Ladakhis are notably tolerant of other beliefs.

Statues & Shrines

To make some sense of the many statues and shrines in the gompas of Ladakh, you will need some knowledge of the various deities and historical personages that are depicted. It is impossible to give anywhere near a full description here, as the various Buddhist sects have different representations of the same god, and within each sect there are regional variations. What follows is a very broad outline and should not be taken to be correct in any one situation.

Dhyani Buddha There are five different representations of the Dhyani Buddha, each in a different pose:
Vairocana This pose shows the Buddha preaching or turning the wheel of the doctrine of Dharma. Both hands are held in a circular pattern in front of the chest and the Buddha is seated on the throne of a lion.
Aksobhaya Also known as the Miskyotpa posture, in this pose the Buddha is touching the earth with the fingers of the right hand and the palm facing inward as a gesture of calling the earth goddess to witness the Buddha's fitness for enlightenment. The Buddha is seated on the throne of an elephant.
Ratnasambhava (Rinjung) In this pose the Buddha's right hand is held low and he is seated on the throne of a peacock.
Amoghasiddhi (Tonyot Dugpa) The Buddha is in the gesture of fearlessness, which is interpreted as a sign of bestowing confidence or blessing. The right hand is held upwards and the palm outwards, and the Buddha is seated on the throne of a garuda.
Amitabha (Otpakmet) The Buddha is seated in the Vajrasana pose holding the alms bowl of ambrosia. The earthly manifestation of Amitabha is the Panchen Lama, the spiritual guide of the Dalai Lama.

Other Buddhas include:

Amitayus (Tsepagmet) Amitayus is the Buddha of long life and is widely worshipped in Ladakh and Tibet. He holds an urn of elixir and appears similar to the Amitabha.

Manjushri (Jampal Yangs) Manjushri is a

Elderly pilgrim at a Gompa

personification of the Buddha of wisdom. He carries a sword in his right hand, symbolising his power over the cords of ignorance. His book on a lotus signifies the power of learning.

Avalokitesvara Also known as Chenrezig or Chanrazik, Avalokitesvara is the patron saint of Tibet and is said to be incarnated in each successive Dalai Lama. This incarnation of the Buddha is the god of compassion who taught humans the sacred mantra *om mani padme hum*.

Another manifestation of Avalokitesvara is known as Chughsig-Jal and has 11 heads, the top one being that of Amitabha. Chughsig-Jal is the saviour of all living beings and is said to have burst his head at least 10 times when contemplating the suffering of men and animals. Among his 1000 hands there are eight principal hands – the central pair offers a blessing, the second right hand holds a rosary, the third holds a Shokra and the fourth is Veradamutra. The second left hand holds a bow and arrow and the fourth a drinking vessel.

Vajrapani (Chakra Dorje) Vajrapani holds a *Vajra* in his right hand and his left makes the *Korana Mudra*. He wears a tiger skin and has a snake coiled around his arms and feet. He is the god of energy and power and in his wrathful manifestation he represents the chief of the Tantric deities.

Maitriya (Chamba Gonbo) This is a representation of the Buddha to come. He is usually depicted standing or sitting on the throne, never in a meditative pose. In his right hand he holds the wheel of the *dharma*, on a plant, and in his left hand he holds a pot with a cactus plant.

As well as the various Buddhas and near Buddhas of Tibetan Buddhism there are the historical figures of Tibet and Ladakh who have influenced the way Buddhism has developed, often dividing it into various sects:

Nagarjuna (Lhundub) Nagarjuna was born the son of a Brahmin in south India and became a great Mahayana Buddhist scholar of the Nalanda University.

Padmasambhava Padmasambhava is the great master of the *Tantra*, the Nyingma school of Tibetan Buddhism. He is depicted in paintings and statues with his right hand holding a Vajra and the left hand holding a skull cap with ambrosia.

Rinchen Zangpo Born in western Tibet, Rinchen Zangpo is celebrated as one of the great religious figures of Tibet. He showed such extraordinary skill at learning Buddhist texts that he was sent to Kashmir for higher studies. After several years of study he travelled to the eastern regions of India where he studied under famous Buddhists, saints and scholars.

On his return to Tibet he was recognised as the spiritual teacher of the land and he started work on the translation of Buddhist texts from Sanskrit into Tibetan. His work covered so many areas of Buddhist philosophy and thought that he is credited with being the father of the Buddhist religion in Tibet.

He is depicted as seated on a lotus in the meditation pose and covered by a long yellow robe. He is said to have been responsible for the construction of 108 monasteries and shrines, including those at Alchi, Sumdo and Mangyu.

Milarepa Milarepa was born about 800 years ago in Lo in western Tibet. A disciple of Marpa, the first Mahamudra Guru of Tibet, he was a great scholar and is renowned as a poet.

Tsongkhapa Tsongkhapa founded the Gelugpa or yellow-hat sect of Buddhism.

TIBETAN CALENDAR

The Tibetan year is lunar; that is it has 13 months and normally 360 days. In order to keep it in line with the moon's phases, one day is occasionally omitted. As it is the irregularly occurring 'unlucky' days which are dropped, the Tibetan year and months do not always correspond exactly with a normal lunar year or the Chinese months and years.

Another complication is that, to keep the calendar in line with the solar cycle of the seasons, seven months are inserted every 19 years!

This makes comparisons between our calendar and theirs rather difficult. Nevertheless, gompa festivals fall at around the same dates each year, with the important Hemis festival usually in late June.

The year begins in February with the rise of the new moon. The months, or *Da-Wa* (which means 'moon'), are named First, Second, etc with *Da-Wa* prefixed. So, the first month is *Da-Wa-Tang-Po*.

The week is divided into seven days (*Za*) named after the sun, moon and five planets. The days and their associated celestial bodies are:

Sunday	*Nima* (Sun)
Monday	*Da-Wa* (Moon)
Tuesday	*Mig-Mar* (Mars)
Wednesday	*L'ag-Pa* (Mercury)
Thursday	*P'ur-Bu* (Jupiter)
Friday	*Pa-San* (Venus)
Saturday	*Pen-Ba* (Saturn)

The days of the week are associated with the elements – Sunday and Tuesday with fire, Monday and Wednesday with water,

Tibetan calendar in Tikse Gompa

Thursday with air and Friday and Saturday with earth.

Each hour and day of the week possesses a lucky or unlucky character, and the days of the month according to their order introduce other sets of unlucky combinations. Thus each hour of each day has some sort of astrological significance for the Ladakhis.

Every large monastery has a *Tsi-Pa* or astrologer lama, recruited from the cleverest of monks. Some monasteries also have an oracle lama. The astrologer lamas always have a constant stream of visitors asking for prescriptions as to what deities and demons require appeasing and the remedies necessary to neutralise these evils.

Like the Chinese calendar, the Tibetan years are named after animals in a cycle which repeats every twelve years. On the Tibetan calendar 1989 is the year of the earth-serpent or, on the Chinese calendar, the year of the snake – we'll then have the years of the horse, sheep, monkey, sparrow, dog, pig, rat, ox, tiger (or cat), rabbit and dragon before coming back to snake again. There is also a 60-year cycle of Jupiter which combines the 12 animals with the five elements: wood, fire, earth, iron and water. Each element is given a pair of animals, the first being considered male and the second female.

LANGUAGE

Ladakhi differs substantially from Tibetan although they belong to the same family of languages and Ladakhi is written in the Tibetan script. Dialects in nearby villages are very distinct and preserve their individuality to this day – a typical result of a society where few people travelled and where there was little exchange of information. In more widely separated towns, such as Leh and Kargil, the speech is so different that the inhabitants of one can hardly speak the dialect of the other.

There is one Ladakhi word you should learn even before you arrive since you will use it many, many times each day. That is *jullay* – the all-purpose greeting that covers hello, goodbye, how are you and greetings. The Ladakhis are friendly, outgoing, spontaneous people and they call out jullay to everyone they meet – local or foreigner. In a region where passing travellers have traditionally been the most important source of news from the outside world everyone is eager to be friendly to visitors, friend or stranger.

The Ladakhis use a 35-letter alphabet known as *ka-ga* (ka and ga are the first two letters of the alphabet).

Pronunciation Guide

The vowels *a*, *i* and *u* can have two sounds. *A* can be as in f*a*ther or in *a*m. *I* can be as in s*i*n or the *ee* in s*ee*n. *U* can be as the *oo* in p*oo*r or as the *u* in p*u*re. Generally *e* is pronounced as in th*e*m and *o* as in m*o*re.

Usual Compound Letters

ai as y	in m*y*
au as ou	in *ou*r
kh as koh	in *koh*lrabi
ng as ng	in si*ng*
ch as ch	in *ch*urch
ny as ny	in la*ny*ard
th as t	in *t*ub
ph as p	in *p*uppy
ts as ts	in ca*ts*eye
ds as ds	in win*ds*urfer
zh as z	in *z*ephyr
dj as dg	in e*dg*e

Useful Phrases

hello, welcome, etc
   jullay
please
   katin chey
thank you
   thukjechey
good
   gella
What is your name?
   khyoranggi ming la chi tzerchen?
How far is it to . . . ?
   thi na cham shik thak ring yot . . . ?

What time does the bus go?
bus chuchot cham pey ka chat?
Does this bus go to . . . ?
tje bus po cha nog ga . . . ?
Is this the road to . . . ?
tje lani bo tjenaggah . . . ?
How much does this cost?
tje bey rin cham in nak?
Can I buy some . . . ?
nya-chi tong rig no na diggah . . . ?

Give me food.
nya kharji sal
Give me chang.
nya chang sal
Give me meat.
nya sha sal
Give me hot water.
nya chu-stante sal
Please take tea.
solja don

Food

bread	*tagi*
potato	*alu*
tomato	*tamatar*
peas	*kanu*
white radish	*nungma*
red radish	*labuk*
corn, wheat	*zong*
barley	*nass*
barley flour	*tsampa*
cauliflower	*pulgubbi*
carrot	*shanma*
kohlrabi	*kuschutman*

Questions & Commands

Where can I get water?
nya chu kane thobin?
Can I stay in your house?
nya nerang ghi nang la thuk na diggah?
Where can I find a room to sleep?
na nit lok sey nang ka ne thobin?
What is your name?
nyan rang-ni ming-na-chaizer?
Where do you live?
nyanrang karwar zuksat?
Where is the post office?
dakkhana-kaga yotkyak?
Where is the medical shop?
manai hati karwayot?
Where is the hotel?
hotel karwayot?
Where is the tea shop?
cha-hati karwayot?
Where is the gompa?
gompa karwayot?
Where is the dak bungalow?
dakbangla karwayot?
Give me tea.
nya chha sal

People

boy	*nono*
brother	*acho*
father	*abba-laiy*
girl	*chocho*
sister	*achay-laiy*
mother	*ama-laiy*

Extras

wood	*shing*
matches	*machi*
candles	*moom-bati*
kerosene	*sammar*
stove	*stobv*
blanket	*kambal*
paper	*shugo*
monastery	*gompa*
monk	*lama*
nun	*tschomoh*
flag	*tartscho*
flute	*geihling*
horn	*thung*
smoking sticks	*spoz*
prayer flags	*tarchan*

Numbers

1	*chig*
2	*nyis*
3	*sum*
4	*dji*
5	*nga*
6	*tok*
7	*dun*
8	*gyet*
9	*gu*
10	*chu*
11	*chu-chig*
12	*chu-nyis*
13	*chu-sum*

14	*chu-dji*
15	*chu-nga*
16	*chu-tok*
17	*chu-dun*
18	*chu-gyet*
19	*chu-gu*
20	*nyis-chu*
30	*sum-chu*
40	*dji-chu*
50	*nga-chu*
60	*tok-chu*
70	*dun-chu*
80	*gyet-chu*
90	*gu-chu*
100	*gya*
1000	*stong*
100,000	*bum*

first	*dang-pa*
second	*nyis-pa*
third	*sum-pa*
fourth	*dji-pa*
tenth	*chu-pa*

Om Mani Padme Hum

On thousands of prayer flags and mani stones in Ladakh you will see the phrase 'om mani padme hum' written, carved or painted. You'll hear the phrase murmured by the monks and believers in all monasteries. The generally accepted translation runs: 'Oh, thou jewel in the lotus.' It is usually addressed to Buddha or to Avalokitesvara, his Tibetan incarnation.

It is interesting to read the interpretation of this mantra by the clergyman Phuntsog, who trained as a Buddhist lama before his conversion to Christianity:

Om – the syllable which represents the basis of all being in Indian thought, in Buddhist thought represents the trinity of speech, body and soul; *Mani* – the jewels which the god of the Tibetans holds in his right hand. These are arranged as a garland of roses and symbolise the way to holiness; *Padme* – the lotus flower which the god holds in his left hand. It is the symbol of purity; *Hum* – bless me.

The whole phrase could thus be translated as 'Thou God with the jewel-rose-garland in one hand and the lotus flower in the other, bless my life, soul and spirit'!

Facts for the Visitor

REGULATIONS

Despite the off-putting eagerness of the officials, it's wise to register your name and passport number at the tourist office in Leh (if you arrive by air) or at the office in Drass (if coming overland).

The Indian authorities do not like tourists selling cameras, watches and camping equipment in Ladakh. There are many traders only too ready to make you an offer, but take care in any negotiations.

Finally, remember that much of Ladakh is a highly sensitive border area where India meets China and Pakistan. You are not allowed to go more than one mile (1.4 km) north of the Srinagar-Kargil-Leh road. At Leh the road turns south through Upshi and eventually reaches Manali in Himachal Pradesh. You are not allowed east of a line one mile west of this Leh-Manali road. People who ignore these regulations, so the story goes, may find themselves in an unpleasant jail for a week or three before the authorities get around to telling them how naughty they've been.

MONEY

Although there are banks with facilities for changing foreign currency in Ladakh, India's perennial shortage of change can be particularly bad in Ladakh. Bring as many one and two rupee notes as possible.

Apart from Leh, Kargil and Karu, changing foreign currency will be virtually impossible. Banking hours are quite restricted. In Leh the summer hours are 10 am to 2 pm on weekdays and 10 am to noon on Saturday. In winter the hours are shorter. In Kargil the Muslim holidays are also observed.

Free-spending tourists have created the

image that all foreigners have money to burn. This is not helped by the very high entry charges (by Indian standards) to all Ladakhi gompas, but at least the Ladakhis are putting this new-found monastic income to good use by restoring and renovating the gompas.

Do not be too lavish with tips and donations. The inflation this brings about does not effect tourists only.

INFORMATION

Post & Telecommunications

There are post, telegraph and telephone offices in Leh and Kargil. There are also post offices at some of the smaller towns such as Lamayuru, Khalsi and Sakti, but it is unlikely that they will be able to handle foreign mail.

Trunk and overseas telephone calls are usually very difficult, if not impossible, to make in the region, even from Kargil or Leh. However, there is a radio link facility from Padum in Zanskar to Kargil.

Police

There are J&K police stations in Drass, Kargil and Leh and an office of the tourist police at the Leh Tourist Reception Centre.

HEALTH

Altitude

Remember the effects of altitude! People who fly straight to Leh from Delhi should take it very easy for a few days until they're acclimatised. Even coming from Srinagar (at 1768 metres) you're likely to feel breathless and lightheaded at Leh's 3554 metres.

Take it easy and don't over-exert yourself at first. Bad headaches and nausea are common effects of a lack of acclimatisation, and these are particularly prevalent at night. Severe altitude sickness, which can be fatal, is extremely unlikely to afflict you unless you immediately start rushing up mountains.

There's only one sure treatment for altitude sickness and that is to get down to a lower level. People with heart conditions should seek medical advice before visiting Ladakh as your heart has to work hard at this height. Also, the effects of alcohol are compounded by the altitude here.

Medical

There are district hospitals at Leh and Kargil and primary health centres at Drass, Sanku and Padum in Zanskar. There are dispensaries on the Srinagar-Kargil-Leh-Upshi road at Kharbu, Pashyum, Mulbekh, Khalsi, Chuchot, Tikse and Sakti. A dispensary is a small hospital with five beds and attended by trained medical staff. There are also dispensaries on the Kargil-Zanskar route at Tripson, Tampis and Pannikar.

BEGGING

Begging has become an epidemic amongst Ladakhi children, although they do it more out of imitation and fun than in seriousness. Everywhere you go there will be children calling after you 'one pen', 'one bonbon' or 'one rupee'. Unfortunately this practice has been created by thoughtless and patronising tourists doling out pens, candy and rupees to the children. Ignore them or it will only become worse. It is said that enterprising professional beggars from Calcutta and Bombay are also beginning to make a summer appearance in Ladakh.

PHOTOGRAPHY

It is prohibited to take photographs of any military or strategic equipment or installations. This includes military camps or vehicles, soldiers, bridges and even places or objects that in our eyes could be civilian installations, such as the radio broadcasting station in Leh. This prohibition is strictly enforced and infringing it can result in the confiscation of cameras and film.

In the gompas you can generally photograph whatever you please, apart from very holy places, such as the Gonkhang room of Matho Gompa, where only monks are permitted to set foot.

Nevertheless, you should exercise great restraint during prayers since flashes of light and the clicks of camera equipment are very disturbing.

FOOD

The staple food in Ladakh is *tsampa* which is made by lightly roasting barley, mixed with sand to prevent the barley from catching alight, in a large metal pan. The barley is then sieved to remove the sand and the roasted grain is ground in a watermill. The resulting meal is sprinkled with *gurgur* (salt water) or mixed with a small amount of liquid to form cakes. Salted butter tea or chang (a locally made beer) is often drunk with the tsampa and these dishes are called *cholak*.

If you eat in a local restaurant in Leh you will probably be offered these dishes, apart from tsampa:

Pava – peas and barley flour boiled in water for a long time until the peas are hard.
Cholak – a mixture of tea, butter, sugar and tsampa.
Khambish – bread made from wheat flour.
Thukpa – water and wheat flour made into noodles and dropped into boiling water and then served with a flavoured meat sauce.
Gugur chai – salt tea made from green tea, salt, soda from the Nubra Valley, butter and milk.
Curd – made from yak milk.
Moe moe – steamed tsampa dough, usually with meat in the middle like dumplings.
Gyatug – a dish of long, vermicelli-like strips of tsampa over which minced meat and a flavoured sauce is poured.
Skir – a hotpot of meat, potatoes, grain and sometimes vegetables.
Kambir – small round breads, sometimes sweet.
Holkur – Ladakhi biscuit made of sugar, nuts and grain meal, normally baked by the host to be served to the patrons.

The Tibetan influence is strong, so you will find many Chinese-Tibetan dishes like chow mein or *kothay* – meat or vegetables wrapped in a thin dough and fried or steamed.

You may be surprised to see potatoes served in Ladakh. These were brought in by Moravian Christian missionaries from Germany in the last century. There are still about 200 Christians in Ladakh today.

Food can get a little boring in Ladakh as the variety of locally grown produce is very limited. Barley, potatoes, peas, onions and turnips are virtually the only local vegetables on sale, although apples, mulberries, apricots, walnuts, mustard and a variety of herbs also be grown in some areas.

A lot of food and produce comes up from Kashmir, but only in summer when the passes are open, of course. Prices are understandably inflated. In the last few weeks before the summer season commences with the opening of the road, and when tourists are already flooding in by air, the supplies of food can be limited. It's worth bringing in a few menu brighteners like bars of chocolate or cans of apple juice. The usual Indian glucose biscuits are available everywhere, and in Leh it is possible to buy dehydrated soya bean meal or biscuits, which provide a very useful and energy-giving carbohydrate supplement to your diet, especially at this altitude.

Cultivation in Ladakh is by means of manuring and irrigation, and despite food production being limited, what does grow there can be quite outlandish. The long daylight hours and the extra strength of the ultra-violet rays at this altitude create wondrous garden produce, like five kg turnips or radishes and potatoes that weigh up to two kg!

Ladakh is as unsanitary as anywhere else in India so take care where you eat and beware of fresh fruit and vegetables. There is no piped water system in Leh so drink water at your own risk! Even boiling water isn't such a positive method of purifying it at this altitude since the boiling point is much lower. Remember to keep your fluid intake up as you can easily become dehydrated.

DRINKS
Tea & Butter Tea

The tea habit initially came to Ladakh, as to all Tibet, from Imperial China but due to the closing of the Tibetan border tea now comes from India. You may find Chinese/Tibetan tea smuggled over the border from Tibet on sale in the bazaar in Leh. It's more rare than expensive and the quality is not too high. The tea is often transported in pressed blocks which can frequently be seen as offerings in monasteries.

Traditional Ladakhi tea is made with

Making butter tea

Top: Women from Temisgang, Ladakh at the Hemis festival (BP)
Left: Brokpa woman (NT)
Right: Ladakhi woman (NT)

Top: Gujar man and woman (GW)
Left: Woodcutter at Phyang Gompa (BP)
Right: Bakharval shepherd with hennaed beard (GW)

butter and tastes more like a soup than our idea of tea. The tea is initially made very strong, brewed for a long time, then diluted to a drinkable strength. It is then put into a butter churn, a wooden vessel about 15 cm in diameter and 80 cm long and bound with brass at the top, bottom and in the middle. A spoonful of salted butter is added and churned into the liquid. This broth is then reheated and drunk continually until it is gone.

Every Ladakhi, no matter how poor, has his own tea vessel. In rich families the tea is served in three-part silver cups. The lower cup stands on a small pedestal and the cup itself is covered with a lid. The tea is generally drunk warm and during the colder season the lower cup serves as a handwarmer. If you are invited for tea anywhere in Ladakh you will find that your cup is refilled as soon as you take a sip. Tea drinking continues until all the tea made is finished.

Tea is usually drunk during prayer ceremonies at gompas and you may be offered some, in which case you will be expected to have your own cup, an item all Ladakhis carry everywhere they go. Cups are on sale at all the street stalls in Leh and at the general stores.

In monasteries and for an average family's breakfast, the tea is accompanied by tsampa, which is either sprinkled into the warm brew, or kneaded into lumps and dipped into the tea.

Chang

Beware of the effects of the native beer – chang. High altitude and too much alcohol do not mix well! Nevertheless you should try some of this local alcoholic beverage. There are chang 'pubs' in Leh and the price is around Rs 1 per bottle. You should also try chang in a village as it usually tastes much better. Chang is home-brewed from barley and millet, partially seasoned by the addition of pepper and sugar. It is not filtered before serving so dregs and grains are found swimming in the liquid. In short, chang is a most unusual pleasure for the palate.

In Ladakh, as in the other Himalayan states (except Tibet) with a population which belongs to the Tibetan group, there is no manufacture of spirit liquors.

THINGS TO BUY

You may dream of antique dance masks and tankas but you are not allowed to buy them! Antique dolls, swords, monastic antiquities such as buddha figures, dance masks and tankas are all banned from being purchased, dealt in or taken out of Ladakh. Antiques are defined as being 100 or more years old.

Since demand for authentic items has outstripped supply you cannot be certain that anything is of any age. Antiques in Ladakh are likely to be instant antiques. In any case authentic items should be left where they belong – in Ladakh.

There has been a terrible drain of the accumulated treasures of the gompas due to the greedy actions of some over-wealthy and thoughtless tourists. The Government has, belatedly, recognised the danger of Ladakh losing much of its cultural heritage and departing visitors have their baggage searched at Ladakh airport.

New tankas are now being produced. In fact there really aren't any old tankas for sale, no matter what some fast-talking salesman may tell you! The new tankas are generally painted in Darjeeling or Nepal.

There are many other items which you are free to purchase and export but first of all it is wise to identify whom you are dealing with. There are three groups of traders in Ladakh: Kashmiris come from Srinagar or Delhi just for the tourist season and bring with them inflated prices and hard bargaining techniques. Tibetans come from Dharamsala and operate many of the street stalls near the tourist centre in Leh on behalf of Kashmiri traders. Finally there are the Ladakhis themselves, of whom there are very few. Naturally you have to be most careful when dealing with the Kashmiris but don't believe that the Ladakhi or Tibetan merchants are above the art of overcharging. Always shop around and bargain hard.

There is a very small but growing local handicrafts industry, mostly based at the Tibetan refugee camp at Choglamsar, where the main craft is Tibetan carpets. Visit Choglamsar and buy them direct, or at the street stalls in Leh. They are cheap, compared to Kashmiri or Persian carpets, and also very durable although somewhat bulky to carry. It is possible, though difficult, to find some old Tibetan carpets in good condition in Leh.

You can also look for chang and tea vessels, silver cups and butter churns or the mussel shells which serve as ornaments. For a few rupees you can buy a prayer flag or for a very large number of rupees you could invest in a new perak (these cost up to $10,000) – the headgear with hundreds of turquoise stones and silver pieces, worn at festivals and on special occasions. Or you may be satisfied with a tea kettle from the bazaar or prefer to search for silver-worked articles from China.

In most gompas during the tourist season monks will have a variety of items for sale, ranging from bells and locks to small drums and musical instruments. There are many items which are easy to carry such as prayer wheels or *dorjes*.

Prices in Ladakh are generally quite high. Although there is a lot of Tibetan and Ladakhi clothing, Tibetan jewellery and other Tibetan curios on sale, you should familiarise yourself with prices in Kashmir, Nepal, Dharamsala or other Tibetan centres before spending in Ladakh.

WHAT TO BRING

Bring a sleeping bag. Even in summer it can get very chilly at night and if you spend the night at a monastery or village you'll definitely need warm bedding. If you use public transport from Leh there

Butter lamp vendor

are gompas which can only be visited if you stay overnight and return the next day, due to the bus timetable. If you're planning to do a lot of travelling around Ladakh a tent is also worth having, for similar reasons. If you're trekking it's a necessity.

Be prepared for dramatic changes in temperatures and watch out for the sun's surprising intensity at this altitude. On a warm day the temperature can drop with striking speed when a cloud obscures the sun. You will find yourself putting on and taking off a sweater a dozen times a day. The burning power of the sun in Ladakh is phenomenal. If you want to avoid sunburn and a peeling nose you'll find a sun screen cream is essential. A hat also helps.

Ladakh in Winter

Winter is not the time of year to go to Leh, but we very much wanted to include at least a short visit and, of course, the rest of India is at its best at that time. Providing (as at other times of year) conditions are right, Indian Airlines operate flights to Leh in the winter. Although one will probably not encounter other tourists on flights into Leh they are still likely to be fully booked so be as careful about booking – and reconfirming! – as for any other flights with Indian Airlines.

Whether the flights are more spectacular in the winter than at other times of the year I don't know, but certainly it's difficult to imagine finer flying weather than we experienced during our two flights in early January – beautiful blue skies and crystal-clear views of the white peaks of the Himalaya stretching as far as the eye could see in every direction. Although the route via Chandigarh is magnificent the Leh-Srinagar flight is even more awe-inspiring.

To the best of my knowledge, while we were there only one hotel was open in Leh – the Khangri. The family who run this small and simple hotel is very friendly and hospitable. Everyone did all they could to make us feel comfortable. Leh was particularly cold during our visit and even the Ladakhis were minding the cold. Our friends in Leh informed us that it had been –45°C one night. At any rate soft drinks left on the window sill inside the room at the hotel were frozen solid in the morning. In addition to the stove which was set up and lit in

the middle of our room late in the afternoon (a fascinating ritual), the hotel supplied us with hot water bottles and lots of blankets and heavy quilts.

If on a tight schedule, like we were, you tend to worry the whole time about whether or not the plane will arrive for the return flight. We heard many stories about winter visitors being stranded in Leh for 12 to 14 days. If you had an unlimited travel 'Discover India' ticket it might be interesting to fly in to Leh and straight out again, just for the superb views of the Himalaya and of Leh and its surrounding gompas from the air.

We experienced no problems finding taxis to take us to Tikse and Shey and enjoyed participating in an important religious festival at Spitok, otherwise attended by only the local inhabitants. If you decide to visit Leh in winter bring plenty of warm clothing and be prepared to still be bitterly cold much of the time. If you're lucky, as we were the day we arrived, the temperature will not be unreasonable during the day (it was – 10°C at noon) and there will be brilliant sunshine. All in all a winter visit is an exhilarating experience.   – John Berridge

Getting There & Away

AIR

In 1979 Indian Airlines began flying into Leh, which is one of the highest airports in the world to be used regularly by jet airliners. Since then the original route from Srinagar to Leh has been supplemented by direct flights from Chandigarh. During summer there are four flights a week into Leh – starting from Delhi one goes via Chandigarh, the other three via Srinagar with various stops between Delhi and Srinagar. One-way fares are:

Srinagar-Leh	Rs 334
Chandigarh-Leh	Rs 477
Delhi-Leh (via Chandigarh)	Rs 750
Delhi-Leh (via Srinagar)	Rs 900

The short flight from Srinagar (less than half an hour) is spectacular as it goes right across the Himalaya with superb views of

Nun and Kun almost directly below and K2 (Mt Godwin Austin), the second highest mountain in the world, away to the north in Pakistan.

Flying to Ladakh does have a few hassles. The weather in Leh is very changeable and the high winds that blow up virtually every afternoon mean that flights can only be made in the morning.

Also, the approach to Leh is difficult and requires clear visibility. When arriving, the jet flies up the Indus Valley with the mountains rising above on both sides, then turns left to the runway. Leaving Leh, the jet banks right as soon as it's airborne because the Spitok monastery, perched on its hill, is not far to the left of the runway end. Approaches and departures can only be made in one direction because the runway runs steeply uphill away from the Indus.

The result is that flights to Leh are frequently cancelled or aborted after crossing the mountains. To compound these difficulties, Indian Airlines' tight scheduling and limited aircraft numbers means that it is difficult to put on extra flights or replace cancelled or aborted flights. Particularly at the start of the tourist season flights can be absurdly heavily booked – a 737 can be flown in fully loaded but due to the altitude only a partial load can depart Leh. Fortunately, at the beginning of the season, the rush is into Leh, not out.

If you arrive in Srinagar planning to fly to Leh without a reservation, or worse have a reservation but the flight is cancelled, you may have to do some hard work to get on a flight. Your houseboat/hotel owner or a local travel agent with some clout may know how to do it. On the other hand, several travellers have written to report getting on the flight despite seemingly impossible positions on the waiting list. Indian Airlines' booking

Street scene, Kargil

system is not always super-efficient and the waiting list can sometimes be quite meaningless.

At the start of the tourist season a typical week of flying to Leh went like this: Monday flight – aborted. Tuesday – extra flight put on but aborted. Wednesday, Thursday, Friday – no extra flights but the unlucky Monday/Tuesday passengers had to keep reporting back to the IA office to find out what was happening. Saturday – regular flight goes OK but there was no room for any of the Monday/Tuesday passengers. Sunday – extra flight but again it's aborted! Monday – regular flight gets through OK but with only a dozen or so of the previous Monday/Tuesday passengers. Tuesday – no extra flight. Wednesday – extra flight gets through and finally gets passengers, many of whom have been waiting in Srinagar for 10 days and have flown to Leh (unsuccessfully) on three occasions, to their destination. Some passengers had crossed the Himalaya seven times before finally landing on the other side!

Still a few years back it was not unknown for unlucky Ladakhis to make a last-minute trip down to Srinagar in October only to get stuck there when the snow came unusually early. In that case you just had to sit and wait for six months before you could get home. Today they can fly back although winter flights are, of course, even less predictable. The Indian Air Force flies to Leh from Chandigarh every day with a large transport aircraft, and their flight always gets in, bad weather or not.

BUS

Buses depart from Srinagar for Leh every day during the season. Officially this is from June to October but it's not unusual for the road to be closed until mid-June although on occasion it may be open by mid-May.

Because of its strategic importance, the army always tries to have the road open by mid-June. The Zoji La Pass is the last pass to be opened because, although it is not the highest, it gets the heaviest snowfall. The pass is usually closed about October/November each year when the heavy snowfalls begin. The Namika La and Fatu La passes within Ladakh experience very light precipitation.

Fares to Kargil and Leh from Srinagar are:

Leh – super deluxe	Rs 153
Leh – A class	Rs 78
Leh – B class	Rs 58
Kargil – A class	Rs 39
Kargil – B class	Rs 29

While the super deluxe and A-class buses operate from Srinagar to Leh twice weekly, B-class buses run daily. Also, the B-class bus from Srinagar to Kargil operates on alternate days.

Travellers often discuss which is the best class of bus to/from Ladakh. I think A class is just as comfortable as super deluxe – A's clear glass windows giving unspoilt views of the scenery win me, and with my long legs, the cramped and crowded B class is definitely not my choice. For those on a shoestring budget, though, a sore bum and aching joints are a small price to pay.

The trip takes two days with an overnight halt at Kargil. The 434 km covers a winding and often steep road, and at high altitudes the buses crawl uphill at a snail's pace. There are often lengthy stops at road blocks because some stretches of the road are one-way and vehicles travel in convoy.

JEEP

Hiring a jeep to make the trip will cost about Rs 2000, but it will easily accommodate six passengers if you tie packs on the roof. If you take a jeep it's worth spreading the trip out by another day and making short forays off the main road to see some gompas.

If you ask around Srinagar it is sometimes possible to hitch or buy a ride on a private vehicle going to Leh.

Rides in trucks are also possible although trucks tend to go over the edge with much greater frequency than buses. After a tourist was killed in a truck accident the J&K Government banned trucks from taking tourists. However, the ban was soon forgotten.

Before the Road Opens In the last few weeks before the Srinagar-Leh road opens it is possible to get to Ladakh by walking over the Zoji La Pass. The pass marks the boundary to dry Ladakh and is the last to be cleared of snow.

The *chowkidhar* at Sonamarg is the person to ask about the condition of the road. From Sonamarg the pass is reached by 26 km of winding road and is 800 metres higher up.

To get to the pass you can either hire a jeep from Srinagar (say Rs 500) or stay overnight in Sonamarg and in the morning try to get the 7 am Beacon Patrol Truck up to the pass.

It's wise to try to latch on to a party of locals to ensure you follow the correct path across the pass. There will usually be someone crossing every day and it's often possible to hire ponies or porters.

Porters from Sonamarg are likely to cost Rs 70 a day and you can double that since they also charge for walking back. Ponies are likely to be Rs 100 a day, with extra for the pony man and perhaps for feed for the ponies.

There's usually transport across the pass since tourists start flying into Leh in increasing numbers shortly before the pass is open and food must follow. Supplies are driven up to the pass, carried across by yak and pony train, then loaded back on to trucks for the trip to Leh.

Towards the end of the melt the walk may be only a couple of km, taking a few hours, but early birds at the start of the melt may have to walk for more than a day, sheltering at an army hut on the way. In 1980, a month before the road opened, walking across the pass entailed a 20 km trudge through the snow. In these early conditions the patrol may insist that you're adequately equipped and prepared before letting you cross.

You must take sunglasses and a good skin barrier cream. The deep snow and intense sunlight can easily lead to temporary snow-blindness or very bad sunburn.

Late in the melt, or late on a hot day,

you can get very wet from the slushy snow. Once over the pass you need to get a ride down to Drass. How easy this is depends on how many people are up at the pass working on the snow clearance. You'll quite possibly have to wait all day and if you're wet it will be an uncomfortable wait.

At Gumri, which marks the Ladakh end of the pass, there is a Beacon lodge or camp. This is usually operating from May when bulldozers and snowploughs have begun their heavy work of clearing the road and reforming its surface.

The pass is actually cleared of snow for some time before the road is open to traffic, but there are always road repairs to be done and debris, brought down with the snow, to be cleared. Jeeps can often cross the road before it is officially cleared for buses.

Matayin is the first village, about 10 km from the top of the pass at an altitude of 3179 metres. There is a PWD Rest House here.

About 15 km further on at Drass there is a tourist hut. If you stay here, the next day you should be able to get a ride down to Kargil. From Kargil there are buses on to Leh but only on two days each week during winter.

Leh

The capital of Ladakh is about 10 km north-east of the Indus at the exit of a fertile side valley, and from the town to the Indus river, the landscape is almost completely barren.

Leh (3505 metres) has a population of 20,000 and a large military camp stands between the town and the airfield, which is also towards the Indus. There are many places to visit in and around this fascinating town yet it is equally interesting just to wander the back streets of old Leh.

Once Leh was a main stopping point on the Asian silk route and a commercial

available for hire and the staff help out with basic queries. The office is at the back of the Dak Bungalow.

Post & Telecommunications Leh's post office and poste restante are on one side of the main street with the telegraph office on the other.

Banks There are two banks: the State Bank of India is up the road from the vegetable market or down the road from the mosque, and the J&K Bank is at the start of the main street. They are open Monday to Friday from 10 am to 2 pm, (winter 10.30 am to 2.30 pm), Saturday from 10 am to noon, (winter 10.30 am to 12.30 pm), and closed Sunday.

Bookstores Artou Travel's bookstore has a good selection of the many guides and coffee table books on the region. Another store, opposite the vegetable market, sells paperbacks.

Ali Shah's Postcard Shop You can browse through and buy some superb photographs/postcards shot over the past 30 years or so by Mr Shah. It's well worth a look.

Libraries The Centre for Ecological Development has a good library, mainly concentrating on the subjects of ecology, Buddhism and the Ladakh region.

Airlines Leh's usually chaotic Indian Airlines office is opposite the popular Dreamland Restaurant, upstairs and next to the Snow Lion Restaurant. The office is run by a handling agent, not the airline itself, which can often result in the staff being unable to cope with the problems created by cancelled and overbooked flights.

capital in its own right. Today, it is important primarily for its military base and, more recently, for tourism.

Orientation
Leh is small enough to make finding your way around easy. There's one main street with the Leh Palace rising up at the end of it. The bus station and jeep stop is on the airport side of town. The airport, with its steeply sloping runway, is several km out of town near the Spitok Gompa.

Leh has grown in size quite considerably in recent years and continues to do so. The town now reaches what were outlying villages, such as Changspa, Tukcha and Skara.

Information
Tourist Office This has a helpful wall map of Leh and the surrounding area and a useful noticeboard where you can communicate with other travellers for trekking companions, taxi sharing, etc. Some climbing and trekking gear is

Leh Palace
The old palace of the kings of Ladakh (open 6 to 9 am and from 5 pm) overlooks the town from the south-west slope of the Tsemo hill. It has eight storeys and was

built by King Singe Namgyal in the 16th century, at much the same time as the famed Potala of Lhasa which it resembles.

The damage to the palace – one side is gaping open – stems from the Dogra invasions of the last century. Also, beware of the many holes in the floors while you're wandering around the palace. Like the Shey Palace the Leh Palace still belongs to the Ladakhi royal family, who now live at their palace in Stok.

Few of the palace wall paintings are worth looking at since they have been scratched and smeared over the years. The small Khar Gompa within the palace is also of little interest. In fact the main reason to make the short, steep climb up to the palace is for the superb views from the roof. Here the coloured prayer flags wave in the wind, the lines of which begin on the Tarchock mast. In good weather the Zanskar Range, snow covered until early summer, appears close enough to touch although it rises from the other side of the Indus.

If you can, get a monk to unlock the preserved but now unused central prayer room – a dusty, spooky place with huge faces looming out of the dark and two walls lined with religious texts written on rice paper, allegedly 600 years old.

Leh Town

The old town of Leh, with its houses for the aristocrats and servants of the royal household, is clustered at the bottom of the hill under the palace. The new city spreads away from the hill on land which once belonged to the royal family.

At one time Leh had a city wall with three gates, one of which still stands close to the market – to the right and uphill towards the palace. The gate is called Kingsgate because only the king and his family could use it. The chorten above the city is the remains of a royal leisure site.

Due to steady growth in recent years, Leh is becoming increasingly westernised.

Left: Looking towards Leh Palace

Leh Gompa

The Leh Gompa stands high above the palace and also overlooks the ruins of the older palace of the King of Tagpebums. The Red *Tsemo* Gompa was built in 1430 by King Gvags-Pa-Bum-Ide and has a fine three-storey buddha figure which is seated, flanked by Avalokitesvara on the right and Manjushri on the left. The walls have been brightly painted and the gompa is open from 7 to 9 am.

There are three gompas at the top of the hill. The topmost one is ruined but offers extremely fine views over Leh and the surrounding countryside. To the right of the palace you can see a buddha painted on the rocks, a remnant of an earlier monastery.

Other Leh Gompas

There are a few lesser gompas in the old town of Leh, such as the *Guru Lakhang* to the left of the palace, beneath the large chorten. The *Chamba Lakhang*, south of the palace, and the *Chenrezig Lakhang*, to the south-east, are similarly neglected since they contain little of interest compared to other, more splendid gompas around Leh.

In the centre of Leh the recent *Gompa Soma* or *Jokhang* was built by the Buddhist Association of Ladakh in 1957. It contains an image of the Buddha Sakyamuni that was brought from Tibet. The association meets at this monastery.

Mani Walls

Near the Leh radio station are two long mani walls. The one in the centre of the open plain is known as *Rongo Tajng* and was built as a memorial to Queen Skalzang Dolma by her son Dalden Namgyal at about 1635. It is about half a km long and contains many hundreds of thousands of mani inscriptions carved in stone in Tibetan. At its end is the Stupa of Enlightenment and the Stupa of Victory.

The second long mani wall, further down the hill, is said to have been built by Tsetan Namgyal in 1785 as a memorial to

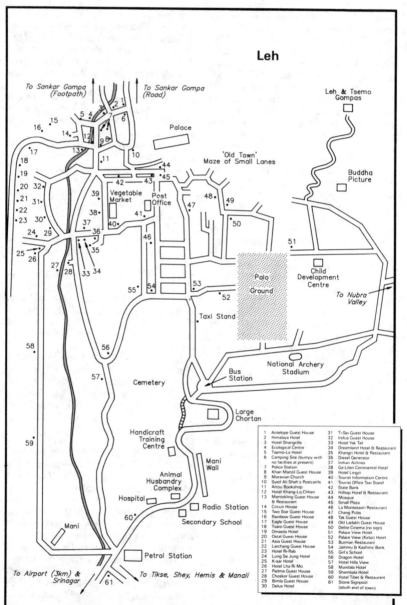

Leh

To Sankar Gompa (Footpath)
To Sankar Gompa (Road)
Leh & Tsemo Gompas
Palace
'Old Town' Maze of Small Lanes
Buddha Picture
Vegetable Market
Post Office
Polo Ground
Child Development Centre
To Nubra Valley
Taxi Stand
National Archery Stadium
Bus Station
Cemetery
Large Chortan
Handicraft Training Centre
Mani Wall
Animal Husbandry Complex
Hospital
Radio Station
Secondary School
Mani
Petrol Station
To Airport (3km) & Srinagar
To Tikse, Shey, Hemis & Manali

1 Antelope Guest House
2 Himalaya Hotel
3 Hotel Shangrilla
4 Ecological Centre
5 Tsemo-La Hotel
6 Camping Site (bumpy with no facilities at present)
7 Police Station
8 Khan Manzil Guest House
9 Moravian Church
10 Syed Ali Shah's Postcards
11 Artou Bookshop
12 Hotel Khang-Lq Chhen
13 Mentokling Guest House & Restaurant
14 Circuit House
15 Two Star Guest House
16 Rainbow Guest House
17 Eagle Guest House
18 Tsaro Guest House
19 Omasila Hotel
20 Ostal Guest House
21 Asia Guest House
22 Larchang Guest House
23 Hotel Ri-Rab
24 Lung Se Jung Hotel
25 K-sar Hotel
26 Hotel Lha Ri Mo
27 Padma Guest House
28 Choskor Guest House
29 Bimla Guest House
30 Delux Hotel
31 Ti-Sei Guest House
32 Indus Guest House
33 Hotel Yak Tail
34 Dreamland Hotel & Restaurant
35 Khangri Hotel & Restaurant
36 Diesel Generator
37 Indian Airlines
38 Ga-Ldan Continental Hotel
39 Hotel Lingzi
40 Tourist Information Centre
41 Tourist Office Taxi Stand
42 State Bank
43 Hilltop Hotel & Restaurant
44 Mosque
45 Small Plaza
46 La Montessori Restaurant
47 Chang Pubs
48 Tak Guest House
49 Okt Ladakh Guest House
50 Delite Cinema (no sign)
51 Palace View Hotel
52 Palace View (Kidar) Hotel
53 Burman Restaurant
54 Jammu & Kashmir Bank
55 Girl's School
56 Dragon Hotel
57 Hotel Hills View
58 Mandala Hotel
59 Shambala Hotel
60 Hotel Tibet & Restaurant
61 Stone Signpost (south end of town)

his father King Tsewang Namgyal, and is about 350 metres long.

Leh Fort

Built by Zorawar Singh, the fort contains three temples but cannot be visited because it is within the military camp area.

Schools

Besides the monastery schools, the Indian Government has 380 educational establishments including more than 200 primary schools in Ladakh. In 1971 literacy in Ladakh was still only 14%. There are more than 200 Ladakhi students at universities in Srinagar, Jammu and elsewhere in India, and they receive a monthly stipend from the Indian Government.

It's interesting to visit the primary schools. The Tibetan alphabet is learned by the pupils singing it together and the children still use the typical wooden panel on which they write with a wooden stylus and thinned clay liquid. A line for writing on is drawn in an unusual way. They stretch a string, rubbed in chalk, across the board and pluck it like a musical string. The result is a very sharp line.

Centre for Ecological Development

Next door to the Hotel Tsemo-Lah is the HQ of the Ladakh Ecological Development Group (LEDeG) which initiates and promotes 'a development strategy for Ladakh that is carefully tailored to its environment, available resources and culture'. This includes solar energy, environmental and health education, strengthening the traditional system of organic farming and publishing books in the local language. Visitors are welcome to hear what LEDeG is all about, to use the library and to eat in the restaurant (see Places to Eat).

A Few Ecological Words

One of the concerns of the Ladakh Ecological Development Group is the negative effect that tourism can have on the region. The behaviour of some tourists has aggravated many Ladakhis so, although they may not apply directly to you, the following guidelines have been included to increase awareness for all travellers.

To avoid causing offence, try to be sensitive and aware of the feelings of the Ladakhis and bear in mind that the Ladakhis have private lives too. Always ask before entering Ladakhi houses and gardens, and above all, before using your camera. Try to put yourself in the Ladakhi's position.

Remember that the Ladakhis have thought patterns and time concepts that often differ from your own. Of course, that does not make them inferior. Generally, try to be tolerant of differences between Ladakh and your home country.

Whatever your status may be in your own country, in a developing country like Ladakh you are comparatively rich. This leads Ladakhis to form a highly idealised image of life in the west (eg, it looks as though westerners are on a perpetual holiday). At the same time this causes them to see themselves as backward and poor. Try to present a more balanced picture of life in the west and make a point of telling the Ladakhis what you like about their culture.

Try not to encourage begging children by giving money, pens or other items to them. This is how begging started in Ladakh. By giving you are maintaining a vicious cycle. There are other better ways to provide real help.

Try to inform yourself about current rates and prices so as not to contribute to inflation.

Try to take an interest not only in the past and present, but also in the future of Ladakh.

Be aware that the sale and purchase of old tankas, statues and other religious objects is prohibited, and that there are restrictions on the sale of any object more than one hundred years old. Do not rob Ladakh of its cultural heritage.

Try to respect local customs. What is courteous at home may be insulting in Ladakh. Above all, try to dress decently. Shorts, bare shoulders and backs are not appreciated. Public displays of affection of all sorts (holding hands and kissing) are frowned on. The following are cultural norms that you should be aware of.

It is polite to give and receive with both

hands. Point with your whole hand, not with just one finger. All religious objects, including books, statues and photos are kept high off the floor. Be aware that you may cause offence by leaving items such as postcards and guide books on the floor. Don't point your feet at, or step over people, religious objects, tables or food. It is impolite to be too quick in accepting offers of food or drinks, and cooking and eating utensils are not shared.

Monasteries Don't be put off by the entrance fees to monasteries. This money is used for the upkeep and restoration of the monasteries, as well as for the construction of new shrines. Most tourists visit monasteries as they would visit a museum. For them it is not a place of worship. Therefore, there would seem nothing wrong with asking a small fee.

Dress properly. Sometimes in Europe there are guards at churches and cathedrals who check people's dress. In Ladakh there are not (yet), but very similar rules apply. So, please, no shorts or bare shoulders.

Remember that you are visiting a holy place, so always remove your shoes before entering shrines. Refrain from smoking, drinking alcohol and spitting. Never touch the statues, books, tankas or any other religious objects.

Never disturb the monks during prayer. Especially at the monastery festivals, be aware that these are not folk dances, but important rituals.

Never use a camera flash unit in the monasteries since this is likely to damage the colour and paint of the frescoes.

When walking through a monastery, or when passing chortens or mani walls, always circle clockwise, keeping them to your right. Also, never remove stones from mani walls.

Trekking Be aware of the cultural landscape's highly sensitive ecology and economy. Since the villagers generally grow just enough food to provide for their own needs, do not expect to be able to buy food from them. Instead, try to be self-sufficient. This also applies to fuel. Wood is an extremely scarce resource, so don't use it. Always bury excrement. Preferably, bring all waste back with you, otherwise burn and bury it on site.

Make realistic plans. Do not endanger yourself and/or others by pushing yourself too far. You should never rely on others to get you out of trouble.

Repair anything you damage, such as walls or irrigation channels.

Finally, try to be law abiding. Do not trek into restricted areas or climb peaks which are higher than the limit set by the authorities.

Places to Stay

There are an amazing number of hotels and guest houses in Leh and it is also relatively easy to arrange accommodation in private homes. Indeed, many of the smaller guest houses are simply private homes which rent the odd room out.

Prices are extremely variable, dropping right down in the off-season when there are very few visitors in Leh and shooting up in the high season. Many places close down completely over winter. Prices quoted here are for the high season. Cheaper places may halve (or more) their rates during the off-season although the more expensive hotels are less likely to be so variable.

The traditional Ladakhi-style homes are understandably very popular, characterised by wooden-framed windows and kitchens centred around a wood-burning stove with pots and utensils attractively arranged. These factors, along with that wonderful Ladakhi hospitality and quite often a large room with superb views, play no small part in making a stay in Leh so pleasurable.

Top-end rooms appear to be somewhat over-priced. Although the establishments may look fine from the outside and in the public areas, the rooms are usually sparsely furnished and decorated, while the hot water supply and service are generally erratic.

Places to Stay – bottom end

There are many budget-priced places in Leh. The following choices all come with good recommendations so you should look around and see which most appeals to you.

The old town is dirtier and smellier than elsewhere in Leh. Even if your room is clean, the street outside usually isn't. Despite this, many travellers happily choose to stay at the *Old Ladakh Guest*

House with dorm beds for Rs 10, singles Rs 15 and doubles from Rs 30 to Rs 80. *The Tak Guest House* opposite has singles/doubles for Rs 15/30. The larger *Palace View Kiddar* has singles from Rs 10 to Rs 15 and doubles from Rs 20 to Rs 40.

More central and more pleasant, the *Khan Manzil Guest House* is the friendly home of the local director of the Save the Children Fund and has singles/doubles at Rs 30/35.

Moving down past the tourist office and the Dreamland Restaurant, the road crosses a stream to the outlying village of Tukcha. To the right, signs point to a group of very popular guest houses all with great views, lovely gardens and friendly families.

The Christian-owned *Bimla* is one of my favourites in the upper-cheap bracket with singles from Rs 40 to Rs 50 and doubles from Rs 80 to Rs 100. The *Indus* is similarly priced, while the *Delux* is a particular favourite of French travellers with singles at Rs 30 and doubles from Rs 40 to Rs 50. Last in the row is the *Ti-sei* with singles/doubles at Rs 15/35. The newly opened *Jorchung Guest House* is also good.

Follow the stream in the opposite direction and you head towards the *Padma Guest House* which is in the middle of the fields to your right, with more great views and another pretty garden. Isolated but only a short walk from downtown Leh, it has singles at Rs 15 and doubles from Rs 25 to Rs 50.

Up past the *Tsemo-La Hotel*, the *Two Star Guest House* is another Leh favourite with singles from Rs 20 to Rs 25 and doubles from Rs 30 to Rs 60. Just after the Circuit House, the *Eagle* and *Rainbow* have similar prices.

Continue along the road heading away from town to find some nice guest houses to choose from: the *Tsaro* is very basic but is as authentic a Ladakhi home as you could find with a beautifully painted prayer room and singles from Rs 10 to Rs 15, with doubles from Rs 20 to Rs 35. Further on are

the *Otsal*, *Asia* and *Larchang* with singles/doubles at Rs 20/40. These are about a 20-minute walk from town.

Places to Stay – middle

The *Lung-Se-Jung*, down past the Dreamland Restaurant, is a popular middle-priced hotel, if only because of its reliable evening supply of piping hot water. Singles cost Rs 120 and doubles are from Rs 150 to Rs 170.

Similarly priced is the *Khangri*, for a long time Leh's only hotel that stayed open all year. It's down the street from the vegetable market, behind the Dreamland Restaurant.

Below the main town, down the hill from the start of the main street, the *Dragon Hotel* has nicer surroundings and better rooms for the same price. The adjacent hotel, *Hills View*, has singles/doubles for Rs 100/120. There is also the *Dak Bungalow* at the tourist office but you usually need to make reservations and it is generally filled with government officials.

Places to Stay – top end

With singles/doubles at around Rs 425/495, including all meals, Leh's top category hotels include the palatial-looking *Lha-ri-Mo*, the *K-Sar* next door, the *Mandala* further down the road, the *Ga-Lden Continental* across from the vegetable market (not the best location), the *Kang-La-Chen* near to the Moravian Church, and the *Shambala* out of town towards the edge of the valley. The less expensive *Omasila* is about a 20-minute walk from town, just past the Circuit House in the outlying village of Changspa.

Places to Stay – around Leh

There are places to stay in many of the villages and gompas around Leh. The tourist department has *Tourist Bungalows* in Sakti, Saspul and Khalsi as well as in Leh. Each has a minimum of six double rooms and costs Rs 25 for an ordinary double, Rs 45 for a deluxe room and an extra Rs 4 for bedding.

Many villages are now taking advantage of the tourists passing through and have established small cooperative hotels. The following list tells you what's available and where.

Alchi A guest house with eight beds.

Chipkyangchen Between Kargil and Leh near Lamayuru, the six-bed guest house is near the road, not in the town.

Hemis A 10-bed hotel/restaurant with food service. Camping sites are near the monastery.

Khalsi A 10-bed hotel/restaurant and a 10-bed *PWD Rest House*.

Lamayuru Three hotel-come-restaurants with 22 beds; and an excellent camping site.

Nemo A forest rest house with six beds but food is not available.

Nurla A guest house/restaurant with six beds and a good camping site.

Phyang A hotel/restaurant.

Sakti A *Tourist Bungalow* with eight beds.

Saspul Two hotel/restaurants with 12 beds, a *Tourist Bungalow* with eight beds and a good camping site.

Shey Enquire at the tea stall near the foot of the Shey Palace.

Stok A hotel/restaurant with 30 beds in Yurt tents; and an expensive A-class hotel.

Tikse The popular *Shalzang Chamba* hotel/restaurant with 16 beds and doubles at Rs 15; and a forest rest house with four beds but no food.

Places to Eat

For many of Leh's visitors, eating out simply means a regular visit to the *Dreamland Restaurant*, opposite the Indian Airlines office and near the vegetable market. Not associated with the dingy Dreamland Hotel next door, it is central, clean, has friendly staff and nice decor, and the consistently good food is very reasonably priced.

Tibetan Kathay, various chow meins and other noodle dishes, along with western favourites such as french fries, omelettes and superb pancakes make a pleasant change from curry and rice, especially if you've been in India a long time.

While there are now some good alternatives to the *Dreamland*, many people continue to eat only here. This can mean queues and being unable to sit around after your meal which, in turn, puts some people off the place.

The competition over the years has proven inconsistent, with new places opening to great reviews but then having their standards deteriorate within a few months. However, the sparse (no glass in the windows) and tiny *Tibetan Restaurant* has managed to maintain its reputation for great, cheap and nourishing food. Just up the road from the vegetable market or down the road from the State Bank of India, you walk past the kitchen on your way in and out. With only a few tables, you cannot always get in but it's well worth a try.

Next to the mosque and upstairs, the *Patala Hilltop* was doing well but some recent reports suggest that the standards could be declining. Ask around when you are in Leh for the latest reviews. On the main street, again upstairs and just along from the post office, *La Montessori* serves up big portions of very tasty Chinese, Tibetan and some western favourites – to me on a par with the *Dreamland*. Let's see if it lasts.

The *Tibetan Friends Corner Restaurant*, up from the tourist office by the taxi stand, is another long-established favourite. Across from the Moravian Church and the Khang-La-Chen Hotel, the more recent *Mentokling Restaurant* serves up interesting versions of felafel, hummus, cakes, pies and generally unusual dishes for this part of the world. Just up the street, the *Ecological Development Centre* offers nice coffee, herb teas, cookies and cakes. In the busy season they also have more substantial meals with health food prepared using solar energy.

For more basic and cheaper ethnic food, try the *Nepali Restaurant*, off the main street, or the *Burman Restaurant* which serves Indian favourites such as curd and masala dosa. After these places, standards drop rapidly.

The *Ibex Hotel*, between the Dak Bungalow and the Tibetan Friends Corner Restaurant, boasts the only licensed bar in Leh. Here you can enjoy India's bottled beers served chilled in silver tankards along with spirits such as rum, whisky and vodka, also made in India. For those interested in tasting chang, try to find one of the unofficial (illegal) chang pubs in the street behind (parallel with) the main street.

Alternatively, you can buy fresh vegetables from the pavement market at the top of the main street. There's a more official vegetable market too.

Also, early in the morning you can get delicious hot, freshly baked bread from the cluster of little bakery stalls in the back streets by the mosque. They're on the road that leads up to Ali Shah's Postcard Shop or the Hotel Kardungla. The bread is cooked middle-eastern style in hole-in-the-ground ovens and is great for breakfast with honey – bring the latter with you from Srinagar. Most hotels and guest houses will provide a basic Tibetan breakfast of bread, jam and tea, and sometimes eggs if you ask. Some will also provide evening meals.

Wedding Ceremonies

A visitor to Ladakh rarely has a chance to see a Buddhist wedding performance in accordance with the old customs and ceremonies. Today too much foreign influence has crept in and European clothing is slowly replacing the traditional dress. But in 1975 we were fortunate enough to be guests at a wedding performed in accordance with the old rites.

The celebration began at 10 pm in the house of the bride. The all-male party celebrated with chang which, according to custom, must be taken in three consecutive draughts. As a special sign the host improved the chang by adding butter. A celebration meal was served at 2 am, but again only men partook.

The bride remained in her mother's kitchen, symbolically indicating where her place was! Clothed in a wedding gown with a silver-embroidered cape, decorated with old family jewellery, the bride is covered with lucky white ribbons (*kataks*) and given gifts of money by her relatives and friends. While the men sing and the mother laments, the bride goes to the family of the bridegroom, where she is met, in front of the house, by lamas.

Now the celebration properly begins. In a long ceremony, in which the bride must firstly refuse the food which is offered to her, the bride is led from her father or a friend of the family, to her husband, with whom she then symbolically partakes of a meal. She is then shown the house, with particular emphasis on the kitchen. By sunrise the ceremony is concluded, but not the celebration which is a social occasion for the families with musicians, food and much, much chang.

Funeral Ceremonies

Near to the palaces at Stok, Shey and Leh you may notice a large number of chortens, the old 'pleasure gardens' of the kings of Ladakh. If you go into the side valley, to the north-east of Leh, from the eastern slopes of which the road to the Nubra Valley begins, you may find (particularly with the help of a local) a large stone where a curious funeral practice was once conducted. The bodies of the dead were hacked to pieces and ground up with stones then left to be devoured by vultures. This practice was also followed in Tibet and is still followed in the Mustang region of Nepal.

Today the site of dismemberment is used for cremations. After a ceremony in the house of the dead person the corpse is tied to a sedan chair and covered. Accompanied by lamas the procession makes its way into the side valley near Leh. A few hundred metres north-west of the chortens the procession halts and the chair is placed in a walled oven. This is really only a vertical tube with a firehole underneath. The fire is started with many prayers and during the long ceremony oil is frequently thrown into the oven until the cremation is complete. The ashes are scattered into a holy river or, in the case of a person of high standing, placed in a chorten.

Getting There & Away

See the Getting There & Away section for information on getting to Ladakh by air or land.

Getting bus tickets for the return trip to Srinagar can be rather confusing as the operators are reluctant to sell tickets to Srinagar until they know the buses have turned up from Srinagar.

To travel by truck, the truck park is next to the bus stand. Prices are generally Rs 60 or Rs 80 but the tourist office does not approve of visitors using trucks and may make it difficult for you. The trucks driven by Sikhs are probably the best.

For jeep or taxi hire from Leh to Kargil or Srinagar, the official rates are:

	Kargil	Srinagar
taxi	Rs 840	Rs 1890
jeep	Rs 966	Rs 2173
jonga*	Rs 1008	Rs 2268

*six seater

If the road from Kargil to Padum is open a jeep from Leh to Zanskar will cost Rs 3500 one-way or Rs 5100 return.

Getting Around

Airport Transport The bus service to the airport costs Rs 3 whereas a jeep or taxi will cost about Rs 25.

Bus One of the easiest ways to get around the Indus Valley is to use the local bus service. The buses are extremely crowded, run down and look as though they will never get to where you want to go, but they always do. This is one of the better ways of getting close to the local people. You will share the bus with Ladakhis, Zanskaris, Dards, monks, goats, chickens, bales of hay and piles of wood. The local custom is that everyone, including women and children, stand up to give their seats to a monk.

However unreliable they might look, the buses are cheap and usually run on time. The main problem is that there are not enough of them and there may be only one service a day to the more remote parts where you want to go.

Another local custom is to get to the bus stop in Leh almost an hour before the bus goes if you want a seat. This has its advantages and disadvantages. If you are on a very crowded bus, jammed into a seat by an aisle full of people, you may not be able to get out when you want to, or even to get fresh air. On the other hand, the roofs of the buses are very low and it is impossible for an average-sized westerner to stand. In this case your journey can be quite uncomfortable.

If you are unsure if you are on the right bus, just ask. Ladakhis are very friendly and helpful people and they will soon tell you what you want to know, as best they can.

In the tourist season the J&K Tourist Office may offer bus tours of the area.

The main services from Leh are:

A young school girl in Pharka

Top: Flying over the Himalaya to Leh, with Nun and Kun below (TW)
Left: Window shopping in Leh (TW)
Right: Main street of Leh (TW)

Top: Leh Palace with Leh Gompa above it (NT)
Left: Tikse Gompa (TW)
Right: Looking towards Leh Gompa (NT)

route	distance	buses daily	fare
Choglamsar	8 km	4	Rs 1.20
Chushot	25 km	3	Rs 3.30
Hemis	45 km	1	Rs 6.00
Khalsi	98 km	1	Rs 12.95
Matho	27 km	2	Rs 3.75
Phyang	22 km	3	Rs 3.10
Sabu	9 km	2	Rs 1.35
Sakti	51 km	1	Rs 6.95
Saspul	62 km	1	Rs 7.90
Shey	16 km	2	Rs 2.10
Spitok	8 km	2	Rs 1.20
Stok	17 km	2	Rs 2.85
Tikse	20 km	3	Rs 3.00

Trips further afield: daily buses to Kargil cost Rs 59 (A class) or Rs 44 (B class). For Lamayuru (124 km) – Rs 12.10, take a Kargil bus; for Lekir (54 km) – Rs 7.10, take a Khalsi or Kargil bus; and for Karu (40 km) – Rs 4.85, Alchi (65 km) – Rs 8, or Nimmu (36 km) – Rs 4.50, take any of the Khalsi or Kargil buses operating along the Kargil Rd. The tourist office in Leh will have the full story on bus fares and timetables. Services are much less frequent in winter.

Jeeps & Taxis An easy and convenient way of getting around Ladakh is to band together with other travellers and hire a taxi or jeep. These are not cheap and the drivers have formed a union and now refuse to bargain, especially in Leh, but if you cannot stand the crush and endless delays of the buses, these are the only way to go. There are set fares for some longer journeys and for certain local trips, but other destinations must be by negotiation.

In general, taxis charge Rs 4 per km or, on return trips, Rs 4 per km on the way there and Rs 3 per km on the way back. In most cases a loading of 30% is added for longer routes and sightseeing tours.

The charge for the long tours to monasteries and places of interest usually includes a wait of one hour. Beyond the one hour wait the charges are at the rate of Rs 10 an hour. For local routes in and around Leh there will be no waiting charge for the first half hour, then Rs 6 for the

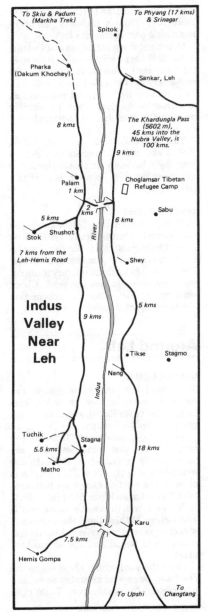

To Skiu & Padum (Markha Trek)
To Phyang (17 kms) & Srinagar
Spitok
Pharka (Dakum Khochey)
Sankar, Leh
The Khardungla Pass (5602 m), 45 kms into the Nubra Valley, is 100 kms.
8 kms
9 kms
Palam 1 km
Choglamsar Tibetan Refugee Camp
Sabu
2 kms
5 kms
6 kms
Stok Shushot
River
7 kms from the Leh-Hemis Road
Shey
Indus Valley Near Leh
9 kms
5 kms
Indus
Tikse
Stagmo
Nang
Tuchik
Stagna
18 kms
5.5 kms
Matho
Karu
7.5 kms
Hemis Gompa
To Upshi
To Changtang

next half hour and Rs 12 an hour thereafter. This is probably the most negotiable part of the taxi trip.

Overnight stays are charged at the rate of Rs 96. Where a village name is given as the route destination the fare will be to the monastery of that village. The best deal will probably be to try and negotiate an all-in cost for the places you wish to visit in one day. Count on around Rs 400 to Rs 600 for a day.

You can easily visit the Shey, Tikse, Hemis and Spitok Gompas in a day by jeep. Split between six people the cost is not excessive. Six, however, is a bit of a tight squeeze.

Leh-Manali Road

In 1988 the 475 km long Leh-Manali road was opened to tourist traffic for the first time. The highest pass is the Tanglang La (5429 metres), 65 km beyond Upshi. Previously only local and military transport were permitted to use the road. Check with any tourist office for information about transport schedules.

Around Leh

SANKAR GOMPA

This small but interesting gompa can easily be visited on foot (three km from Leh, entrance fee Rs 10), and is an under-gompa of Spitok Gompa.

At the most, only about 20 monks live here at any one time and few are permanently in residence, although the monastery is fairly active. The gompa is open to the public (except on holidays) from 7 to 10 am and from 5 to 7 pm only. It is, however, well lit, so an evening visit is worthwhile. At these times the monks will welcome you and may offer yak butter tea, tsampa and boiled and spiced mustard plant.

From the yard, climb the steps to the *Dukhang*, or general assembly room, and pass through the double doors. To the right

of the doors and under three green drums, which immediately attract the eye, is the place of the *gyeskos*. From the seat of the head lama, the Venerable Kushok Bakula, is a good view of the richly painted wall and entrance door. Kushok Bakula is also the head lama of Spitok Gompa and all of Ladakh's Gelugpa or yellow-hat sect.

The upper floor of the gompa has the *Dukar Lakhang*, a temple with a Dukar figure – a most impressive representation of Avalokitesvara (Chenrezig) complete with 1000 arms, all holding weapons, and 1000 heads. The walls are painted with mandalas, a Tibetan calendar and rules for the monks. Above a wooden stairway you can see the residence rooms of the head lama next to the guest rooms and the library.

A wooden stairway leads to the rooftop where, if you are early enough, you will see the monks playing the long trumpets to rouse the lamas to morning prayer. The rooftop also provides a view across the endless valley and the town of Leh.

A concrete path which leads from Leh to the front door of the gompa can be found by going past Ali Shah's Postcard Shop, turning left at the Antelope Guest House and right at the first path which runs alongside the stream.

SPITOK GOMPA

There are 125 yellow-cap monks at this monastery (10 km from Leh, entrance fee Rs 13) which stands on a small mountain above the Indus. The gompa is passed on the way into Leh on the righthand side of the road and it's also very close to the end of the Leh airport runway. You can walk to the monastery from Leh in two hours but take care not to wander into the military zones.

The Spitok head lama is the head lama of the Sankar Gompa, the Venerable Kushok Bakula, who also represents Ladakh in the Indian Parliament. Gurphug in Stok and Pashi Gephel in Sabu are under-monasteries of Spitok.

The gompa has three chapels of which

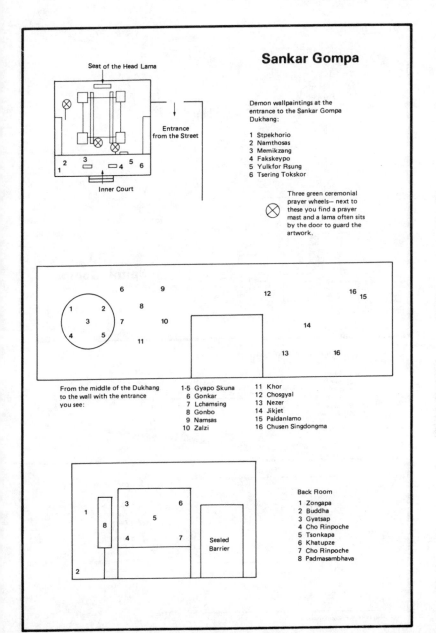

Sankar Gompa

Seat of the Head Lama

Entrance from the Street

Inner Court

Demon wallpaintings at the entrance to the Sankar Gompa Dukhang:

1 Stpekhorio
2 Namthosas
3 Memikzang
4 Fakskeypo
5 Yulkfor Rsung
6 Tsering Tokskor

⊗ Three green ceremonial prayer wheels— next to these you find a prayer mast and a lama often sits by the door to guard the artwork.

From the middle of the Dukhang to the wall with the entrance you see:

1-5 Gyapo Skuna
6 Gonkar
7 Lchamsing
8 Gonbo
9 Namsas
10 Zalzi
11 Khor
12 Chosgyal
13 Nezer
14 Jikjet
15 Paldanlamo
16 Chusen Singdongma

Sealed Barrier

Back Room

1 Zongapa
2 Buddha
3 Gyatsap
4 Cho Rinpoche
5 Tsonkapa
6 Khatupze
7 Cho Rinpoche
8 Padmasambhava

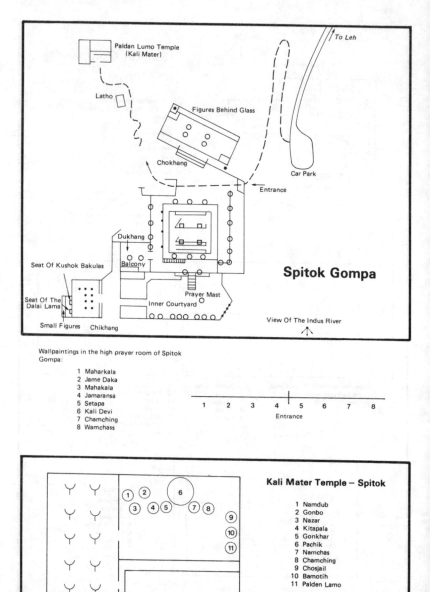

Paldan Lumo Temple
(Kali Mater)

Latho

Figures Behind Glass

To Leh

Chokhang

Car Park

Entrance

Dukhang

Seat Of Kushok Bakulas

Balcony

Seat Of The
Dalai Lama

Small Figures   Chikhang

Prayer Mast

Inner Courtyard

Spitok Gompa

View Of The Indus River

Prayer Mast

Wallpaintings in the high prayer room of Spitok
Gompa:

1 Maharkala
2 Jame Daka
3 Mahakala
4 Jamaransa
5 Setapa
6 Kali Devi
7 Chamching
8 Wamchass

1 2 3 4 5 6 7 8

Entrance

Kali Mater Temple – Spitok

1 Namdub
2 Gonbo
3 Nazar
4 Kitapala
5 Gonkhar
6 Pachik
7 Namchas
8 Chamching
9 Chosjail
10 Bamotih
11 Palden Lamo

Hall With A Prayer Wheel

the highest, *Kali Mater*, or the Paldan Lamo Temple, is the most impressive. This temple, or *gonkhang*, is more than 1000 years old.

From Paldan Lamo Temple, a small path leads past a red *Latho* (god house) to the monastery proper where the built-in Dukhang is well worth seeing. The area around the wall paintings, where there are tankas, prayer flags, bookshelves and books, is well illuminated.

Near the Dukhang are several other chapels of which the new *Chokhang* is above some stairs. Funeral ceremonies can be witnessed here.

Many of the small, old prayer rooms, the head lama's room and the rooms of the monks are, unfortunately, no longer shown to foreigners because a thoughtless tourist once took objects as souvenirs. These rooms contain some wonderful wall paintings, tankas, silver chortens, buddha figures, statues of other deities and hundreds of books.

From the Dukhang, 19 steps lead up to the inner courtyard where there is a flagpole around which, on the 28th and 29th days of the 11th month of the Tibetan calendar (mid-winter), the *Spitok Gostor* is celebrated with mask dances.

The monastery has a statue of *Kali*, the face of which is only shown once a year. *Kali*, one of the fiercest of the Tantric gods, is the darker side of Parvati, the beautiful consort of Shiva.

From the highest point on the Spitok hill there is a good view over the Indus Valley, of the village of Spitok at the foot of the hill, of Pharka lying opposite, of the mountains (usually snow-covered even in summer) which divide the Indus Valley from Zanskar and, lastly, Leh. Don't take photographs looking back towards Leh because the airport, between the monastery and Leh, is a military area.

PHYANG

An access track to the right of the main road leads to the monastery (24 km from Leh towards Srinagar, entrance fee Rs 10). Phyang village (or Fiang) is in the river valley, a few hundred metres walk away. Take care when photographing as the barren mountainside opposite Phyang is a military zone! Also, Phyang Lake, to the north of the gompa, is in a restricted area and therefore off-limits.

The Phyang Gompa has 50 lamas and seven novices of the red-cap sect and possesses five chapels. The monastery is interesting for its museum containing some old Chinese, Tibetan, Mongolian and possibly Serasan weapons and armour. The museum room is said to be nearly 900 years old. The monastery has had several renovations recently, including the addition of a large house for the head lama and a new entrance hall with a large prayer wheel. The 650-year-old Dukhang Temple was renovated in the late '70s.

Phyang's large and colourful festival rivals that of Hemis in the crowds it attracts. However, until recently it has always been held in winter. The lamas decided to move it to summer to take advantage of the tourist season and have built new rest houses.

If you go down into the village of Phyang from the monastery or the main road you may be able to see a wonderful kitchen in a Phyang farmhouse. The summer kitchen in the upper storey is so lavishly equipped with dishes inherited over the generations that you feel like you are in a living museum.

The sturdily built farmhouses generally have three storeys. The stables and store rooms are found on the ground floor. Above these is the so-called 'winter kitchen', which also serves as the living and sleeping room for the entire family during the winter. These close living arrangements, plus 'floor heating' from the stables beneath, conserves precious fuel (usually wood or dried cattle dung). A small animal may also be kept in this collective living room over the winter.

In the summer the family moves up to the top storey, which is often just a summer kitchen set on the roof. They sleep under the stars in summer. In Leh you may also see houses on whose roofs groundsheets are spread out, under

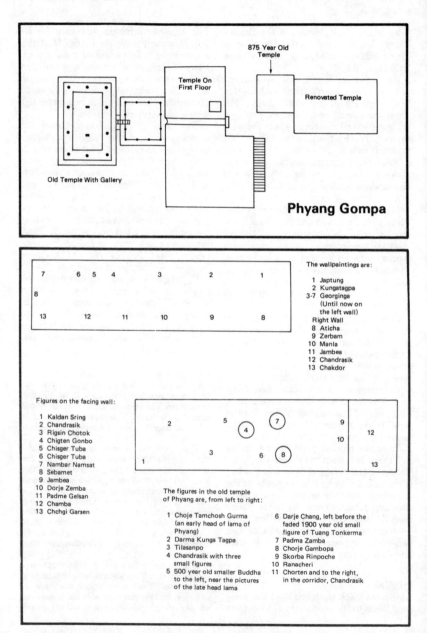

875 Year Old Temple

Temple On First Floor

Renovated Temple

Old Temple With Gallery

Phyang Gompa

The wallpaintings are:

1 Japtung
2 Kungatagpa
3-7 Georginga
   (Until now on the left wall)
   Right Wall
8 Aticha
9 Zerbam
10 Manla
11 Jambea
12 Chandrasik
13 Chakdor

Figures on the facing wall:

1 Kaldan Sring
2 Chandrasik
3 Rigsin Chotok
4 Chigten Gonbo
5 Chisger Tuba
6 Chisger Tuba
7 Nambar Namsat
8 Sebamet
9 Jambea
10 Dorje Zemba
11 Padme Gelsan
12 Chamba
13 Chchgi Garsen

The figures in the old temple of Phyang are, from left to right:

1 Choje Tamchosh Gurma (an early head of lama of Phyang)
2 Darma Kunga Tagpa
3 Tilasanpo
4 Chandrasik with three small figures
5 500 year old smaller Buddha to the left, near the pictures of the late head lama

6 Darje Chang, left before the faded 1900 year old small figure of Tuang Tonkerma
7 Padma Zamba
8 Chorje Gambopa
9 Skorba Rinpoche
10 Ranacheri
11 Chorten and to the right, in the corridor, Chandrasik

View from Phyang Gompa

which the house owners live, as if they are camping in tents.

The summer night temperatures are low enough to make westerners reach for their sleeping bags, but they don't bother the Ladakhis at all. They're a hardy race! At a festival in Bodh Kharbu we saw a cook who, in the absence of a drinking vessel, took a draught of boiling butter tea in his cupped hands and drank from that as if it had been no more than a handful of cold water. Rich farmhouses will have special drinking vessels for butter tea or chang.

BEACON HIGHWAY

Unfortunately off-limits to foreigners, the Beacon Highway leads from Leh into the Nubra Valley over a pass at 5606 metres – probably the highest road in the world and where, according to the road builder's sign, *You can have dialogue with God*! The road is only open in September and October as at other times ice covers the road on the northern side of the Nubra Valley.

TIBETAN REFUGEE CAMP

Near Choglamsar, on the left side of the Leh-Shey road and close to the Indus, is the Sonam Ling refugee camp, nine km from Leh. Since the early '60s more than 2000 refugees have lived here under primitive conditions. They have managed to grow some vegetables on this rocky ground but live mainly on the donations of international aid organisations. However, they earn some money from handicrafts, particularly the manufacture of Tibetan carpets. The Tibetans are known as fair dealers and have only slowly infiltrated the Kashmiri dominated artefacts business in Ladakh.

Choglamsar is the main training place for Buddhist monks in Ladakh. Since the Chinese invasion of Tibet, the School of Buddhist Philosophy, on the righthand side of the road from Leh to Hemis, has become an important centre for the study of Tibetan literature and history and of

Signpost for the Beacon Highway

Buddhist philosophy in its pure form. Many westerners, interested in Buddhist learning and meditation, have studied here. Choglamsar has an extensive syllabus and its library is worth seeing, even for the casual visitor.

In 1977 the old bridge at Sonam Ling was replaced with a new one able to take heavy vehicles. Cross the road and turn right to reach the village of Palam where there are mani stones. Palam has a mixed Buddhist and Muslim population. The Hemis-Stagna-Palam road is very rough and river crossings must be made, but there is a regular bus connection.

SHEY

The old summer palace of the kings of Ladakh, Shey (15 km from Leh towards Hemis, entrance fee Rs 5) was built more than 550 years ago by Lhachen Palgyigon, the king of Ladakh. It stands next to the remains of a larger construction on the east side of a hill which runs south-east towards the Indus. From the palace you can see over the fertile Indus plain north-east to the Tikse Gompa and over the Indus to the Zanskar mountain range. Hundreds of chortens of the most diverse form and size stand on the barren plains to the north, separated from the fertile riverbank land by the Hemis Rd.

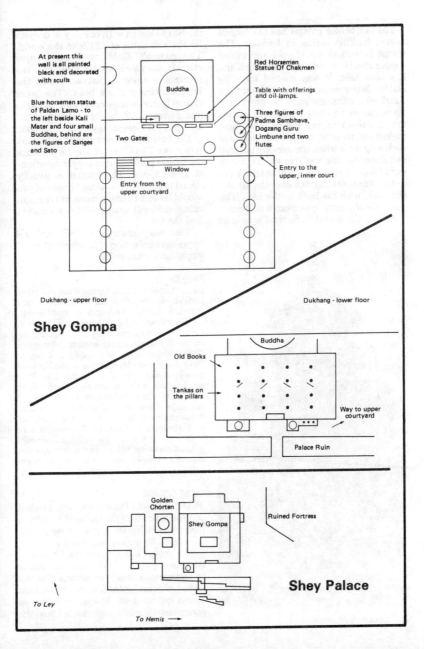

At present this wall is all painted black and decorated with sculls

Blue horsemen statue of Paldan Lamo - to the left beside Kali Mater and four small Buddhas, behind are the figures of Sanges and Sato

Buddha

Red Horsemen Statue Of Chakmen

Table with offerings and oil-lamps.

Three figures of Padma Sambhava, Dogzang Guru Limbune and two flutes

Two Gates

Window

Entry to the upper, inner court

Entry from the upper courtyard

Dukhang - upper floor

Shey Gompa

Dukhang - lower floor

Buddha

Old Books

Tankas on the pillars

Way to upper courtyard

Palace Ruin

Golden Chorten

Shey Gompa

Ruined Fortress

Shey Palace

To Ley

To Hemis →

The old palace gompa has the largest golden buddha statue in Ladakh. The statue is worked out of gold and gilded copper sheets, stands 12 metres high and has blue hair. It was erected by King Dalden Namgyal in the mid-17th century. Sacrificial offerings such as grain and jewels, as well as holy signs and mantras are contained in the figure. The most important moment in the construction of such a figure is when the eyes are painted and the statue can 'see'. No artist or monk would dare to look the Buddha in the eye so the pupils are painted over the artist's shoulder, with his back to the idol. The palace is officially open from 6 to 9 am.

In July the Metukba festival is held at the Shey Gompa with one day of prayers for the well being of all life in the world. The gompa's *Dukhang-Chung* (upper chapel), used for everyday functions, is a mezzanine balcony that surrounds the huge buddha statue's head. The lower chapel houses a large collection of tankas and a library. All the old tankas bear the stamp of the Gompa Association, Ladakh.

The best time to visit the Shey Gompa is between 7 and 9 am or 5 and 6 pm since the monks perform their prayer devotions at these times. The gompa is usually closed to the public at other times but you should be able to find a monk in the small village before Shey who will know where to find the key.

Near Shey there is a field with an impressive collection of hundreds of small stupas and mani walls.

Shey Oracle

As in Mulbekh, Tikse, Matho, Stok and other Ladakh villages, Shey has an oracle. During the Shey Shublas, the August harvest festival, the Shey oracle rides on a horse and stops at various places around Shey to prophesise the future. The oracle, a Shey layman, starts at the Tuba Gompa where he engages in a two or three-day prayer while in a trance, in order to be possessed and become an oracle. The Shey oracle is held in the highest regard and viewed as a god who has achieved the highest level of existence. Other oracles, especially those in Tikse and Stok, are not so well regarded, but are at the same time feared and revered because of their spiritual state. It is said that if one asks a question of an oracle, but disbelieves the answer and goes to another oracle, no answer will be given.

TIKSE GOMPA

The 500-year-old Tikse monastery, perched on a hill high above the Indus, (17 km from Leh towards Hemis, entrance fee Rs 10) has about 100 yellow-cap monks.

The gompa's new-found tourist wealth is being put to good use in major improvements and renovations. On the right of the entrance to the main courtyard a new chapel houses an enormous 15-metre high seated buddha

Zan La temple at Tikse

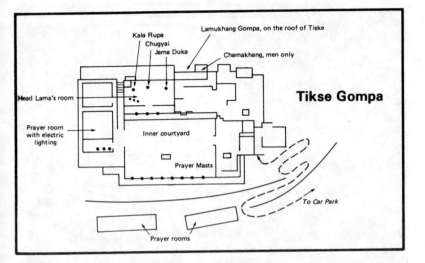

Tikse Gompa

Kala Rupa
Chugyai
Jama Duka

Lamukhang Gompa, on the roof of Tiske

Chamakhang, men only

Head Lama's room

Prayer room
with electric
lighting

Inner courtyard

Prayer Masts

To Car Park

Prayer rooms

Wallpaintings in the high prayer room of Tikse Gompa:

Left
1 Gonbo Ping
2 Gonbo Chakjipac
3 Gonbo Chhak Tukpa
4 Gonkar
5 Sangdu

Right
1 Chamsing
2 Lamo
3 Chosgialckhor

Figures:
Flag pole (Gyaltsan) in the middle, to the right of Chosgial,
left of Tsepakmet.

In the prayer room there are two seats, one for the Dalai
Lama who visited Tikse in 1973 and 1976, and one for the
head lama of Tikse.

Behind the prayer room:

1 Sharipu
2 Buddha
3 Mongalpu
4 Shikdan and Chamsing
5 Chandajik

Above: Library at Tikse Gompa   Below: Pages from a book

figure. The outside of the gompa is painted red and is visible from far away.

If you get to the gompa by 6.30 am you can witness the daily morning prayers but there are also prayers closer to noon, preceded by long, mournful sounds from the horns on the roof. The monastery mountain is best ascended on foot although there is also a new 1½ km sealed road up to the monastery. The small temple of *Zan-La* is beside the car parking area on this road.

On the walls in the gompa courtyard are some interesting Tibetan calendars. In the chapel is a picture, near the central Chamba statue, of Tsung-Khapas, the founder of the *Tugend* (Gelugpa) sect. Some steps run up to a roof balcony from which there is access to the rooms of the head lama. Above everything is the roof top *Lamukhang* chapel, to which the *Chamakhang* also belongs, where only men may go. If you remain very quiet you may see mice nibbling at the offerings of grain and drinking the water.

Whereas a few years ago travellers could buy a printed prayer flag for a few rupees, today the monks wait in the monastery yard with portable stands from which they sell monastic souvenirs!

Below the monastery are more chapels which are not very attractive. The houses of the monks stretch out towards the foot of the hill. The important *Tikse Gostor* festival with mask dances is held on the 18th and 19th day of the 12th month of the Tibetan calendar.

There's a popular small hotel at Tikse and from here it's a beautiful walk through the fields and villages, instead of along the road, between Shey and Tikse. In October, when they're busy threshing the barley, the villagers will sing in the fields. They have different traditional songs for each task.

Monks

When asked what criteria are used to choose lamas, or which sons in a family will become monks, a monk of Tikse told us that he came from a family with four sons. His eldest brother is a farmer, the second eldest a teacher and his youngest brother a monk like himself. In principle, all could become monks but the father must give his consent. This he will certainly not give to all his sons because some must stay to run the farm and look after the rest of the family.

Tikse Oracle

The Tikse oracle is the most important oracle in Ladakh. An old man in the village is supposed to have supernatural powers. In a trance this layman, for he is not a lama, is possessed by a spirit and speaks Tibetan, a language which he cannot normally understand. He is said to be able to perform miraculous cures on beasts and men. With the help of a small tube he can 'suck' diseases from the bodies of the ill. He also gives advice for healing and can predict the future. In 1975 a new oracle appeared, the young wife of a Leh carpenter. Even in her youth there were special indications of her status as an oracle.

Printing

Tikse Gompa possesses a rich and beautiful library with many handwritten and painted books. Recent editions are produced by block printing, as in old Tibet. This procedure is also used today for the printing of the holy books *Kandshur*, *Tibetan gka-hgyur*, the translated word of Buddha and Tandshur, and the translated teachings of the Lamaist religious teachers Bu-Ston (1290 to 1364). The latter consists of a 225-volume commentary on the Kandshur!

Wooden printing plates are made up for each page and pressed by hand. The many hundred volumes indicate how much space the printing plates must take up in the monastery. Older and more highly regarded editions are often printed, not black on white, but painted with gold ink on black lacquered paper. These are decorated with buddha figures. The individual pages are not bound up but kept as collections of loose sheets, wrapped in cloth between two wooden boards, tied up with a strap and stored on the shelves.

Tikse Gompa has the most beautiful library. In Hemis Gompa there are some rarities such as bilingual books in Tibetan and Sanskrit. You may meet one of the porters who has to lug the heavy books from the gompa to a village for a

Hemis Gompa

festival – the monks themselves follow on much later.

HEMIS GOMPA

The Hemis Gompa (45 km from Leh, entrance fee Rs 10) is famous far beyond the borders of Ladakh for its festival (*Hemis Setchu* or *Mela* of the Hemis Gompa). This takes place every year from the 9th to 11th day of the fifth Tibetan month which usually falls in the second half of June, although it sometimes goes into the beginning of July. Hemis also has a gigantic tanka, one of the largest in the world, which is only displayed to the public every 12 years at the festival. It will not be shown again until 1992.

The festival features mask dancing and draws pilgrims, dressed in their finest costumes, from all over Ladakh and, since 1975, tourists from all over the world. Apart from being one of the largest religious festivals in Ladakh it is one of the few which is held in summer, when the passes are open. However, other monasteries are considering switching their festivals to the summer months.

Hemis Gompa is the largest and one of the most important in Ladakh quite apart from its annual festival. It was founded about 360 years ago by Stagtshang Raspa, who was invited to Ladakh by King Singe Namgyal who also established the monasteries of Chemre, Hanle and Themisgang.

You can gain an impression of the extent of the monastery area on the climb to the eyrie, a hermitage known as Gotsang or Kotsang Gompa which is reached by a one hour, three km climb to 3900 metres, 300 metres higher than Hemis. The 13th century monastery predates the Hemis Gompa and was built by Syalwa Gotsang-Pa, who meditated in a cave nearby. A small shrine has been built around the cave, where you can see his foot and hand print in the rock.

About a dozen monks live at this small gompa which serves as a retreat for many of the lamas from Hemis. It also services many of the monasteries in Ladakh by printing religious texts using carved wooden blocks, yak oil, lamp black and rice paper imported from Burma. The climb is quite strenuous because of the altitude, so you should not undertake it lightly. While the Ladakhis, who are used to the scarcity of oxygen, will virtually sprint up the mountainside, you will need quite a few rest breaks.

The 1000 square metre courtyard of the Hemis Gompa is entered from the northeast. The two prayer flags in front of the first steps up to the Dukhang (the general assembly room) form the middle point during the festival. A few places are reserved for guests but it is sometimes possible to buy tickets to the gallery from business-minded monks! The day before the two-day festival is devoted to demonstrations.

On the first day of the festival the ceremonies which foreigners can watch begin at 10 am in the courtyard. After

Spectators at the Hemis festival

prayers in the Dukhang the *Rimpoche*, or head lama, climbs the steps to the courtyard accompanied by musician monks, crosses it and takes his place underneath the gallery.

Shortly afterwards the dances begin. Their theme is the struggle against evil and infidels and the inevitable victory of good and of Buddhism. The *Padmasambhava* dance, which shows the conquest of the *Ruta* demons, is part of this. Other figures which the dancers represent are *Yama*, the god of death and *Guru Trakpo*, the black-hatted sorcerer and vanquisher of all demons.

The sequence of the dances changes with time, often to present a different finale for the benefit of distinguished guests! The dancing continues to late afternoon, with a brief stop at midday. Locals and foreigners find time to patronise the many small stands outside the monastery walls where tea, soup, tsampa, sweets and other refreshments are sold. If you wish to take photographs, take into account the position of the sun when selecting your vantage point, because the crowded conditions during the dancing make it virtually impossible to leave your place.

If you visit the gompa outside the festival time you will be impressed by the stillness of the valley. You will also have the opportunity to see the various chapels. In the Dukhang, the throne of the Rimpoche, the spiritual overlord of Hemis, dominates the sitting places of the monks. Near the Dukhang is the Lakhang, which is the first chapel after a small set of steps from the yard. The side walls of its front room are covered with partially damaged frescoes of the watchers of the heavenly directions.

In the Lakhang is a large gilded statue of the Buddha Sakyamuni with blue hair, surrounded by several silver chortens which, as in Spitok Gompa, are decorated with semi-precious stones. There are also beautiful frescoes in the *Lakhang Nyingpa* which is otherwise practically empty.

Dancer at the Hemis festival

The hands of the artists who prepared the Hemis Gompa's giant tanka are revered as holy relics. Hemis also has many lesser, but still interesting tankas, as well as an excellent library, some particularly well preserved wall paintings and many good buddha figures.

On the second and third storeys, near the *Zankhang* chapels are the *Kharrabgysal*, the rooms of the Rimpoche. Hemis' head lama is considered to be a reincarnation of the monastery's founder, Stagtshang Raspa. The last Rimpoche was undergoing training in Tibet when the Chinese invaded in 1959. The monastery had no communication with its own Rimpoche, who was five years old at the time, from then until a new head lama was chosen in 1975. In the meantime the *Chakzot* (manager), a brother of the late King of Ladakh, has conducted the business of the gompa.

During the 1975 festival, Drugpa Rimpoche, a 12-year-old youth, became the new Rimpoche as a new incarnation. He is also overlord of the *Drugpa Kargyupa*, one of the six divisions of the red-cap sect which, before the Chinese invasion of Tibet, possessed influence practically only in Bhutan and Ladakh. In Ladakh the Stagna and Chemre monasteries belong to this order, while Spitok belongs to the yellow-cap sect. Drugpa Rimpoche lives in Darjeeling where he is completing his training.

Most of the 500 monks who were once based at Hemis have moved to other monasteries throughout Ladakh. Consequently the monastery is maintained almost entirely for tourism and is growing rich from the proceeds of its festival – for tourists it costs Rs 20 for each day of the festival. The monks have been building a new shrine with a two-storey statue of the Sakyamuni Buddha.

Getting There & Away

Hemis is easily reached by car or jeep as a day trip from Leh, but is more time-consuming to visit by public transport. By car, follow the Upshi Rd past Shey and Tikse (this is the Manali Rd which follows the Indus). Past the TCP checkpoint at Karu (where foreigners must show passports), turn right to cross the Indus over a new bridge and follow the winding road up towards the gompa. Unlike many other gompas, Hemis is not visible from afar – it only comes into view when you're right beside it.

During summer there is one bus a day to Hemis. Departure and arrival times are variable which means you must stay overnight if you want to see the monastery. There is plenty of good camping space in the woods nearby, which is usually full of campers during the festival time. The woods are extremely beautiful and are well maintained and cared for by the monks. A small stream feeds the trees, the grass and propels a water wheel in a small stone house near the centre of the wood. This grinds the grain for the monks' tsampa.

There is also a restaurant/rest house with four bedrooms, where you can buy cheap meals and plenty of tea. You cannot, however, buy any other supplies, so if you are camping overnight, you must bring most of your requirements from Leh. The 'parachute' restaurant near the bus stand has cheaper food and good accommodation. The monastery has a diesel generator, housed in the stone structure that looks like a garage. Don't camp near it.

If after an afternoon's exploration and a night's camping you want to return to Leh, walk down to the Upshi Rd before 7 am and catch the bus up from Sakti at Karu. During the festival there are several buses from Leh to Hemis and back each day, but you will be missing something if you do not camp with the many hundreds of people who flock to the gompa for the festival.

Dancer at the Hemis festival

Top: Monks at Tikse Gompa (TW)
Bottom: Wall painting at Tikse Gompa (TW)

Top: Hemis monks chanting pujar prior to the festival (BP)
Left: Guru Padmasambhava makes his final appearance at the Hemis festival (BP)
Right: A Ladakhi woman offers yak butter oil at the Hemis festival (BP)

TAGTHOG GOMPA

Also known as Bragthog, this is the only monastery (entrance fee Rs 10) of the *Nyingma* school of Buddhism in Ladakh. Tagthog means 'the place with the rock ceiling' and it is built around a cave which, as legend has it, was used by the Padmasambhava (Guru Rimpoche) in the 8th century. He is believed to have stayed in the cave for meditation and thereby blessed it with his presence.

There are three main shrines. The cave hall is the oldest and from time to time sacred water drops from the cave ceiling. Within this temple, the statues of Padmasambhava include one in the wrathful *tantra* form. The tantra deity is the Buddha Heruka and the wall paintings show 100 deities in their peaceful and wrathful forms.

The original Lakhang (chapel) was built 100 years ago while the new one, completed in 1966, was conceived and planned by the Stakling Rimpoche, who was abbot of Dorje Tag in Tibet for several years before coming to Tagthog. The statues in this temple are different forms of Padmasambhava and the frescoes have images of renowned spiritual personalities of the various schools of Buddhism.

In summer there is a bus from Leh to Tagthog and back. The bus stays overnight in the village of Sakti and leaves Tagthog the next day at about 7 am, passing through Sakti 10 to 15 minutes later. It is possible to catch this bus at Karu, if you walk down from Hemis, between 7.30 and 8 am. However, it is the first bus down the valley to Leh for the day and will be very full.

Festivals

Most of the great religious festivals of Ladakh fall in the winter. The main exception is the Hemis Festival, the biggest of them all. Other summer gompa festivals include the Phyang monastery's festival in mid-July. The monasteries at Thagtog and Chemre usually hold theirs in November, before the real depths of winter.

More festivals, which used to be associated with certain religious, cultural or agricultural meanings, are now being adjusted to coincide with the June to September tourist season. Festival dates tend to vary by several weeks from year to year due to the 13-month Buddhist calendar's variation from the western calendar.

In addition to the monastery festivals, practically all the villages have harvest thanksgiving festivals and archery events during summer. There are also private parties in which dance plays an important role. In these slow, sustained dances the dancers appear to be between dream and trance. Many of the dances, which have a musical accompaniment of drums and flutes, show interesting elements from the daily life of farmers. Hand movements, for example, are unmistakably taken from the actions involved in sowing seeds.

In general, men and women dance separately. If they are together on the same dance floor they will still do their own, unrelated dances. We experienced a special feature during a celebration at Bodh Kharbu – a dance master selected from the crowd some women and young girls to dance. After initial reluctance they seemed to quite enjoy it.

Ladakhi archery contests, which are followed by more dancing, are only a pale reflection of similar festivals in other Himalayan states. Whereas in Bhutan specially designed and fashioned bows are used for such a contest, in Ladakh the bows are much cruder. Nevertheless these contests have their own charm and they do give the opportunity to see the making of chang, butter tea and tsampa. No matter what else happens at a festival, these three ingredients must be included. Festival musicians are generally paid in local produce. After a good meal they receive a cup of butter tea, a cup of tsampa meal, sometimes sugar and a piece of butter. The whole lot is wrapped in a piece of cloth and knotted for transport.

Anyone wishing to tape record festival music should keep their microphone concealed, otherwise the result will be a wild medley of noises as the Ladakhis are fascinated by these strange technological instruments. They will point it out to the audience and comment loudly! A cassette recorder with an inbuilt microphone can be kept out of sight, even inside a carrying bag.

In Leh, especially during summer, there are often cultural nights with dancing, singing and other entertainment put on by the people from the Tibetan refugee camp at Choglamsar. The tourist office in Leh is also organising festivals with archery contests, polo games and wedding and dance feasts. The Dalai Lama's birthday on 6 July is a festival in Leh, mostly for Tibetans. Leh also has a picture theatre in the town and another at the army base. They usually show Indian movies.

CHEMRE GOMPA

Turn left at the Karu TCP and after five km you will reach Chemre Gompa on a ridge above the village of Chemre. Like Hemis it was founded by Stagtshang Raspa but in contrast to Hemis the mask dances are held at the turn of the year in the Tibetan calendar, in mid-winter. The Dukhang and the three chapels above it are not really worth visiting.

The small but noteworthy Trak Tok Gompa is 10 km further on. The old Trak Tok Rimpoche, who came from Tibet, is highly revered by the Ladakhis. The old cave chapel, reminiscent of Dakum Khochey, is especially interesting. Although they both lie in a restricted zone, tourists may visit the Chemre and Trak Tok gompas.

MATHO GOMPA

Matho lies five km from Stagna in a southern side valley. The monastery is above the village on a long ridge surrounded by a small forest. The gompa was founded in the 16th century by Tungpa Dorje but was almost destroyed during the war between the Muslim invaders and the Ladakhis in the late 16th century. It was saved a few years later by the arrival of another lama, Chokyi Lodo, who renovated the monastery and restored its activities. Now it has 60 monks and 30 novices from the larger monasteries and belongs to the *Sakyapa* sect.

Near the chapels, which were renovated for the visit of Sakya Trinzin Rimpoche, overlord of the sect, is a small, interesting room called *Gonkhang* which is filled 50 cm high with grain. According to an old custom every family from Matho brings a small bowl of grain from the first harvest for this

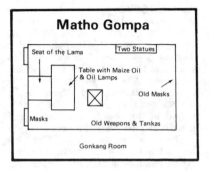

room. This is not accompanied by any special ceremony. The lama responsible for the Gonkhang room is changed every three years. The room has a special significance during the two-day *Nagrang* Festival (for the Tibetan New Year in February) and a one-day festival on the 8th day of the second Tibetan month (usually March) called the *Nispetsergyat*.

During these two festivals two special monks (called *Rongzam*) go into a trance in this room and then, adorned with old weapons, run over the mountain ridges in the area and over the roofs of the monastery.

During the Nagrang Festival the lamas are evil-minded on the first day (they hit spectators) but are very peaceable on the second day! At the Nispetsergyat, the two Rongzam ride the stretch which they went over on foot at the beginning of the Tibetan year. Both of these festivals are accompanied by mask dances. High in the mountains there are two *Lathos*, special red chortens from which prayer flags flutter, dedicated to these two monks. They're about five or six km from the monastery, close to a glacier.

The monks, also known as *Luyar*, are like other monks at other times of the year, but if someone in the village doesn't believe in or has lost faith in the powers of Buddhism, these two monks batter themselves on the arms, feet and tongue with their old weapons. The wounds do not bleed and their injuries are said to heal so quickly that they are able to dance a short time later. They do this in order to show that they possess divine powers. This ritual is still practised on the 14th and 15th days of the first month of the Tibetan calendar.

Like the lama of the Gonkhang room the Rongzam are replaced every three years. The monks are chosen, following a prayer, from four or five candidates. All 60 monks write their selection on a small piece of paper. The head lama draws two names and those monks become the Rongzam for the next three years.

In front of the door to the Gonkhang room is a prayer mill made out of oil cans – a sign of the times – but still adorned with the mantra *om mani padme hum* in addition to other prayers. These are written on a paper roll. The Gonkhang room, in which meditation takes place, is ascribed its own spiritual power. Thus one cannot in any circumstances take photographs here because pictures of the room would take away a part of the power.

Matho is famous amongst Ladakhis because of its oracle. The Lhaba of Matho is, in contrast to the oracle of Tikse, a priest and lives in the monastery. On special days (in winter on the 8th day of the second month of the Tibetan calendar) the oracle runs over the mountains near Matho. He is blindfolded and 'sees' only with a painting on his breast and back. The oracle speaks to the audience of village dwellers by a small spring at the foot of the monastery mountain.

STAGNA GOMPA

This gompa lies on a sugarloaf mountain on the west bank of the Indus River. The hill is said to be shaped like a tiger jumping up to the sky and since the monastery is built on the tiger's nose it took the name *stagna* or tiger's nose. As it cannot be reached directly from the Leh-Hemis road because there is no bridge, you must use the Choglamsar or Karu bridge.

The most important image in the monastery is one of Avalokitesvara which is said to have come from Assam. In the chapel are three new paintings – a large picture of Choshikzal, the red figure of Standin and the blue figure of Dorje Chang. In the wooden cupboard is a large standing figure of Dorje Phakma beside eight Sashan Gyat. Under this main chapel is another chapel which may only be entered by lamas.

Stagna has 25 red-cap monks and the head lama can offer his visitors a European sofa with two easy chairs, of which he is more than a little proud.

Under-monasteries of Stagna are those of Mut, Karu and Stakrimo in Ladakh and Bardun and Sani in Zanskar.

STOK PALACE

Eight km towards the Indus from Stagna, then four km over a rubble slope at the

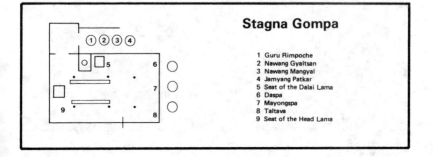

Stagna Gompa

1 Guru Rimpoche
2 Nawang Gyaltsan
3 Nawang Mangyal
4 Jamyang Patkar
5 Seat of the Dalai Lama
6 Daspa
7 Mayongspa
8 Taltava
9 Seat of the Head Lama

Royal Palace at Stok

outlet of a side valley brings you to the Palace of Stok (entrance fee Rs 20). Coming from Leh you cross the Indus at Choglamsar then travel a km towards the Indus and turn to the right. The palace is about 200 years old and is the only Ladakhi royal palace which is still inhabited. The last king, Raja Kunsang Namgyal, died in 1974 and, as is customary for personalities of high standing, a chorten was erected in the village where he was cremated.

One of his brothers is the manager of the Hemis Gompa. Only his widow, the Rani of Stok, and his youngest son live in the palace. The widow, who was formerly revered as the *Gyalmo*, Rani Parvati Davi Deskit Wangmo, the 18th Queen of Ladakh, was born in 1936. She has four children and the eldest son will become the next King of Ladakh when he is between 20 and 25 years old. The exact date will be set by lamas and people of high standing.

Gyalpo means king, Gyalmo means queen, *Gyallu* means prince and *Gyalmo Chhunun* means princess. The King of Ladakh formerly had a cabinet of five ministers and the influence of Ladakh's kings once reached from Demchok (on the present-day Chinese-Tibetan border) to Mulbekh and in the north over the Nubra Valley. Now political power rests with the Indian Governor, the District Commissioner.

The Palace of Stok has 80 rooms, only 12 of which are used. There are 25 servants working for the Rani, but because the palace is so difficult to heat the Rani moves south to Manali for the winter months.

Three rooms, which make up the museum, are open to the public. It is also possible to visit the small gompa with the lama's permission. A guide with reasonable English unlocks the museum which contains the royal family's jewellery, noted for its turquoise and red coral, and a superb collection of 35 400-year-old tankas, coloured by using paints made of crushed semi-precious stones. Some visitors feel that unless you have a distinct interest in the Ladakhi royal family visiting the palace is barely worth the Rs 20 entrance fee, but others find it very interesting.

Apart from the palace, Stok's only other attraction is the July archery contest. As in Matho you can see the small water mills in which the roasted grain is ground into meal. There are two lay oracles in Stok and they perform at the *Lchagrang Festival* on the 9th and 10th days of the third month of the Tibetan calendar. There is a variety of accommodation available at Stok and you can camp. There is also a small tent restaurant.

PHARKA

The village of Pharka is on the opposite side of the Indus from, and in sight of, the

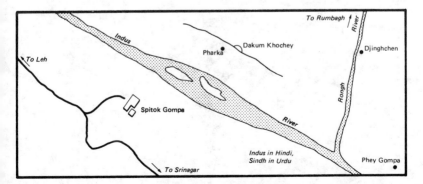

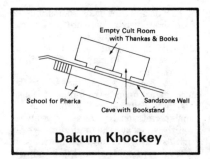

Empty Cult Room
with Thankas & Books

School for Pharka
Sandstone Wall
Cave with Bookstand

Dakum Khockey

Spitok Gompa. You can only reach Pharka by the Choglamsar route. The last few km must be made on foot but up to that point the road is jeepable. At the village of Pharka is a cave in the sandstone bank of the Indus. The cave gompa, Dakum Khochey, was built by Lotsava Rinchen Sanghpo and is older than Spitok Gompa. In front of the gompa cave is a building housing a small primary school. The teacher enjoys painting modern tankas in his spare time.

Rafting
Experienced by organised groups visiting Ladakh for several years, rafting the Indus River can now be enjoyed by independent travellers. Contact Rigzin Jora of Indus Expeditions at the Hotel Mandala in Leh for reservations.

Basically there are two trips to choose from: Easy – Hemis to Choglamsar, 'scenic floating' with four to five hours on the water; and White Water – Spitok to Nimmu, which rates two to three in the international river grading of one to six.

The rafts used carry eight passengers comfortably plus the captain. A minimum of four are required per trip which costs about Rs 500 per person. You leave Leh around 8.30 am and arrive back between 3.30 and 4 pm with all transport and a packed lunch provided. You can certainly find more spectacular river rafting routes in the world, but nowhere takes you through the incredible landscapes that you see here with their deep gorges of awesome beauty, towering snow-caped peaks, gompas and the occasional herd of ibex.

Trekking in Ladakh

Ladakh offers many possibilities for trekking and mountain climbing. The Suru Valley (reached from Kargil) and Zanskar are especially good for trekking. Zanskar can only be reached along the Suru Valley from Kargil. It is possible to trek from Nimmu directly into the Zanskar Valley, but only with the greatest difficulty. The Zanskar Valley can be reached in about a week of walking from Kargil and less time if the road from Kargil is open. Treks into Zanskar or within Zanskar are covered in the Zanskar chapter. There are also numerous mountain climbing possibilities in Ladakh.

MARKHA VALLEY TREK

The Markha Valley is a popular trekking route, adjacent to the Indus Valley and south-east of Leh. This is an eight day or more round trip trek from Leh. Part of this excellent trek follows the same route as the trek from Leh to the Markha Valley and on to Zangla and Padum in Zanskar. See the Zanskar chapter for details on the route into Zanskar. The trek can be made in either direction.

The views throughout the trek are superb and the local people are very friendly. They generally offer accommodation and food but don't depend on it. Be sure to leave a small donation if they do. There's no need for guides or porters as local people always tell you the way. Within the valley the best known peak is Kang Yissay at 6401 metres, but there are many unnamed peaks between 5000 and 6000 metres.

Day 1: Leh-Spitok

There are several buses each day or you can take a taxi. It's possible to stay in a villager's house in Spitok, otherwise camp by the Indus.

Day 2: Spitok-Rumbagh

This is a long day's walk. You start by bearing north-west along the Indus from Spitok until you reach a good suspension bridge which leads to the southern bank. Next walk eastwards to the flanks of the foothills directly ahead. Sketchy paths traverse these flanks parallel to the Indus. Follow these across a large dry ravine until you hit a very well defined path and river running south-west.

This is the path to Rumbagh. The path follows the river valley all the way through via Jingchan (Zinchan) before turning south to Rumbagh. It's possible to overnight with villagers at Jingchan or Rumbagh, which is in a side valley to the left of the main valley. The day's walk is strenuous – a steady ascent throughout.

Day 3: Rumbagh-Skiu

Another long day starts with returning down from Rumbagh to the main valley. You continue south for a short time before turning west (right) up the first side valley. This path leads up to the village of Yuruche then to the Ganda La at 5000 metres. The long ascent to the path takes up most of the day. After the pass the walk is straightforward. Head south-west down the obvious path, following the river valley to Shingo then Skiu. Accommodation is possible with the villagers at either place.

Day 4: Skiu-Markha Village

The true Markha Valley is joined at Skiu. The easy day's walk follows the Markha Valley upstream to Markha. There are many paths in the main valley and no steep gradients. The Markha River has to be crossed twice but bridges might be completed by now. There is abundant wood and water and the people are very friendly. Accommodation is possible in old buildings below the village or you can camp by the river. Markha village is the

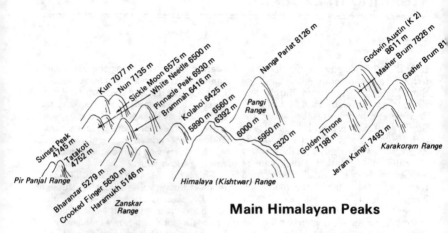

Main Himalayan Peaks

starting point for the trek to Zangla in Zanskar.

Day 5: Markha Village-Longmaru La

This is another long day's walk but by this time you should be well acclimatised. Start by following the Markha River upstream past the villages of Umlung and Hankar. It's very important to turn north-east (left) away from the Markha Valley soon after Hankar, where an obvious path leads up a narrow side valley and over a wooden bridge from where a good path follows the side river up towards Nimaling and the Longmaru La. Nimaling is reputedly very small and very old – if you can find it! You can camp by the river below the Longmaru La, but it's very cold although the views of the Himalaya are superb.

Day 6: Longmaru La-Chokdo

The ascent northwards to the pass at 5200 metres takes about two hours through the snow. It's easier than the Ganda La. The views from the top are good, but the pass is followed by a tedious descent northwards towards Larsa. The rocks here are very loose. Continuing north down the river valley the path is very ill-defined, but as you follow the main stream down and say

'Hemis?' to anyone you meet you won't go wrong! At the end of the day you reach Larsa. Chokdo is only half an hour further on. There are friendly people and accommodation is possible at either place.

Day 7: Chokdo-Hemis Gompa

A leisurely last day starts with an easy morning clambering downriver to Martseland and the Indus Valley. The path is still poor, so just follow the river valley. From Martseland to Hemis bear north-west above and parallel to the Indus Valley for three km or so. There's accommodation and food available at Hemis and transport back to Leh.

KONGLACHA PEAK

The Konglacha Peak (6700 metres) lies south-east of Leh and is reached via Rumbagh, the first day's walk on the Markha Valley trek. From Leh go to Stok where you can hire porters and donkeys. From Stok go past the Gurphuk Gompa and on to the 4800-metre Namlung Pass then descend to the village of Rumbagh at 3270 metres. From there it's another day's walk to the base camp of Konglacha Peak. It takes another two days to climb the peak.

At Stok, it is also worth visiting the small

but well maintained Gurphug Gompa which is attached to the Spitok Gompa.

STOK BASE CAMP

This trek starts out like the Konglacha trek. You can hire donkeys at Stok for about Rs 17.50 to Rs 20 per day, inclusive of the donkeyman if you hire two. They're not really necessary as you can make this trek without them, but it does ensure you have a good guide.

The first day's walk out of Stok follows a river valley for about five hours, keeping to the left of the valley and ascending about 1000 metres. You pass some summer dwellings and the eroded landscape is very beautiful. There's a good camping place at the end of the day.

The second day continues up the valley and is easier walking than the first day. In a four-hour walk you ascend about 600 metres to the Stok base camp at about 5200 metres. The sun at this altitude is very strong and at night the fast-flowing mountain stream nearby may freeze over.

You can spend another day or two around the base camp, perhaps ascending to nearly 6000 metres. Animal life to be seen includes the Ladakhi desert rat. From the base camp you can descend all the way back to Stok in one day, and perhaps even back to Leh if you arrive early enough to catch the bus.

KOCHTET PEAK

The Kochtet Peak (7015 metres) is in the restricted zone. From Leh to Changla is 79 km along a jeepable road. You leave Leh on the Indus Road to Hemis Gompa. At Karu turn left into the restricted zone. The ascent takes four days. Note that north of the Srinagar-Leh road and east of the Leh-Manali road is a restricted area, so all treks must be confined to the other side of these roads. You should be well-equipped with mountaineering rations.

LEH-MANALI

Before setting out on this 14-day trek you must obtain a permit from the District

Porter carrying books

Commissioner in Leh, otherwise your trek will come to an end at the control post before Upshi. Follow the Indus Valley as far as Upshi where you turn into a side valley over the Miru, Gya and the Tanglang La Pass to Rukchen. Next go over the Marang La Pass, past Sutak, over the Lachalang La (5070 metres) and the

Baralacha La Pass (5100 metres) and cross the Rothang Pass to Manali. Kargil-Manali is covered in the Zanskar chapter.

Other Treks

Other treks in Ladakh include the eight-to-nine day trek over Shang from Leh to Sihumar. The Alchi to Chiling and Sumdah trek takes four days.

MOUNTAIN CLIMBING

Ladakh was practically shut off from the outside world between the end of WW II and 1974, so the mountaineer will find many 5000 to 7000 metre peaks which have not been climbed. Some have not even been named. Since the Ladakh valleys are at altitudes of 3500 to 4000 metres, the mountain ascents are only 1000 to 3000 metres and sloping sides and deep ravines make them comparatively easy to climb. The next decade is likely to see a large influx of western mountaineering enthusiasts. Japanese teams have already started conquering some of these virgin peaks.

All foreign climbing expeditions to India require permission in writing from the Government of India through the Indian Mountaineering Foundation. Violation of this regulation may entail arrest and prosecution. Intending climbers should contact the foundation for application forms and other details. The address is: The Secretary, Indian Mountaineering Foundation, Benito Juarez Rd, New Delhi.

Karakoram

The range of mountains north of Ladakh, and thus north of the Himalaya, has 10 peaks over 7000 metres including, at 8611 metres, the world's second highest peak, Mt Godwin Austen, also known as K2. It stands in the Pakistani held part of Kashmir. Because the mountains in the Karakoram rise from a base altitude averaging close to 3000 metres they do not look as impressive as the Himalaya. This region is outside the permitted zone.

Around Leh

Across the Indus to the south of Leh, beyond the village of Stok, is a range of mountains that is popular with climbers. The base camp for climbing in this region is about two day's trek from Stok, along the trail towards the Ganda La, one of the entrances over the range to the Markha Valley.

Most of the peaks in this area are unnamed but Stok Kangri at 6150 metres, Gulap Kangri at 5900 metres, Mashiro Kangri at 7537 metres and Kantaka at 5275 metres are among the named peaks.

Around Kargil

The Suru and Zanskar valleys provide some of the more spectacular and difficult climbing in Ladakh. The Nun-Kun Massif is one of the most frequently used climbing areas of the region and is booked out for months ahead, sometimes years, by climbing expeditions. The approach to the twin peaks is from the Kargil-Padum road, about 70 km south of Kargil. The main approach is either from Tangole or Gulmadong. Some expeditions have also approached from Parkutse along the Kangri Glacier. To reach the base camp for Kun it is necessary to cross the Suru River, but at present there is no bridge.

The Nun-Kun Massif, which lies on the Great Himalayan Range, is the highest peak in Ladakh at 7077 metres (Kun) and 7135 metres (Nun). Other named peaks within the Suru and Zanskar areas are Pinnacle at 6930 metres, White Needle at 6500 metres, Z1 at 6400 metres and D41 at 5600 metres. In this region, along the Great Himalaya to the south of the valley and the Zanskar Range to the north, are many peaks between 5500 and 6500 metres which are unnamed. Zealous climbers could even claim some of these higher peaks for their own although all claims must be registered with the Indian Mountaineering Foundation.

Zanskar Range

This range is north of the Suru River along

the Kargil-Padum road. The most frequented area is around the village of Trakkur, just over the 4400-metre Pensi La Pass from Padum and near the foot of the Turung Drung Glacier. Named peaks of the region are Z2 at 6175 metres, Z3 at 6270 metres and Z8 at 6050 metres.

Pir Panjal
This mountain range is south of the Himalaya. The Vale of Kashmir is between the Pir Panjals and the Himalayas. The Lahaul Valley, north of Manali and south of Ladakh, is similarly sandwiched between the two ranges.

Zanskar

Zanskar, the region between Kishtwar and Manali in the south and Kargil and Lamayuru in the north is ideal for trekking. Surrounded by the main Himalaya on one side and the Zanskar Range on the other, it is the most remote district of Ladakh. Few inhabited valleys in the world are so isolated.

You won't find many hotels in Zanskar but neither will you find the military installations and soldiers so common in the rest of Ladakh. The most you'll come across is a mounted patrol or pony caravan of the J&K Police. As for foreigners, they are still few and far between in this far 'off the beaten track' Himalayan valley.

Padum, the capital of Zanskar, has a population of about one thousand people, of whom about 300 are Sunnite Muslims. Padum has several hotels, a few shops and a tourist office. A wide variety of supplies are becoming available and there are many interesting short treks which can be made from here.

Facts About the Region

HISTORY

Zanskar became an administrative part of Ladakh under Senge Namygal. He had three sons whom he installed as rulers of Ladakh, Guge, and Zanskar and Spiti, respectively.

After Ladakh's war with Tibet this order gradually fell apart and Zanskar's royal families split, one side assuming jurisdiction of Padum and the other of Zangla. This continued until the Dogra times when both families were reduced to having only nominal powers.

This was a period of great unrest in Zanskar and the records testify to wholesale destruction of many of the villages. Thereafter Zanskar's political history was again very much intertwined with Ladakh.

GEOGRAPHY

Zanskar consists of two populated valleys, the Stod (Doda Chu) and the Lunak (Tsarap Chu), which converge below Padum, the capital. The Zanskar River flows across the plains from Padum to Zangla, where it penetrates the huge Zanskar Range en route to the Indus, creating some of the most spectacular gorges in the Himalaya.

The valley is about 300 km long and is unusual in that access is only by high passes from the sides. A unique feature of Zanskar is the twin peak of Nun and Kun.

The entire Ladakh region is extremely arid but the Zanskar Valley gets more snow than other areas, with falls for seven months of the year. The people spread gravel on the snow to make it melt.

Passes are often under heavy snow for more than half the year and winter temperatures of $-20°C$ and below make Zanskar one of the coldest places in the world. In the depths of winter all the rivers freeze over. Even the Zanskar River freezes on the surface and the Zanskaris walk along it to reach the Indus River near Nimu – an otherwise inaccessible route.

Until a few years ago it took villagers a week or more to reach the roadhead out of the valley, but these days a jeep track links Kargil and Padum. Despite this link with the outside world, life in the valley has changed little. Yak trains still plod their way over the wild and remote passes to Lahaul, Kulu and the Indus Valley.

The new road over the Pensi La from Kargil to Padum has brought some of the trappings of civilisation to the Zanskar capital, but one severe winter proved how tenuous a connection that road is.

RELIGION

Zanskar's uninterrupted Buddhist heritage is mainly due to its extreme isolation and can be traced from when the Buddhist monks first crossed the Himalaya from Kashmir.

While the Mohammedan influence stretched right through Baltistan to the northern borders of Zanskar, Islam did not spread over the Pensi La. There are Mohammedan communities in Padum, but these mainly date from the time of the Dogra invasion in the 1830s.

The foundation of Sani in the 11th century is recognised as the earliest monastic siting, while the original sites at Phugtal and Karsha are also attributed to this period. In many respects the development of Buddhist sects was on a par with Ladakh.

The *Delgupta* order was established in the 15th century and the later foundations of the well-preserved monasteries at Karsha, Lingshot and Mune date from this period. The *Drukpa* order established Bardan and Zangla and colonised the monastery at Sani in the 17th century.

Today the Delgupta monasteries have established ties with Lekir monastery, the head lama being the younger brother of the late Dalai Lama. Similarly, Bardan, Sani and Zangla have administrative and financial links with the monastery at Stakma in the Indus Valley.

Religious Festivals

Mune Gompa *Anchog* takes place on the 15th day of the 11th month but it is only prayers.

Karsha Gompa *Gostor* is from the 25th to 29th days of the 11th month of the Tibetan calendar – usually from mid-December to the first week in January – and features *cham* dance with masks.

Thonde (Stongde) Gompa *Gostor* from the 29th day of the 11th month of the Tibetan calendar, following the *Karsha* Gostor.

Tagrimo Gompa A one-day prayer festival on the 29th day of the 11th month, at the same time as the Karsha Gostor.

Phuctal Gompa *Gostor* is on the 29th and 30th day of the 12th Tibetan month and features prayers but no mask dances.

Bardan Gompa *Gertsa* is on the 15th day of the fourth month (usually the first week in June) and features cham dance with masks. This is the main Zanskar summer festival. The Hemis Festival in Ladakh takes place at the same time.

Zongkhul Gompa *Zongkhul Huchot* takes place on the 16th and 17th days of the fourth month but there are no mask dances.

Sani Gompa *Nungnes* has no fixed date but usually takes place in July.

Sani Gompa *Sani Nasjal* takes place between the 15th and 20th days of the sixth Tibetan month, which is usually the first week in August. The festival takes place during the blooming of the Guru Neropa Flower.

Padum The Padum *Hurim* or *Skurim* is on the 28th and 29th days of the 10th month of the Tibetan calendar and features cham dances with masks.

Zangla The Zangla *Hurim* is on the 28th and 29th day of the 10th month (first week in December). On the 29th day there are mask dances in front of the Zangla Palace.

Lingshot Gompa *Monlam* takes place on the 15th day of the first Tibetan month (February) and consists of prayers.

Visiting Gompas

At present most of the monasteries in Zanskar do not charge an entrance fee. However, the monks prefer tourists to arrive early in the morning or late in the evening.

Facts for the Visitor

TREKKING

In the routes which follow, remember that daily trekking schedules are influenced by a great many things and may vary enormously from trekker to trekker or season to season. Where you get to each day will be affected by when you start, how fast or slow you walk and how fit you are.

River levels in Zanskar are even more likely to cause variations in the itinerary. Many treks in Zanskar, the Padum-Markha Valley trek in particular, involve numerous river crossings.

If, due to heavy snow from the previous winter, the river levels are high then crossings will take longer and distance covered will be shorter. Also, the rivers tend to be higher later in the day, as the snow melts faster. Thus if the rivers are high you are likely to be stopped by a high water level earlier in the day than in a year when the river levels are lower generally.

So take the trek reports as a general guide and don't think that your trek will duplicate day to day itineraries.

Trekking in Zanskar is not easy. The trails are often rough, the rivers are often deep and the passes are always high. This is not a place for beginners. Certain precautions will, however, make a Zanskar trek an easier proposition.

Survival

Intending trekkers should be completely outfitted in Srinagar or, at the latest, Kargil. Very little will be found in Padum, and at the small villages along the trail it is not always easy to buy even tsampa meal. If you have porters or pony leaders, ensure that they feed themselves.

Most importantly, take sufficient kerosene (and ensure the containers do not leak!) since there is very little fuel for burning.

Food

Westerners should take along tinned meat (unless they're vegetarians) and other food suitable for strenuous walking at altitudes from 3000 to 5000 metres. A larger group could take along a sheep as live meat.

If you want or have to survive Zanskari style you should bring tsampa (roasted grain) with tea, water and chang. A type of noodle known as *pakthuk* can be prepared for a change and tsampa can also be baked as a flat bread called *takir* or, in Tibetan, *pakleb*. *Chuli pak* is a real Zanskari appetiser, consisting of apricots (*chuli*) cooked in butter (hopefully not rancid), which is eaten with flat bread for breakfast.

Packing

Clothing and equipment should be packed in a rucksack or kitbag, the latter being easier to transport on pony back. Waterproof individual items by putting them in dustbags sealed with rubber bands.

Shoes

Light running shoes with rubber soles are recommended for trekking as they dry quickly after crossing streams. The rocky trails, however, are very hard on running shoes which may not stand the abuse. Some trekkers feel that trekking boots are better. In no circumstances try to cross streams or rivers barefoot.

Other Equipment

A sturdy walking stick is important, especially for crossing streams, snowfields or ice. Take a sun hat but ensure it stays firmly in place or it will soon be blown away. A chapstick is important if you want to avoid burnt, dry lips. Sunglasses are very important in the high mountains – good quality and with an 85% filter factor. Have some safety pins on hand, not packed somewhere far away or where they could be lost in a fall.

Your parka and sleeping bag should both be good quality since the nights can get very cold. Make sure your tent is waterproof as some monsoon rains creep

One of Zanskar's many terrifying suspension bridges

over the mountain barrier and bring heavy downpours.

Ponies

Ponies are indispensable for riding and haulage in the Kashmir Valley, particularly on the Pahalgam-Amarnath trek although many westerners manage without them on that route. They're also useful in Ladakh, particularly on treks into Zanskar, although in many places you find donkeys instead ponies.

Locally supplied saddles tend to be very uncomfortable. In Pahalgam these are often made of iron – hard, inflexible and awkward – with just a little leather on top. In the Suru Valley the saddles are made of wood. In either case, riding rapidly becomes impossible. The bridle and stirrups are equally bad. In fact stirrups are often completely lacking on Suru Valley and Zanskar ponies and the bridle may be simply a loose rope tied around the animal's neck. A tall westerner, with his legs reaching almost to the ground, looks like Don Quixote!

The reason for this poor equipment is quite simple. Apart from water crossings, ponies are primarily used as beasts of burden and rarely ridden. If you wish to use your own saddle it is not necessary to bring it with you since saddles are sold near the Shah Hamdan Mosque in Srinagar. They can easily be resold once you complete your trek.

In choosing a pony, if you should be so fortunate as to have a choice considering the limited number available, pay close attention to the rear and withers. Otherwise you will have an uncomfortable time riding. Forget whatever you know about horses when viewing these animals as they fly in the face of our preconceptions and are unbelievably nimble and surefooted.

If you decide to entrust yourself to such a 'disguised deer' do not try to steer them as they find their own way with remarkable certainty. If you do want to direct the pony with the reins (they do not seem to understand hints on the shanks),

give a gentle indication and allow one or two seconds reaction time. They're not machines with instantaneous reactions! Over-strenuous tugging at the reins leads to defensive resistance.

Allow the ponies sufficiently long rest stops and opportunities to relax. The animals don't always find enough food at overnight halting places (at least in Zanskar) so they are allowed to wander in search of food at night. Don't blame the pony drivers if it takes time to round them up in the morning.

The midday stop should, if possible, be at a place where ponies can graze. Unload them at this time and remove the saddles. You will see the ponies roll on their backs to reduce the flatulence caused by the tight belly band. The pause should not be too short or else, further down the trail, the docile beasts may suddenly decide to throw off their load or rider and settle down to some serious grazing.

Bear in mind that the smell of westerners is still unusual to Zanskari horses, so a local pony leader can be very reassuring for the animals. If you ride alone it is important to tether your pony during stops, otherwise it will gallop off home at the first opportunity.

The lightly tinkling bells around the necks of Zanskari horses drown out the noise of falling stones and reassure the animals. Despite such precautions against panic, ponies sometimes fall, as happened on our trek from Zangla to Nerag (see Padum-Lamayuru trek) when our horse was drowned. This is naturally seen as a bad omen for the trip and porters and pony drivers may desert you after such an accident. Financial compensation (reckon on between Rs 1000 and Rs 2000) for the dead animal will help as it is often the pony driver's sole possession.

In general, Zanskari horses and porters are more reliable than those from Kashmir. For example, the rope suspension bridges at Padum constitute an insurmountable obstacle for Suru Valley horses on a trek to Zanskar. You will have to switch to

Zanskari horses which come from Thonde or Zangla, as these can get across frightening bridges. Also, many porters from the Kashmir valleys are unwilling to go beyond Padum since they are unused to the high altitude passes (5000 metres) on the treks to Lamayuru, Leh or Manali.

At Rangdum, porters (who will carry 15 kg) cost about Rs 30 a day and ponies about Rs 45 plus Rs 5 for the pony man. The ponies will carry about 50 kg. At Sanku and Pannikar porters and ponies are slightly cheaper. Kargil will probably be cheaper again although the price there is variable.

Getting There & Away

It is possible to visit Zanskar without trekking by using different modes of transport on the Kargil-Padum road.

The bus service can be very erratic but basically a (usually crowded) bus does the trip twice a week. Check with the tourist office in either place for information about schedules and fares. It cost me Rs 56 each way.

Finding a private truck can mean a faster and more comfortable trip. Again the tourist offices might help you find one, otherwise ask around. Expect to pay between Rs 70 and Rs 100 and be sure that you are paying for a seat in the cabin and not simply a space in the back of the truck.

Hiring a jeep is very expensive due to the high fuel cost – about Rs 4000 for a round trip.

Depending on the condition of the road and other delays, the trip takes from one-and-a-half to two days.

Treks to/from Zanskar

Zanskar is often pronounced as Zanhar and still appears on many maps as Zaskar

– one of those Victorian era errors which cartographers have perpetuated. There are many routes leading into Zanskar, despite the region's isolation. The two most used routes are those from Kargil and from Manali to Padum, but there are other routes less well known.

PAHALGAM (Kashmir)-PANNIKAR (Suru Valley)

An eight-day trek continuing on from the Amarnath Cave trek and described in the Trekking in Kashmir chapter.

DRASS-SANKU (Suru Valley)

A three-day trek from the Drass Valley directly into the Suru Valley, bypassing Kargil. It is suitable as a Zanskar trek, a Drass-Sanku-Pannikar-Pahalgam trek or simply as a Drass-Sanku-Kargil mini-trek.

KARGIL-PADUM

Although the Kargil-Padum road was completed in the early '80s the severe

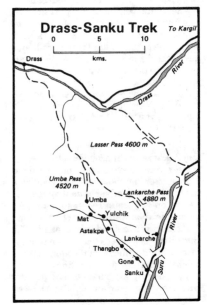

winter of '83 knocked much of it out. Even at the best of times it's a rough road suitable only for the hardiest of vehicles. If the road is not under repairs and the bridges over the tributaries of the Stod are OK, the route will be passable from early June to late October.

If the road between Namsuru and Parkachik is open, and a vehicle is available, it is possible to go from Kargil to the Pensi La in one day and thus shorten the first four days of the trek detailed, to one. (See Ladakh & Zanskar map in Ladakh chapter.)

Day 1: Kargil-Namsuru

The first day consists of preparation in Kargil, then a bus or jeep trip to Namsuru. Beyond Kargil do not follow the Leh road, which crosses the Suru at Chanchi over a metal bridge, but turn right into the Suru Valley. The route goes past the Hotel d'Zojila and for 15 km is surfaced, continuing over Grantung to the village of Rispong (20 km), which has a mosque.

The route continues past Martodas, Skininurai and Sanskritwe (Sanskarwe) to Sanku (Sankoo). Sanku was once the end of the bus route, 42 km from Kargil, and has a school and Dak Bungalow. The road switches to the righthand side of the river four km past Sanku and continues for 7½ km before changing back to the lefthand side towards Namsuru. From Sanku to Namsuru you pass through the villages of Kur, Phokra, Partik and Yoljok.

Day 2: Namsuru-Pannikar-Parkutse

Horses and porters can be hired in Namsuru or Pannikar but it is a good idea to book horses in advance as they may all be out on the trail. The road continues along the river valley, but the trekking route cuts off the wide river bend. The Suru River is crossed over a large wooden bridge near to Namsuru (3480 metres).

The route climbs over the town of Pannikar in zig-zag curves to a ridge, from which the Nun and Kun massif can be seen

to the south-east. Note that on the road to Pannikar roads marked 'impassable' may only be partially blocked by landslides and can be carefully crossed.

Most of the horses hired in the Namsuru-Pannikar region for trekking in Zanskar will be hired from Kashmiris because this is where the last main settlement of Indo-Aryans and Muslims is to be found.

Beyond the ridge of Pannikar the trekking route winds down to Parkutse where there is a good camping spot with fresh grass. Here you meet the road again, and until the Rangdum Gompa the road runs along the northern river bank.

Day 3: Parkutse-Parkachik-Yuldo-Rangdum Gompa

Parkachik is the approach base for the Nun Glacier and the last Muslim village en route to Padum.

Between Parkachik and the next camping place at Gulmatang there is some absolutely breathtaking scenery in this practically uninhabited valley. On the other side of the river the Ganri Glacier extends directly from the Nun and Kun saddle to the river below. It's coloured green from the high copper content in the subsoil (Zan means copper, skar means valley). The Kargil region is rich in other minerals too – chromite, sulphur, limestone, borax, soda and gold have been extracted from certain rivers.

Closer to Gulmatang, opposite the Shafat Glacier, is a fantastic view to the right of the Nun and Kun massif. The Nun peak is approached from the village of Tangole, the Kun peak from Shafat. Past Gulmatang the road continues through Zulichok, then past the ruins of the village of Shakar on the left – depopulated some years ago by smallpox.

Yuldo, six km before the Rangdum Gompa, is the first town with a Zanskari population (there are about 10 houses). Travellers are likely to get a friendly welcome. If you do not wish to continue by car to Padum or Karsha, leave your vehicle here and take native Zanskar ponies. Prices start from Rs 25 a day.

The journey from Yuldo to the gompa, visible in the distance perched on a steep, sugarloaf mountain, can be shortened by cutting across the many corners along the road, especially where it runs on the northern slope of the wide, gravel plain. You have to cross a network of rivers which meander through this plain and here, as elsewhere on this trek, the river crossings are easier early in the day as melting snow raises the rivers later in the day. About 40 Gelugpa (yellow-cap) monks live at the gompa.

According to an inscription the monastery was built about 250 years ago by Gelek Yashy Takpa during the reign of King Tsewang Namgyal of Ladakh. As in other monasteries, travellers are expected to make a donation.

The small mani walls here and towards Padum are more ornate than in Ladakh. Buddha reliefs are arranged on the stones and some of the stones are carved not only with the usual 'om mani padme hum' mantra but also with pictures of chortens and mandalas.

A field suitable for camping is about 1½ km from the gompa towards the Pensi La pass. Gnats from the nearby swamp can be a nuisance but, in compensation, edelweiss grows in profusion.

Day 4: Rangdum Gompa-Pensi La

By vehicle you can get to the Pensi La from Kargil in one day. It's about 25 km from the gompa to the 4401-metre Pensi La Pass into Zanskar. The road runs along the north-eastern slopes, giving beautiful views of the mountains to the west. If you have come all the way on foot and are reasonably acclimatised to the altitude, the climb to the Pensi La will be relatively easy. On your way to the pass you will come across stone heaps with prayer flags. Travellers often add their mani stones or small flags with a picture of a horse's head and the usual mantra.

There are 20 or so ponds at the top of the

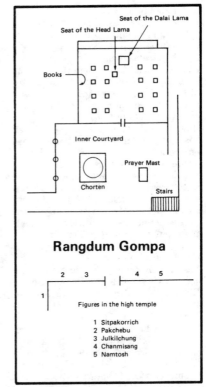

Rangdum Gompa

Figures in the high temple

1 Sitpakorrich
2 Pakchebu
3 Julkilchung
4 Chanmisang
5 Namtosh

pass where you should have no difficulty in finding a good camping place. The pass is an alpine high plain with firm, soft grass, rosemary and other alpine flowers and many red-brown marmots which pop up out of their holes to survey, warily, any intruders. The view is superb – to the south-east you can see the Takar and many other glaciers.

Several hours walk will take you to a glacier in the south-west side valley but beware of the river which, due to the melting snow, may be fordable in the morning but impossible in the afternoon. The summit at the end of the valley, of which only the peak can be seen, is 7072 metres high while the mountain to the north stands at 6873 metres. There are many unnamed peaks in the area, waiting for intrepid mountaineers to be the first to climb them.

The descent from the Pensi La into the Stod Valley is steeper than the climb up from the Rangdum Gompa, but not too difficult. The road winds about with many hairpin turns, which can be cut across on foot, to the river below. Wild rhubarb can be seen growing on the slopes. The usual trekking route follows the road on the left bank of the Stod (or Doda). There is possibly a bridge over the river now. The grass at the foot of the Pensi La is a good pasturage and this is a fine camping spot, although Trakkur, shortly before the crossing of the Chinzum (Ghinzilin) is also to be recommended. Another good camping place is Chumkurmu (3920 metres).

Day 5: Pensi La-Abran

Past Chumkurmu is a spectacular but short ravine which the Chanu (Chinu) River, coming in from the left (north), has cut through a ridge. A road bridge has been built over the ravine and a temporary bridge leads down to the river and over a bridge to the other bank, up to the river terraces. The left bank route continues through Aksho (3750 metres), Chibra, crosses a tributary of the Stod and finally reaches Abran (3700 metres), the first village of the Zanskar Valley.

Day 6: Abran-Phe

From Abran to Phe, where there is a small, deserted gompa above the village, you pass the interesting villages of Hamiling and Kygam, where there are only a few houses. The route is now generally heading south-east.

Opposite Phe (3600 metres), the Bardur Valley opens into the broad Stod Valley. Because the Stod cannot be crossed at this point you must go further towards Padum to the Tungri Bridge, then back along the other side of the Stod if you wish to visit the Bardur Valley and the Zongkhul Gompa or to trek over the Umasi La to

Kishtwar (see Tungri-Zongkhul Gompa Roundtrip or the Padum-Kishtwar Trek).

From Phe a route goes north-east to the Rulakung La and then turns down to Hanumil on the Zanskar River on the way to Padum or past the Lingshot Gompa and on to Lamayuru (see Padum-Lamayuru Trek) on the Kargil-Leh road.

Day 7: Phe-Padum

The road to Padum leads through the villages of Rantak Shuk, Shamuni and Tarkand to Tungri. A new road will probably be built from Tungri to the Karsha Gompa, currently a three-hour journey on foot. The footpath to Padum runs past Tungri, over the sturdy wooden bridge (with stone supports) to the righthand side of the Stod and then past Sani.

Apart from Karsha, the Sani (Sanee) Gompa is the most important monastery near Padum. The gompa is unusual in that it is not built on a hill or mountainside but on flat ground and is encircled by a stone wall in which chortens are mounted at intervals. You enter this 25-monk, red-cap monastery through a gate chorten with prayer mills. It leads to a Latho, or god house.

The monastery walls have the usual symbols to ward off evil spirits and, for the same purpose, there is a goat's head filled with jewels, fortune-bringing mantras and prayer cards with *om mani padme hum* written on them. The monastery is subject to the control of the Stagna Turku in Ladakh.

If you happen to be there at the right time, or provide a suitable donation, you may see the long ceremony in which the symbols of fortune are consecrated. The ceremony involves a goat's head being sizzled in a large pot. The value of the 'garnishings' which the monks add to the pot during the proceedings depends upon the prosperity of the person who donated the head and for whom it is supposed to bring good fortune. Look out for the goats' heads which hang outside practically

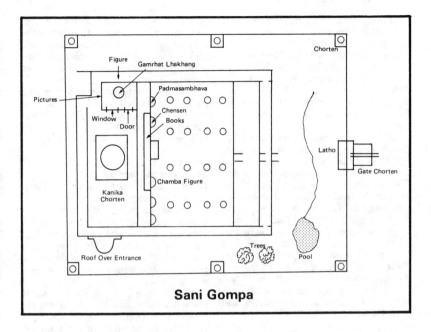

Sani Gompa

every house in Leh and other towns. In the normal course of events this symbol is renewed annually.

A small ditch, leading to a temple, goes through the gompa courtyard and delivers enough water for the trees, a rarity in Zanskar, which grow there.

The Dukhang, with its 16 columns, houses a Chamba, a Chenren and a Padmasambhava figure amongst others. The Gonkhang is a small room behind the altar and is worth seeing for it contains an old figure of the Cho Rimpoche and a new bookshelf in lattice work for the holy writings of *Kandshur*. Upstairs are the rooms of the head lama, a storage room for tankas and, on the left side, the room of Dorje Chan.

More interesting than these first-storey rooms is the old part of the gompa, which can be reached through the corridors which run right around the monastery. In this low and dark passage lie many small

Tsatsas on the floor. The corridor ends in another inner courtyard, past the large *Kanika* chorten where Buddhist relics are preserved.

To the right of the chorten, squeezed between the main building of the gompa and the corridor, is the *Gamshot Lhakhang* in which Padmasambhava is supposed to have dwelt for five years. A door from the inner courtyard leads into the room. If it is locked you can still look through the window and see the Padmasambhava figure in the middle and historical scenes in half-relief on both sides.

North-west, outside the fenced-in area of the gompa, is one of the most important cremation places in Zanskar or Ladakh – well known on account of its two-metre high dark grey boulder – on which a relief of the Maitriya has been carved. It shines from the sacrificial oil which monks and pilgrims pour over the Buddha image. Other smaller, crumbled stones can be seen in the semi-circle and the picture is completed by a prayer mast with fluttering prayer flags.

Ponies can be hired from Rs 30 per day and porters from Rs 10 to Rs 25. In contrast to the ponies of the Kashmir Valley, these are suitable for a trek through Karsha up the left side of the Zanskar, past the Lingshot Gompa to Lamayuru.

An alternative stretch from Pensi La to Tungri leads up the right side of the Stod, at the foot of the Takar Glacier, south-east through Chibra, Chukarpa, Denya and Tangar, then opposite from Phe into the Bardur Valley where the route merges, at the Zongkhul Gompa, described in the Tungri-Zongkhul Gompa Roundtrip and Padum-Kishtwar Trek. Cross the Bardur River, follow it downstream on the right bank and turn again at Ating into the Stod Valley which you can follow to Padum. This route from the Pensi La to the Tungri Bridge is shorter than that on the left bank of the Stod, but is much less travelled and little known.

MANALI-PADUM

The 10-day trek from Manali to Padum can take one of two routes. One goes from Darcha over the 5100-metre Shingo La pass to Kargiakh, while the alternative route continues from Darcha along the Leh Rd to a little beyond Sarai Kilang then turns north-west and crosses the 5345-metre Phirtse La pass, eventually meeting the first route a little north of Kargiakh. At one time it was difficult to take the first route without special permission but this no longer appears to be so.

Manali-Darcha

There has been a summer bus service across the 3650-metre Rothang Pass from Manali to Keylong and on to Darcha for several years but, as on the Srinagar-Leh road, travellers often have to wait for the pass to be cleared and the road opened each summer. In Manali, John Bannon organises tours and vehicles for this trip. The surfaced road ends at Darcha and the gravel road which continues north-east, all the way to Leh, is suitable for four-wheel drive vehicles only and is only open to the military.

From Darcha the 5100-metre Shingo La pass leads directly into the Zanskar Valley – see Alternative 2. To trek right through the Zanskar Valley to Lamayuru or Kargil will take from 16 to 20 days.

Alternative 1
Day 1: Darcha-Mane Bar

Darcha, at 3300 metres, is a control post where the police chief will want to see passes. Westwards, on the bank of the Bhaga, the good road continues to the next rest place at Sarai Valley where there is a small lake (not possible to swim in) to the left of the road with a good view of the ravine. This is a good spot for an early midday rest.

A little beyond here the road crosses to the left bank of the river by a wooden bridge, then continues to Pataiso. The river terraces broaden out to a rolling, grassy plain while the river runs in a deep ravine. Topachani will be reached late in the afternoon. Fast walkers can continue to Zingzing Bar or Mane Bar (4150 metres).

Day 2: Mane Bar-Sarai Kilang

This walk crosses the Baralacha La, but although the route starts almost at the pass height, the climb to the top should not be under-estimated. The Baralacha La is a double pass to the east and south. Even the lower, eastward pass is, at 4891 metres, higher than Mont Blanc, the highest mountain in Europe, and twice the height of Mt Kosciusko, the highest mountain in Australia! To the right the pass is close to the Suruf Lake and in good weather you can see snow-capped peaks rising from 5000 to 6000 metres high. The southern pass is at 5100 metres and gives a view further southwards. The route continues to the left bank of the Yaman River, which has its source in the

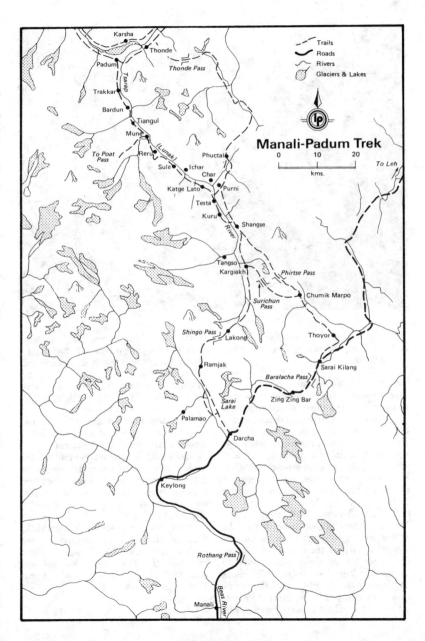

Manali-Padum Trek

Suru Valley, to the Sarai Kilang (4460 metres) camping place, a grassy oasis with a brook.

Day 3: Sarai Kilang-Debni

An early start is advisable. The route, now just a track, fords the river and continues until the Keylong River, entering from the left, obstructs the route. As with all river crossings in Zanskar the earlier you cross, the lower the water level will be. Take no risks as this is a dangerous crossing. Running shoes should be worn for the crossing since they give a more secure footing on the slippery rocks.

Further along the left bank of the Yaman is a wide, grassy plain. If you take a short detour to the right to the edge of the river terraces there is a view of the deep Loess ravine of the Yaman. Beware of the crumbling ravine edge. The route continues over the plain into the valley then gradually uphill towards the Phirtse La pass, the highest pass on the trek. The 4280-metre Thoyer is reached first, then the walk continues on the right bank of the Lingti Chu, following it upstream and across some deep side streams. After some more up and down walking you reach Debni (4360 metres), the next overnight halt.

Day 4: Debni-Chumik Marpo (4600 metres)

Again it is wise to start early in order to cross the Kamirup, which enters the river from the left, at Kyonon. By midday the route climbs over a ridge to the right of the river – it's cut through by a cleft. Past here is the next river crossing as the Trukkar enters from the left of the Phirtse La Glacier.

Trukkar is a rest stop but you should continue on to the overnight stop at the foot of the pass. From here a route branches off to the left over Kurziakpulo and the Surichun La to Kargiakh, but it doesn't gain much.

Day 5: Chumik Marpo-Shingsan
(4460 metres)
Once again you should start early for this fine walk over the Phirtse La (5435 metres). On the pass crest there is a mini-glacier to the left and to the right a mani stone with prayer flags. Past here is a small, rocky peak which gives a better view than the pass itself. On clear days it extends to the Karakoram Range in the north. The route then descends steeply into the valley of the Phirtse Chu to the camping place in front of a rubble slope.

Day 6: Shingsan-Kargiakh or Purni
The rubble slope has to be climbed first. By noon you reach a mountain from where the Zanskar Valley is visible to the west and the valley of the Kargiakh Chu to the south. The latter joins here with the Phirtse Chu at Anokh, one of the three tributaries of the Zanskar.

A smaller path zig-zags steeply down to the valley. The route leads to the right into the village of Shangse, with long mani walls and a small gompa on a slope up to the right. Here the route splits. You can turn south to Kargiakh (4060 metres – see Alternative 2) and over the Shingo La back to Darcha, or continue north to Zanskar.

A wooden bridge crosses to the left side of the river from Shangse and you continue through the villages of Kuru, Testa and Yal before a second wooden bridge, with stone supports, leads back to the right bank. Above the bridges it is possible to camp in front of Purni (3750 metres).

A second route also leads to Purni from Shangse, keeping to the right bank all the way, but it is not so interesting because there are no villages.

Day 7: Purni-Phuctal Gompa
From here the trail again follows the left bank of the Tsarap Chu, the main tributary of the Zanskar, to a swinging but stable suspension bridge – gloves are recommended when crossing. Further along the other bank a surprising view presents itself at a bend in the path – the 500-year-old Phuctal Gompa. The monastery is like a honeycomb, cut into a rock under a gigantic grotto, and has 70 yellow-cap monks. The name means 'through cave'.

The library, three large and one smaller prayer rooms, the kitchens, abbot's chamber, chorten and the grave of Gangsem Sherap Sanpo, who founded Phuctal, Lekir and Rangdum, are all worth seeing. In the caves over the monastery is a waterhole, the level of which never changes. The water is said to have healing properties. There is also a stone tablet left by the Hungarian Alexander Csoma de Koros, one of the first explorers of Tibet. He spent time here from 1826 to 1827.

Day 8: Phuctal Gompa-Katge Lato
There is a route back along the west bank of the river to Char but it is not recommended because the Char bridge is in a dangerous condition. It is better to return along the left bank to Purni, cross the bridge and go further to the right over a ridge, past which is the Katge Lato (3800 metres) camping place with a view over the deteriorated Char bridge, far below.

Day 9: Katge Lato-Reru
There is again a lot of variety on the day's walk. There are many picturesque villages on the bank opposite Char – first Abnop then Dorzong, green oases in the monotonous grey-brown, and finally the Ichar castle, reached by a hanging bridge across the valley. Certain places, with rubble hills and steep, sandy slopes, call for careful treading. Three hours further walking brings you to a camping place opposite Reru (3680 metres), in a side valley to the left of the main route, on green grass with a brook.

Day 10: Reru-Padum
From the camping place the route climbs to a plateau and over a bridge to the town of Reru with an interesting gateway

chorten. The route continues past the town on the wide river terraces towards Mune behind which there is a gompa on a steep hill, but beware of the red-cap monks' ferocious dog!

From here a route leads to the left to the 6150-metre Poat La pass, the highest and most difficult pass in Zanskar. The route crosses a glacier.

Continuing towards Padum (3500 metres), cross Tema and reach the Charmoche Kore camping ground. The route continues past Tiangul to a large rock from where the Bardun Gompa is visible. This gompa was founded by Shabdru, who also founded the Hemis Gompa in Ladakh and later went to Bhutan. There are only a handful of monks working on the reconstruction of the partially ruined gompa. The climb up to the roof is worthwhile. The gompa's principal image is a Gandhara statue of the Buddha Maitriya, which is less than a metre in height and is said to have spoken.

Near the gompa is a good camping place where a spring issues from the rocks. Two-to-three hours further on, with the river always to the right, you reach the wide plains of Zanskar with picturesque villages on both sides of the valley, and ahead Padum, the administrative centre of Zanskar.

Alternative 2
This description covers the route between Kargiakh and Darcha when travelling south. You can also take this route across the Shingo La heading north from Manali to Padum.

It's also possible to make an eight-to-10 day Darcha roundtrip – see Alternative 1.

Heading south, Kargiakh is the last inhabited settlement on this route until you reach Chikka (or Chica), shortly before Darcha. From Kargiakh (4060 metres) you must head upstream as early as possible to the river crossing, above the point where a small stream joins it. You can camp by the mani walls or further

uphill at Lakong (4450 metres). Here the valley branches out and a small valley to the right leads to the Shingo La at 5100 metres.

Day 2: Shingo La-Ramjak
The ascent to the top of the pass should be undertaken early in the morning. There is a superb view of the surrounding mountains from the crest of the pass, on which snow lies all year round. The highest peak, directly to the south, is 6797 metres. The descent from the pass follows the river on its right bank. The route to the next camping place, below the visible south peak at a stone hut called Ramjak (4270 metres), is not difficult.

Day 3: Ramjak-Darcha
Set out early in the morning to the Barai Nallah which comes from the right, and cross the Shingo La River at this point. If the snowfall in the last year has been heavy it is possible to cross by snow bridges as late as July but if the snow has melted you must wade across. The river is wild and rapid so this is probably the most difficult point of the trip.

Continue along the left side of the high valley to a good camping place where the highest trees grow at 3700 metres. A small bridge leads there over a raging mountain brook. Another brook, with a waterfall, branches off and here you can find another camping spot. Yet another can be found past a wooden bridge over a deep ravine. From here it is only about three hours to Darcha. Chikka, a couple of hours before Darcha, is the first habitation after Kargiakh.

PADUM-LAMAYURU
Alternative 1 – via Zangla & Nerag
A local guide is an absolute necessity on this route.

Day 1: Padum-Thonde Refer to Day 1 of the Padum Roundtrip later in this chapter.

Souvenir seller at Lamayuru Gompa

At Kharmapu you can camp by the river, a few km from growing willows so that burning fuel need not be brought. You can also camp at the foot of the double pass of Nerag La, beyond Kharmapu, but although this allows you to reach Nerag in one day the camp is at 4900 metres, just below the pass, and at this height fuel for the fire and fodder for the horses is not readily available.

Day 4: Kharmapu-foot of the Nerag La
This route is very difficult and Zanskari guides and porters are essential. At several places you have to wade across rivers and the trail crosses steep rubble hills above wild mountain brooks. Paths must be cleared (don't forget shovels) for the horses to find their footing. At one point the route leads through a tunnel-like rock passage in the bed of a brook and subsequently under an ice cornice, even in high summer. Past this rough stretch the actual ascent to the pass also requires some skill.

Day 5: Nerag La-Nerag
The view from the Nerag La, over the village 1500 metres below and to the mountain range on the other side of the Zanskar, is superb. Shortly before Nerag you can again find burnable wood and there are some suitable camping spots above the village. Pasturage for the horses and fresh water are also on hand.

Day 6: Nerag-Yulchung-Singi La-Photosar
Two km below Nerag is a wooden bridge across the Zanskar which is suitable for horses. Immediately on the other side of the Zanskar (3400 metres), which here flows eastwards in a deep-cut bed towards Nimmu, the ascent towards the Singi La begins. The first saddle is at 3990 metres, the second at 3930 metres. Near Yulchung the route bends left to the Lingshot Gompa (see Padum-Lamayuru trek, Alternative 2).

At Yulchung one can marvel at the irrigation techniques of the Zanskaris.

Day 2: Thonde-Honia
As far as Zangla the route is the same as for the Padum Roundtrip. From Zangla past Honia to Nerag is difficult, especially for horses, and should be traversed in late summer if the previous winter had heavy snow. Rain can also make this route impassable. Above the small village of Honia is a small spring and you should overnight here whether you have come in a one-day march from Padum or have already spent a night at Thonde.

Day 3: Honia-over the Shing La-Kharmapu
The steep ascent to the Shing La pass begins after Honia. The first stretch can be dangerous due to a deep cut brook which leads directly along the steep slope. In '77 I lost my packhorse with all my personal luggage here. Past the 4500-metre high Shing La you enter a valley with coarse limestone formations.

Above the village, melted ice-water from the mountain brooks is collected in ponds and warmed through insulation, then conducted into the struggling small fields with their poor soil.

There is a grand panorama to the east with waterfalls cascading down the rock walls on the other side of the Singi La (Lion Pass) at 4850 metres. The trekking path wanders around the western valley slope through many side valleys. Mountain wanderers can take a shortcut on the northern rubble slopes by cutting across the serpentine curves on the route leading to the valley.

The valley floor is quite marshy due to the brook flowing eastwards from Photosar into the Photang River. In summer it is richly grown and provides good grazing pasture. The route leaves the western side of the valley and crosses a small pass, then through a mountain ridge between the valley it came out of and the Photang Valley in which lies Photosar. If you arrive late do not go straight into the village but camp on the southern slope of the Photang River, opposite Photosar, where there is also pasturage for horses.

Day 7: Photosar-Shirshi La-Hanuputta

According to our Zanskari guide, Photosar means salt cave. It stands at 4100 metres on a small plateau on the other side of the eastward flowing Photang River. The name touches on the fact that during the rain so much salt is washed out of the rock wall past Photosar that the fields around the village slowly become infertile due to this mineralised irrigation.

Sited 50 metres above the river, Photosar is an attractive place even when the peace is disturbed by loudspeakers, playing music from All India Radio. Upstream from Photosar, to the west, is the bridge over the Photang River.

The route to Lamayuru follows the Photang-Drogpo to the west, first on the southern banks then, after three km, on the northern. The route leads through terraced fields then turns north-east into

a side valley of the Photang River. En route to the pass you can see marmots and rock ptarmigans. It's only a short trek to the Shirshi La (or Sirsir La) and only the last hundred metres is steep and strenuous.

Above the top of the pass you find, as on every pass in Ladakh and Zanskar, a Latho (god house) with coloured prayer flags and mani stones. The flags show the head of a horse in the middle, and every Buddhist traveller will leave behind a flag with a mantra printed on it. Do not collect these as souvenirs under any circumstances! The descent from the pass into the valley of the Tang is steep but not very difficult. From here there are two routes to Lamayuru: the first is via Hanuputta and Wanla while the second is through the valley of the Shillakong to Wanla.

The route via Hanuputta descends from the Shirshi La through the valley of the Tang on the right river bank, high on the slope to the north-east. After several km it crosses a bridge to the left bank where the river is wider and the path better. As in most Zanskari villages it is difficult to obtain food supplies in Hanuputta.

Day 8: Hanuputta-Wanla-Shilla-Prikiti La-Lamayuru

The route from Hanuputta to Wanla is difficult and not always passable, especially for pack animals. Past Hanuputta the route leads down to the river and forces through a narrow spot to where you can ford the river. A little later it climbs above the river to a place where it cuts deeply through the rock. At times the path ends at the water and you must continue along the bank to find a place shallow enough to cross to the other side. The path then winds steeply up the rocks where the ponies clamber like deer.

Heading north-west there are dangerous stretches where the ponies must be unloaded and led across step-by-step. The process repeats itself for a couple of hours – unload, lead the ponies across, carry the loads across, load the ponies, continue on. Finally the mountains open and the path becomes much more hospitable.

The next village offers the inviting shade of apricot trees and the route then leads along a precipice and descends to the bottom of the valley. Here one goes past field after field and large settlements until Wanla is reached.

A left turn takes you into the Shillakong Valley and shortly past the village of Shilla you turn right (north). Early in the morning a part of the route in the narrow, barren valley to the 3900-metre Prikiti La (Lizard Pass) is still in shadow – for both trekker and pony this is very pleasant. By noon the climb in the strong sun can become an ordeal. From the Prikiti La the route leads north-east into the Lamayuru Valley then, once cultivated fields have been reached, a short way to the west.

The Lamayuru monastery is first seen to the right on a sugarloaf mountain. The trail leads westwards from the monastery hill through the village of Lamayuru to the Fatu La-Nimmu-Leh road, on which from the Prikiti La you can already see trucks crawling. Be careful – Zanskari horses are not accustomed to traffic and scare easily. The noise from movie cameras can also frighten them! You should unload the horses as quickly as possible on the road. From here you can take a bus or truck to Leh or to Kargil and Srinagar.

Alternative Route – Day 7 to 9: Photosar-Shirshi La-over the Tang River-Niuche La-into the Shillakong Valley-Shilla-Prikiti La-Lamayuru

If the Hanuputta-Wanla route is impassable then this route may be an alternative as it crosses the Tang River (4500 metres) past the Shirshi La, whereas the Hanuputta route follows this river.

Cross the river as early as possible in the morning since the river is very rapid after midday. The trail then goes north-west into the side valley opposite. If you get here in the afternoon you should seek a camping spot with pasturage for the horses as the last few km to the 5050-metre Niuche La are barren and terrible for camping.

On the other side of the pass, to the north-west, is another camping possibility at 4450 metres. The route continues down into the Shillakong River Valley which it follows to Shilla. This 20 to 25 km route is unique since the valley is so narrow that at times you have to go along the river bed! The mineral layers in this ravine indicate the dislocation caused by the creation of the mountain range.

Shortly before Shilla there are three unstable wooden bridges, one of which is particularly bad. The route crosses a stone bridge with a Latho to a warm spring which is said to have healing properties. From the top of the pass you can reach Shilla (3300 metres) in one day, from where the route is the same as the Hanuputta-Wanla alternative.

Alternative 2 – via Lingshot Gompa
Day 1: Padum-Pishu

You can go via Rubruk to Yalong (Yulung) then Karsha or via Sani, the Tungri Bridge and then downstream along the Stod which is altogether a six-hour trek to Karsha. From Karsha continue on the left bank of the Zanskar to where the Stod joins with the Tsarap Lingti Chu and goes through Ridam to Pishu. Pishu is six hours from Karsha and there are camping spots with grass for the pack animals by the river.

Past Karsha the fields stop and the infrequently travelled path is bordered by sandstone. The mountains creep closer to the trail – constant erosion has carved them into fantastic shapes and the geological layers are easy to observe. Before the village of Pishu the banks get narrower and narrower and at Pishu you can cross the river by a rope bridge, as related in the Padum Roundtrip.

Day 2, 3 & 4: Pishu-Lingshot Gompa

Past Pishu the route leads at first along the bank of the Zanskar until the village of

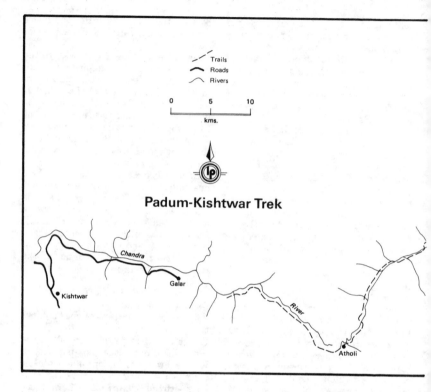

Padum-Kishtwar Trek

Pidmu (Pigmu or Pittu) is reached after four to five hours. Some tributaries of the Zanskar must be crossed but they should present no problem. The path then runs very close to a brook, so close that you can bargain on getting wet feet at some stage. You can stay overnight near the small village of Hanumil (Hanomul) past where the route runs through grassland. A route branches off to the left towards Rulakung and over the Rulakung La to Phe (see Kargil-Padum trek).

Here the valley narrows, the path is hewn through rocks, the bank is steep and at one point, which the rocks overhang, ponies can only be led unloaded. Once past this difficult point a short climb leads

over a rubble hill while to the right the Zanskar River storms past the practically vertical bank. The trail continues along the steep slopes, over which the native ponies go with great certainty.

After a few hours the path leads left to a small pass which is indicated on some maps as the Purfi La. The pass is only steep over the last one hundred metres. On the north side the trail makes tight bends through grass slopes and bushes, then turns right and continues over broken rocks and rubble. At a sharp bend the river and a ruined bridge can be seen far below.

Using a climbing rope and poplars, which grow on the bank, you can build a

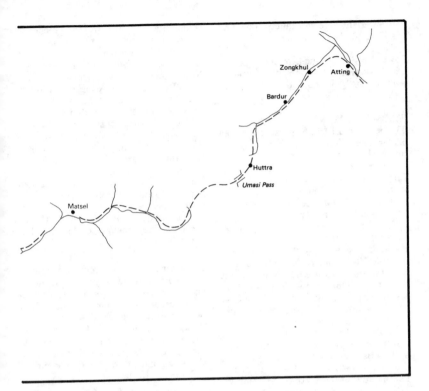

makeshift bridge at a narrower point. The pack animals can, unloaded, swim the river at a wider, less rapid point. On the other side the climb begins at a small pass and at this point the trail leads along a steep canyon wall then gradually gets easier. There is grass and a good camping spot in the valley below.

Continuing upstream towards Lingshot there are snow bridges which can still be crossed in mid-summer. After a while the valley widens and the horses have no more strenuous climbing. The path then turns right and soon the pass saddle is visible with the usual mani stones and prayer flags. From the top of the Hamalun La (or Hanuma La) there is a fine view of the Lingshot Gompa on the other side of the valley. The descent, over sand hills, is steep and several hills and rises must be crossed during the descent into the valley.

After a few hours the village of Lingshot and the Lingshot Gompa are reached. Lingshot (also Lingshed) has 60 monks and is famous in Zanskar for its school of painting. In the gompa are many superb paintings made with bright mineral pigments.

Day 5: Lingshot-Yulchung
Past Lingshot the route leads eastwards over mountains and passes to Yulchung.

Turning right here will take you back to the Zanskar Valley via Nerag.

Day 6, 7 & 8: Yulchung-Lamayuru

The last three days are the same as Alternative 1 for the Padum-Lamayuru trek.

PADUM-KISHTWAR

This trek from Padum, passing over the 5234-metre Umasi La, can only be undertaken with local porters. Since most of the porters do not understand any English it is worth discussing the route with the porters before departure. The tourist officer will interpret. One porter per person is recommended.

Zanskari porters are faster, harder working and generally friendlier than Kashmiri pony drivers so there will undoubtedly be many more trekkers using Zanskaris in the future. The price is about Rs 25 per day for a porter. They will only set out for the Umasi La in good, fog-free, weather so you should also allow Rs 10 per day for waiting time.

No great difficulties are experienced on this trek so long as you are fit, healthy and acclimatised to the altitude. The ascent to the Umasi La pass is steeper from the Padum side but shorter than the Kishtwar side. Leggings are recommended because of the snow on the Umasi La and it is also wise to have a waterproof tent. Bring food supplies from Padum although you can also get some food in Matsel and Atholi.

Day 1: Padum-Ating

Do not hire horses, which are inappropriate for this trek. Instead, see the tourist officer for porters. It's a pleasant march to Ating with a bridgeless glacier river to cross – the earlier in the day the better.

Day 2: Ating-shortly before Ratrat

Turn from the Stod Valley into the south-west side valley of the Bardun and arrive at the Zongkhul Gompa or ravine fortress. The foundations of this monastery are attributed to the abbot Naropa, whose ceremonial dagger in the rocks of Zongkhul attracts many pilgrims. The monastery belongs to the red-cap sect and had 20 monks about 15 to 20 years ago. Now no more than two or three are seldom seen. The route from Ating leads directly to the monastery and takes about two to three hours along a meandering path.

The monastery is built directly on the rock wall surrounded by about 10 stone houses which, from a distance, blend in to the grey background. Like the Hemis Gompa in Ladakh, the Zongkhul Gompa has an eagle's nest which can be reached in about 10 minutes from the gompa. This offers superb views from the roof terrace. It's an easy seven-hour climb to the excellent Ganra rest place which also has a wonderful view.

Day 3: Umasi La-shortly before Bhuswas

A 5½-hour climb takes you over a glacier and a snowfield to the top of the pass with its remarkable crest. On the other side of the somewhat easier descent you go through snowfields and then across another glacier. The walk to the camping spot, about an hour before Bhuswas, takes about 12 hours. There is a spring, a river and grass at the site.

Day 4: Bhuswas-Matsel

It's a pleasant eight-hour descent from Bhuswas to a police station but nothing will persuade Zanskari porters to go further than here and it is difficult to hire porters in Matsel (Machail or Machel). For about Rs 150 you can eventually hire a donkey to Kishtwar. Prices on this side of the pass are significantly higher.

Day 5: Matsel-Atholi

The river valley becomes increasingly narrow and the route more strenuous as it leads over an unbroken sequence of ascents and descents. Atholi is reached in the late afternoon and the police station commandant is hospitable. Beware of the gnats!

Top: Porter (RK)
Left: Campsite at Wadvan Valley (GW)
Right: Kashmiri horsemen (GW)

Top: Fatu La, highest point on the Srinagar to Leh road (BP)
Left: Lingshot Gompa, Zanskar (GW)
Right: Rafting on the lower Zanskar River (GW)

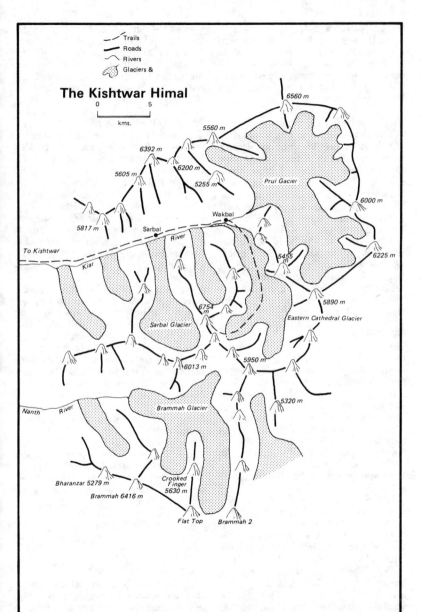

Trails
Roads
Rivers
Glaciers &

The Kishtwar Himal

0   5
kms.

6560 m

5560 m

6392 m

6200 m

5605 m

5255 m

Prul Gacier

6000 m

5817 m

Wakbal

Sarbal

River

5455 m

6225 m

To Kishtwar

Kiar

5890 m

6754 m

Sarbal Glacier

Eastern Cathedral Glacier

Nanth   River

6013 m

5950 m

5320 m

Brammah Glacier

Bharanzar 5279 m

Crooked
Finger
5630 m

Brammah 6416 m

Flat Top   Brammah 2

Day 6: Atholi-Shasho

As on the previous day the route is hard work. It takes from six to eight hours to reach the Shasho rest place – a small, dirty, uncared for site with three or four huts on the mountainside. A stay in the huts is not recommended.

Day 7: Shasho-Galar-Kishtwar

The route continues to climb and drop and the going is quite strenuous. During the monsoon it can be marshy and seem endless. Galar is reached after about seven hours and a road leads from here to Kishtwar. Work is in progress to extend this road from Galar back towards Atholi.

Two or three buses go daily to Kishtwar from Galar, a distance of about 30 km. If you leave Atholi very early and travel fairly fast you can get to Galar in one day. The last bus leaves Galar at about 5 pm. If you miss it you must overnight here and go to Kishtwar the next day. Long-distance buses leave Kishtwar at about 6 am for Srinagar and other places.

PADUM-NIMMU

This is a strenuous and hazardous five-day trek. The first section as far as Hanuputta is covered in the Padum-Lamayuru trek reports. Between Hanuputta and Wanla turn right into a side valley, north of the Zanskar mountain chain, and continue upstream over a pass and then down a brook which is a western side arm of the Zanskar River. You reach the Zanskar a few km to the north of the village of Chiling, with its chorten of Guru Padmasambhava, and follow the river's left bank to Nimmu.

A rope bridge crosses the Zanskar between Chiling and Nimmu so you can turn at Sumdo (the village where three rivers meet) into the Markha Valley. (See the Trekking in Ladakh chapter and the Padum-Leh trek report in this chapter.)

Near Nimmu, towards Leh and above the junction of the Zanskar and the Indus, is a sturdy bridge capable of taking pack animals across the Indus. The route then goes on the right bank of the Zanskar to the Markha Valley. The direct route from Nerag through the Zanskar Gorge to Nimmu is only possible in winter (January and February) on the ice of the river. This strenuous and hazardous trek takes about five days.

PADUM-LEH – Markha Valley

This hard but very rewarding trek takes you from Padum to Zangla as on the Padum-Lamayuru trek. At Zangla turn right to the Charcha La pass (5200 metres) and on to Tilta Sumdo via Tom Tokh. Here a path turns left towards Nimmu but you must turn right. After 12 to 15 km turn left towards Kurna Sumdo. To the right it goes via Lapurbo to Kurna. From Kurna Sumdo the route continues past the Ruberung La pass (5000 metres) for another day or two, to the Markha Gompa.

Here the route diverges: one route goes from the gompa to the right, past Hankar and in two days reaches Chokdo after which comes Hemis and finally along the Indus to Leh; the other route turns left from the Markha Gompa past Skiu, the Ganda La (or Kanda La) pass at 4800 metres and on to Rumbagh. From Rumbagh it crosses the 4880-metre Namlung Pass and on to Leh.

This difficult route is only recommended for the second half of August because from Zangla to Markha many crossings have to be made over large rivers. Often the water is chest high and by September it is once again too cold. See the Markha Valley trek in the Trekking in Ladakh chapter for details of the routes from Markha to Hemis or Spitok.

Days 1-2: Padum-Thonde-Zangla

As for the Padum roundtrip in this chapter.

Day 3: Zangla-Charcha Nullah

From Zangla walk north-east, ascending the Zumling River. During the day you may have to cross the river 20 or more times.

Day 4: Charcha Nullah-across Charcha La

It takes about four hours to ascend the pass which is nearly at 5000 metres and marked by a chorten. Descending from the pass you follow a narrow gorge, crossing a shallow stream several times, sometimes on ice bridges and avalanche debris. At one point the gorge is less than two metres wide for about 50 metres. This could be difficult if the water level in the stream is high. You need to carry additional water for the ascent of the pass. The camp site below the pass is at Tom Tokh Sumdo.

Day 5: Tom Tokh Sumdo-near Tilta Sumdo

This hard day's walk follows a very rough, rocky and unstable trail with many river crossings – between 20 and 30. The walk becomes much more difficult if the river is high or if there have been many recent rockfalls.

Day 6: Tilta Sumdo-below Ruberung La

Another hard day's walk with many river crossings to be made. The first 1½-hour walk to Tilta Sumdo involves a dozen crossings. Here the Khurna Cho flows in to form a main confluence and join the Zanskar River further to the north. Various *nullahs* (streams) join the river trail here. The turn-off for the Ruberung La is the second nullah from the left (north) after Tilta Sumdo.

Day 7: Ruberung La-Markha Valley

The ascent from here is up a narrow gorge with numerous other gorges joining it. It would be easy to take the wrong trail without a guide. The top of the pass, at 4900 metres, is reached after about three hours. From here the path is quite clear and descends to a stream which you follow for four or five hours down to the Markha River.

Day 8-10: Markha-Chokdo-Hemis

The final three days are covered in the Markha Valley trek report in the Trekking in Ladakh chapter.

PADUM

While the locals say Padum, foreigners generally say Padam. The capital of Zanskar, it stands on the southern part of a wide, fertile plain in which the Tsarap Lingti Chu (Lunak River) and the Stod (Doda) River join to form the Zanskar (Cham) River. The small township clings to a hillock, the site of an ancient palace and fort.

Unlike most other Zanskaris, who are practically all Buddhists, about 300 of Padum's roughly 1000 inhabitants are not Ladakhis but Indo-Aryans like the Baltis and Lahulis and are followers of the Sunnite Muslim sect. The division into these two completely different population groups is instantly recognisable by the clothing they wear.

The people are very hospitable but also shy. In the first four years after the re-opening of Zanskar to foreign visitors only a couple of hundred people passed through. Making contact with the children will result in an invitation into a house. If you wish to make a longer trek the administration or the tourist bureau will be happy to answer any questions and are very helpful with the hiring of horses (there are about 40 in Padum) or obtaining accommodation. An overnight stay in a private house in Padum will cost from Rs 10 to Rs 20 per person.

There are a few shops in Padum, like Mohammed Amid's, but only the basics are available and prices are high. The government buildings outside Padum include a morse radio station which, when necessary, can call for a military helicopter from Leh which can land near the Karsha Gompa on the other side of the Stod River.

The local water is milky-white and highly mineralised and even when boiled for tea is not very palatable.

In July and August stray monsoon clouds sometimes creep into Zanskar from the plains of India and heavy showers are not uncommon in the afternoon. Therefore the excursion to Karsha should be made in the morning.

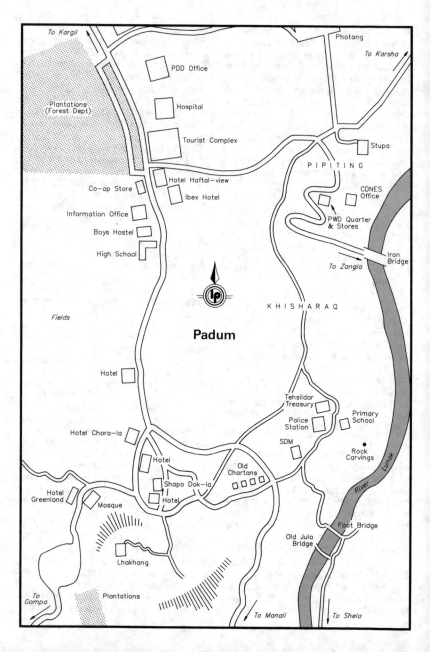

West of Padum, a good half-hour's climb, is the small Tagrimo Gompa with an interesting Dukhang with a stamped clay floor. The paintings on the side walls are, unlike most gompas, not directly on the wall but on tanka cloths.

Information

Padum has several hotels and a wide range of supplies is becoming available. Also, the tourist office is basically helpful with directions to nearby places of interest and for arranging horses. On arrival, you must register with the Tourist Department.

Things to See

Apart from being the administrative centre of Zanskar, sited amidst incredible landscapes, Padum itself offers little of interest. However, it is the base for a few fascinating excursions into the valley and several treks to the south and north of the Himalaya Range.

Monasteries can be visited near the township: Stagrims and Pubitury gompas are merely short walks away while the monastery of Saui involves a six km trip. Karsha, the largest and the most beautiful of Zanskar's monasteries, lies on the other side of the River Dodu, some two to three hours walking distance. This is a treasure-trove of Buddhist art, highlighted by the 500-year-old wall frescoes in the *Ihabrang* (teaching room).

Also a day's excursion to the old residence of the King of Zanskar is well worthwhile. Plans are afoot to develop the site as a museum complex. Enquire at the tourist office.

Places to Stay

Padum's accommodation is limited to a choice of very basic hotels and guest houses, the latter being rooms in private homes. All provide a limited choice of food.

The *Haftal View* and *Ibex* hotels are near the tourist complex with doubles from Rs 30 to Rs 50.

The *Shapodok-la*, in the centre of town,

has dorm beds from Rs 5 to Rs 10. The *Chora-la* opposite has doubles from Rs 35 to Rs 50. Further up the path, beyond the mosque, the *Greenland* is similarly priced.

The *Tourist Bungalow*, near the long mani wall, offers the best deal with doubles for Rs 35 with a bathroom. However, you normally need to have made reservations.

In Karsha there is a hotel with down beds for about Rs 10. Alternatively, Mr Lachok has double rooms in his house for from Rs 30 to Rs 50.

TUNGRI-ZONGKHUL GOMPA ROUNDTRIP

From Padum follow the Stod River to the Sani and then leave the Stod Valley and follow the Sani southwards towards the Muni La pass. About halfway to the pass crest turn west into a side valley, cross a saddle and arrive at the Huttra camping place below the Umasi La.

The trail leads downstream by the Bardur to the Ganra camping place near the Zongkhul Gompa (see Padum-Kishtwar trek) and then back to the Stod Valley. At Chibra Stod head downstream to the east via Ating, Drokund, Shagur, Murkum and Turkum to Tungri. The trip takes about four days.

PADUM-THONDE-ZANGLA-KARSHA GOMPA-PADUM ROUNDTRIP

Day 1: Padum-Thonde

From Padum the route leads over the eastern rope bridge below the town on the right bank of the Lunak, one of the source rivers of the Zanskar. Kashmiri porters are unwilling to transport loads over these rope bridges. Zanskaris are the true specialists and the performance of 'oncoming traffic' can be acrobatic!

The route to Thonde follows the river at a distance above the rubble plain through which the river has carved its path. Thonde (also spelt Stongday or Stongde) is a river oasis with a monastery enthroned above it. Take the direct route to Zangla, which follows the Zanskar

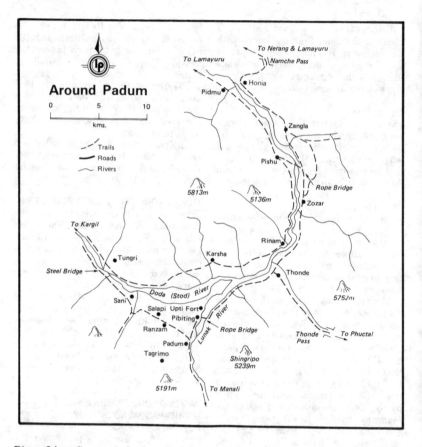

Around Padum

0   5   10
kms.

- - - Trails
─── Roads
∿∿∿ Rivers

To Lamayuru

To Nerang & Lamayuru
Namche Pass
Honia
Pidmu
Zangla
Pishu
5813m
5136m
Rope Bridge
Zozar
To Kargil
Tungri
Karsha
Rinam
Steel Bridge
Thonde
Doda (Stod) River
5752m
Sani
Salapi Upti Fort
Lunak River
Pibiting
Ranzam
Rope Bridge
Thonde Pass
To Phuctal
Padum
Tagrimo
Shingripo 5239m
5191m
To Manali

River. It's a five-to-six hour walk from Padum.

Thonde is an important town for trekking tours towards Lamayuru because it is the first place where horses can be hired on this side of the rope bridge. The horses should be ordered from Padum so that they are ready and waiting when you get to Thonde.

The best view of the irrigated fields, in which the semi-circle of houses lie, is from the monastery which has about 60 monks. It's a strenuous ascent, particularly in the midday heat, but try to see this monastery which exemplifies life in an intact monastic society. Each year sacred dances are held here in conjunction with the festival of Gostor at Karsha Gompa.

At midday the monastery school pupils are fed tsampa balls. You may be lucky enough to view the ritual purification of various ceremonial objects or you may see the manufacture of butter candles.

Descending from the monastery you can see, to the left of the mountains on either side of the Zanskar River, the distant form of Karsha Gompa. A difficult, dangerous and not to be recommended route turns eastward from Thonde through the Shadi Ravine to the Phuctal Gorge – see the Padum-Phuctal trek report.

Day 2: Thonde-Zangla

The route to Zangla follows the Zanskar River further to the north-east. Zozar (Zazar or Tsazar) is the next large town and after this the picturesque trail continues partly on the banks of the Zanskar, which makes it impassable at high water. Halfway between Zozar and Zangla a rope bridge leads across the Zanskar.

Zangla does not have much to offer apart from the rebuilt castle of the one-time kings of Zanskar. Here you will see more newly built chortens than elsewhere in Zanskar, a sign of the living nature of Buddhism in this area. The son of the King, once a monk and an important tanka painter, now wears a nylon wind jacket and sunglasses and spends several months of each year in Delhi. Times are changing. If you should be invited in for a cup of butter tea (or 'sweet' tea) try to have a look at the palace Dukhang. Some of the tankas in this room were painted by the King's son.

The old and decayed remains of the King's fortifications lie on the mountains above the village. The Prince of Zangla compared the site of these ruins to the head of an eagle but they did not impress us enough to want to climb the hill! We did enjoy making friends with the children during our stay with the royal family.

Day 3: Zangla-Karsha Gompa

In Zangla the Markha trek turns towards Leh (see Padum-Leh trek) but if you wish to go to Lamayuru it is best to follow the Zanskar River further along to Honia (see the Padum-Lamayuru trek).

To return from Zangla, crossing over the river to Karsha en route to Padum, you must go several km back towards Zozar and cross the Zanskar by a scenic rope

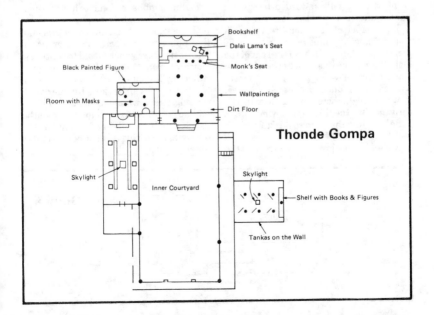

Thonde Gompa

Bookshelf
Dalai Lama's Seat
Monk's Seat
Black Painted Figure
Wallpaintings
Room with Masks
Dirt Floor
Skylight
Skylight
Inner Courtyard
Shelf with Books & Figures
Tankas on the Wall

bridge. The route branches right past the rope bridge and continues past Pishu and the Lingshot Gompa towards Lamayuru (see Padum-Lamayuru) or left towards Padum.

A five-to-six hour ascending walk to the south-west takes you past Rinam towards Yalong and the Karsha Gompa. A direct route also leads to this gompa from Padum and over the river terrace plains to the north towards Yalong. Yalong is on the other bank of the Stod, one of the source rivers of the Zanskar, below the Karsha Gompa.

Karsha is the largest and most important monastery in Zanskar. It has more than 150 yellow-cap monks and is subject to the control of the younger brother of the Dalai Lama. It is said to contain bone relics of Dorje Rinchen. The white-washed walls of the houses and chapels of the gompa, perched like a falcon's nest on the rocks above the Stod and Zanskar rivers, can be seen from a great distance away. A sweat-raising climb is eventually rewarded by superb panoramic views over the valley.

The chapel of the monastery, which contains another three prayer rooms, has places for 35 lamas. Behind the seat of the Dalai Lama's brother is a figure of Lhaso Cho Rimpoche with a golden crown inset with carnelian and turquoise gemstones. It was brought here from Lhasa in the early '60s but the three small windows let little light into the room so it is difficult to see clearly.

Karsha's most important festival is the *Karsha Gostor* with cham mask dances on the 26th to 29th day of the 11th month of the Tibetan calendar – usually mid-December to early January. The library of the gompa is also worth seeing and Karsha's butter tea is widely renowned.

Near the village of Karsha are the monasteries of Khagsar, Purang, Phagspa and a nunnery, Dorjezong, near the top of the valley.

Day 4: Karsha-Padum

Either cross the Stod by a rubber dinghy (cost Rs 5) left behind in '76 by a German party, or take the route over Lami and Kusser towards Rankiut where you can stay overnight, although Tungri is better. A sturdy wooden bridge (the Tungri Bridge) crosses the Stod and the route then follows the river westward (upstream) to Turkum (3550 metres). Above Tungri is a small, but interesting gompa with nuns. From Tungri the route leads back past the Sani Gompa, Salapi and Ranzam to Padum.

Padmasambhava is said to have visited and blessed Sani. It has a large cemetery with trees and springs and in a rock face on the opposite side of the river is a meditation cave which is said to contain a footprint. Sani Gompa also has the great stupa of Kanishka, and an image of Naropa, which can be viewed on the day of the pilgrimage which occurs around the middle of the sixth Tibetan month. People come from all over Zanskar for this pilgrimage, wearing new clothes and their finest jewellery.

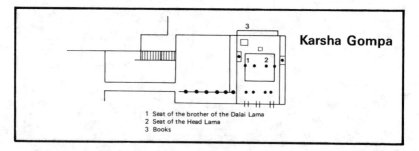

Karsha Gompa

1 Seat of the brother of the Dalai Lama
2 Seat of the Head Lama
3 Books

PADUM-PHUCTAL GOMPA – via Shadi Gorge

This four to five day trek can be extremely dangerous and difficult although it might, superficially, seem like an attractive way of making a Padum-Phuctal-Padum round trip. The route from Padum runs to Thonde then eastwards (to the right) into the mountains and across the 5492-metre Thonde La. To the top of the pass the route is quite easy but from there it's hell through the gorges.

The route has not been regularly travelled for years so the path has deteriorated and a lot of dangerous clambering plus river and mountain crossing is necessary. Horses are unusable! There is only one tiny village, Shadi, on the whole route and even that is in a side valley. Many stretches are dangerous due to the vertical rock walls and the loose rock slopes high above the turbulent rivers winding their way far below the trail. From Phuctal you soon rejoin the usual Padum-Manali route.

Glossary

Amitabha – Buddha of endless life.
Avalokitesvara – the Bodhisattva of compassion.

Bagh – garden.
Bauli – a well.
Bodhi – enlightenment, from which comes the word buddha.
Bodhisattva – a being who compassionately refrains from entering Nirvana in order to save others.
Buddha – the enlightened one.
Bund – an embankment, dyke or embanked road.

Cham – masked dance.
Chang – Ladakhi (Tibetan) beer, brewed from barley and millet.
Chorten – (stupa) a small temple or edifice containing Buddhist relics.
Chowkidar – night watchman or caretaker.

Darwaza – gateway or door.
Dharma – the teachings of Buddha.
Doonga – smaller, usually one-roomed, houseboats; home to many of Srinagar's lake dwellers.
Dorje – thunderbolt symbol, usually made of brass, and used as a weapon against the powers of darkness.
Dri – female yak.
Dukhang – general assembly hall in a monastery.
Dzo – a Tibetan-bred animal, developed by crossing the yak with common cattle.

Gelugpa – (Gelukpa) the Yellow Hat Sect of Buddhism, founded by Tsongkhapa in the 14th century.
Ghat – steps or landing by a river; sometimes a place for cremations.
Gompa – Buddhist monastery or lamasery.
Gonkhang – temple.
Gurdwara – Sikh temple.
Guru – master or teacher.
Gyalpo – leader or king.

Hookah – water pipe for smoking tobacco.

Ka-ga – the 35-letter Ladakhi alphabet.
Kahwa – Kashmiri tea, flavoured with cardamom and ginger and brewed in a samovar with grated almonds.

Kali – this is the terrible side of *Parvati* the beautiful consort of Shiva. In this avatar, or manifestation, she is the fiercest of the gods; she demands sacrifices and wears a garland of skulls.
Kandshur – holy scripts.
Kangri – personal 'central heating', consisting of an earthenware bowl containing hot coals, carried by Kashmiris under their pheran.
Khaushak – head lama of any monastery.

Lakhang – small temple or chapel.
Lama – a Buddhist monk or, more specifically, a priest or monk of Lamaism.
Lamaism – the Mahayana form of Buddhism of Tibet and Ladakh.
Latho – (god house), a red chorten of a special style.
Lingam – the Hindu phallic symbol of the god Shiva.

Mahabharata – the Vedic epics: ancient spiritual texts, the orthodox Hindu scriptures.
Mahayana – a school of Buddhism whose followers seek enlightenment not for themselves alone, but for all living beings; *maha* – 'great', *yana* – 'vehicle' or 'path'.
Mandala – mystic circle, design or cosmogram used in meditation and initiations; a symbol of collective consciousness.
Mani – the mantra *om mani padme hum*, a phrase usually addressed to Buddha or to Avalokitesvara, his Tibetan incarnation.
Mani stone – a stone carved with the mantra *om mani padme hum*.
Mani walls – walls made of mani stones, often constructed by pilgrims.
Manichorkor – a prayer-wheel containing the mantra.
Mantra – prayer formula, chant or spell.
Marg – meadow.
Muezzin – one who calls Muslims to prayer from the minaret.
Mulla – a Muslim priest.

Nirvana – the ultimate aim of Buddhist existence, this is the final release from the cycle of reincarnation, attained by the extinction of all desires and individual existence, culminating in absolute blessedness.
Noon-chai – pink, salted Kashmiri tea.

Numdah – an embroidered rug made from coarse felt.

Padmasambhava – great master of the Tantra.
Perak – the distinctive top hat worn by Ladakhis.
Pheran and poots – traditional Kashmiri clothing consisting of two gowns worn one on top of the other.

Rad – floating garden.
Raj – rule or sovereignty, but specifically applied to the period of British rule in India prior to 1947.
Rimpoche – a monk who has become a master; the word means 'precious', 'blessed' or 'jewel'.

Sadhu – a wandering holy man, usually a Hindu layman who has given up all worldly possessions to seek religious salvation.
Samovar – a metal urn for making tea, in which the water is heated by hot coals held in an inner container.
Sarai – (serai), a place of accommodation for travellers, originally a *caravanserai* where camel caravans once stopped.

Sathu – bund, or embankment.
Shikara – gondola-like boat used for transporting people and goods around the lakes of Srinagar.
Shiva – one of the two main Hindu gods also revered by Buddhists; Shiva is 'the destroyer', and the god who presides over personal destinies.

Tanka – a rectangular Tibetan painting on cloth.
Tantra – a teaching or system of Vajrayana Buddhism.
Tantric Buddhism – see Vajrayana.
Tiratha – a holy place, or place of pilgrimage.
Tschomoh – a Buddhist nun.
Tsi-Pa – an astrologer lama.

Vajra – a dorje (thunderbolt) or diamond-like substance.
Vajrayana – an esoteric form of Buddhism that employs radical shortcuts to obtaining enlightenment; *vajra* – diamond, *yana* – path.

Wallah – person; added to all sorts of things – dhobi-wallah (clothes washer), taxi-wallah (taxi driver), shikara-wallah etc.

Ziarat – a shrine.

Index

MAPS

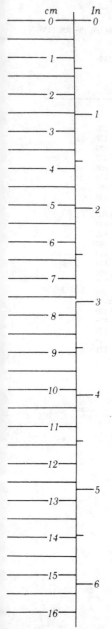

Temperature

To convert °C to °F multipy by 1.8 and add 32

To convert °F to °C subtract 32 and multipy by ·55

Length, Distance & Area

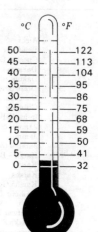

	multipy by
inches to centimetres	2.54
centimetres to inches	0.39
feet to metres	0.30
metres to feet	3.28
yards to metres	0.91
metres to yards	1.09
miles to kilometres	1.61
kilometres to miles	0.62
acres to hectares	0.40
hectares to acres	2.47

Weight

	multipy by
ounces to grams	28.35
grams to ounces	0.035
pounds to kilograms	0.45
kilograms to pounds	2.21
British tons to kilograms	1016
US tons to kilograms	907

A British ton is 2240 lbs, a US ton is 2000 lbs

Volume

	multipy by
Imperial gallons to litres	4.55
litres to imperial gallons	0.22
US gallons to litres	3.79
litres to US gallons	0.26

5 imperial gallons equals 6 US gallons
a litre is slightly more than a US quart, slightly less than a British one

Lonely Planet

Lonely Planet published its first book in 1973. Tony and Maureen Wheeler had made a lengthy overland trip from England to Australia and, in response to numerous 'how do you do it?' questions, Tony wrote and they published *Across Asia on the Cheap*. It became an instant local best-seller and inspired thoughts of a second travel guide. A year and a half in South-East Asia resulted in their second book, *South-East Asia on a Shoestring*, which they put together in a backstreet Chinese hotel in Singapore in 1975. The 'yellow book', as it quickly became known, soon became *the* guide to the region and has gone through five editions, always with its familiar yellow cover.

Soon other writers started to come to them with ideas for similar books – books that went off the beaten track and took an adventurous approach to travel, books that 'assumed you knew how to get your luggage off the carousel,' as one reviewer described them. Lonely Planet grew from a kitchen table operation to a spare room and then to its own office. It also started to develop an international reputation as the Lonely Planet logo began to appear in more and more countries. In 1982 *India – a travel survival kit* won the Thomas Cook award for the best guidebook of the year.

These days there are over 60 Lonely Planet titles. Nearly 30 people work at our office in Melbourne, Australia and another half dozen at our US office in Oakland, California.

At first Lonely Planet specialised exclusively in the Asia region but these days we are also developing major ranges of guidebooks to the Pacific region, to South America and to Africa. The list of walking guides is growing and Lonely Planet is producing a unique series of phrasebooks to 'unusual' languages. The emphasis continues to be on travel for travellers and Tony and Maureen still manage to fit in a number of trips each year and play a very active part in the writing and updating of Lonely Planet's guides.

Keeping guidebooks up to date is a constant battle which requires an ear to the ground and lots of walking, but technology also plays its part. All Lonely Planet guidebooks are now stored and updated on computer, and some authors even take lap-top computers into the field. Lonely Planet is also using computers to draw maps and eventually many of the maps will be stored on disk.

The people at Lonely Planet strongly feel that travellers can make a positive contribution to the countries they visit both by better appreciation of cultures and by the money they spend. In addition the company tries to make a direct contribution to the countries and regions it covers. Since 1986 a percentage of the income from each book has gone to aid groups and associations. This has included donations to famine relief in Africa, to aid projects in India, to agricultural projects in Nicaragua and other Central American countries and to Greenpeace's efforts to halt French nuclear testing in the Pacific. In 1988 over $40,000 was donated by Lonely Planet to these projects.

Lonely Planet Distributors

Australia & Papua New Guinea Lonely Planet Publications, PO Box 617, Hawthorn, Victoria 3122.
Canada Raincoast Books, 112 East 3rd Avenue, Vancouver, British Columbia V5T 1C8.
Denmark, Finland & Norway Scanvik Books aps, Store Kongensgade 59 A, DK-1264 Copenhagen K.
Hong Kong The Book Society, GPO Box 7804.
India & Nepal UBS Distributors, 5 Ansari Rd, New Delhi – 110002
Israel Geographical Tours Ltd, 8 Tverya St, Tel Aviv 63144.
Japan Intercontinental Marketing Corp, IPO Box 5056, Tokyo 100-31.
Netherlands Nilsson & Lamm bv, Postbus 195, Pampuslaan 212, 1380 AD Weesp.
New Zealand Transworld Publishers, PO Box 83-094, Edmonton PO, Auckland.
Singapore & Malaysia MPH Distributors, 601 Sims Drive, #03-21, Singapore 1438.
Spain Altair, Balmes 69, 08007 Barcelona.
Sweden Esselte Kartcentrum AB, Vasagatan 16, S-111 20 Stockholm.
Thailand Chalermnit, 108 Sukhumvit 53, Bangkok 10110.
UK Roger Lascelles, 47 York Rd, Brentford, Middlesex, TW8 0QP
USA Lonely Planet Publications, PO Box 2001A, Berkeley, CA 94702.
West Germany Buchvertrieb Gerda Schettler, Postfach 64, D3415 Hattorf a H.
All Other Countries refer to Australia address.

Guides to the Indian Subcontinent

Bangladesh – a travel survival kit
The adventurous traveller in Bangladesh can explore tropical forests and beaches, superb hill country, and ancient Buddhist ruins. This guide covers all these alternatives – and many more.

India – a travel survival kit
An award-winning guidebook that is recognised as the outstanding contemporary guide to the subcontinent. Looking for a houseboat in Kashmir? Trying to post a parcel? This definitive guidebook has all the facts.

Kathmandu & the Kingdom of Nepal – a travel survival kit
Few travellers can resist the lure of magical Kathmandu and its surrounding mountains. This guidebook takes you round the temples, to the foothills of the Himalaya, and to the Terai.

Pakistan – a travel survival kit
Pakistan has been called 'the unknown land of the Indus' and many people don't realise the great variety of experiences it offers – from bustling Karachi, to ancient cities and tranquil mountain valleys.

Sri Lanka – a travel survival kit
This guide takes a complete look at the island Marco Polo described as 'the finest in the world'. In one handy package you'll find ancient cities, superb countryside, and beautiful beaches.

Tibet – a travel survival kit
After centuries of isolation, this extraordinary region is now open to individual travellers. This comprehensive guidebook has concise background information, and all the facts on how to get around, where to stay, where to eat, what to see . . . and more.

West Asia on a shoestring
A complete guide to the overland trip from Bangladesh to Turkey. Updated information on Afghanistan, Bangladesh, Bhutan, India, Iran, Maldives, Nepal, Pakistan, Sri Lanka, Turkey and the Middle East.
Also Available:
Hindi/Urdu phrasebook, *Nepali phrasebook* and *Sri Lanka phrasebook*

Trekking Guides

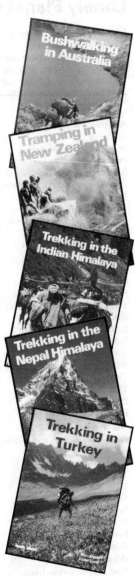

Bushwalking in Australia
Australia offers opportunities for walking in many different climates and terrains – from the tropical north, to the rocky gorges of the centre, to the mountains of the south-east. Two experienced and respected walkers give details of the best walks in every state, plus notes on many more.

Tramping in New Zealand
Call it tramping, hiking, walking, bushwalking, or trekking – travelling on your feet is the best way to come to grips with New Zealand's natural beauty. This guide gives detailed descriptions for 20 walks of various length and difficulty.

Trekking in the Indian Himalaya
The Indian Himalaya offers some of the world's most exciting treks. This book has advice on planning and equipping a trek, plus detailed route descriptions.

Trekking in the Nepal Himalaya
Complete trekking information for Nepal, including day-by-day route descriptions and detailed maps – this book has a wealth of advice for both independent and group trekkers.

Trekking in Turkey
Western travellers have discovered Turkey's coastline, but few people are aware that just inland there are mountains with walks that rival those found in Nepal. This book, the first trekking guide to Turkey, gives details on treks that are destined to become classics.

Lonely Planet Guidebooks

Lonely Planet guidebooks cover virtually every accessible part of Asia as well as Australia, the Pacific, Central and South America, Africa, the Middle East and parts of North America. There are four main series: 'travel survival kits', covering a single country for a range of budgets; 'shoestring' guides with compact information for low-budget travel in a major region; trekking guides; and 'phrasebooks'.

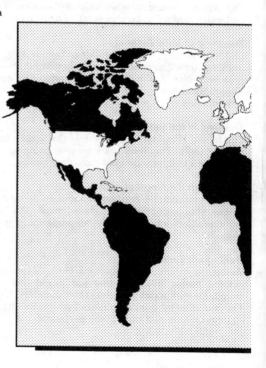

Mail Order

Lonely Planet guidebooks are distributed worldwide and are sold by good bookshops everywhere. They are also available by mail order from Lonely Planet, so if you have difficulty finding a title please write to us. US and Canadian residents should write to Embarcadero West, 112 Linden St, Oakland CA 94607, USA and residents of other countries to PO Box 617, Hawthorn, Victoria 3122, Australia.

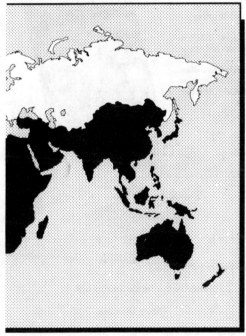

Indian Subcontinent
India
Hindi/Urdu phrasebook
Kashmir, Ladakh & Zanskar
Trekking in the Indian Himalaya
Pakistan
Kathmandu & the Kingdom of Nepal
Trekking in the Nepal Himalaya
Nepal phrasebook
Sri Lanka
Sri Lanka phrasebook
Bangladesh

Africa
Africa on a shoestring
East Africa
Swahili phrasebook
West Africa

Middle East
Egypt & the Sudan
Jordan & Syria
Yemen

North America
Canada
Alaska

Mexico
Mexico
Baja California

South America
South America on a shoestring
Ecuador & the Galapagos Islands
Colombia
Chile & Easter Island
Bolivia
Peru

Lonely Planet Update

We collect an enormous amount of information here at Lonely Planet. Apart from our research there's a steady stream of travellers' letters full of the latest news. For over 5 years much of this information went into a quarterly newsletter (and helped to update the guidebooks). The paperback *Update* includes this up-to-date news and aims to supplement the information available in our guidebooks. There are four editions a year (Feb, May, Aug and Nov) available either by subscription or through bookshops. Subscribe now and you'll save nearly 25% off the retail price.

Each edition has extracts from the most interesting letters we have received, covering such diverse topics as:
- how to take a boat trip on the Yalu River
- living in a typical Thai village
- getting a Nepalese trekking permit

Subscription Details
All subscriptions cover four editions and include postage. Prices quoted are subject to change.

USA & Canada – One year's subscription is US$12; a single copy is US$3.95. Please send your order to Lonely Planet's California office.

Other Countries – One year's subscription is Australian $15; a single copy is A$4.95. Please pay in Australian $, or the US$ or £ Sterling equivalent. Please send your order form to Lonely Planet's Australian office.

Order Form

Please send me

☐ One year's sub. – starting current edition.   ☐ One copy of the current edition.

Name (please print) ....

Address (please print) ....

....

....

Tick One

☐ Payment enclosed (payable to Lonely Planet Publications)

Charge my   ☐ Visa   ☐ Bankcard   ☐ MasterCard   for the amount of $ ....

Card No .... Expiry Date ....

Cardholder's Name (print) ....

Signature .... Date...

US & Canadian residents
Lonely Planet, Embarcadero West, 112 Linden St,
Oakland, CA 94607, USA
Other countries
Lonely Planet, PO Box 617, Hawthorn, Victoria 3122, Australia